VISUAL TEAMS

GRAPHIC TOOLS FOR COMMITMENT, INNOVATION, & HIGH PERFORMANCE

THIS FIELD IS MOVING FAST! LET'S GO!

This book is dedicated to my inspirations, Arthur M. Young and Allan Drexler, and for all the young people worldwide who are working in teams and believe that collaboration is not only an effective but also a necessary competency in our times.

Contents

III. Visual Team Startup
Creating Trust, Focus, & Commitment

IV. Sustaining Results
Innovating for High Performance

V. Growing a Visual Team Culture
Thinking BIG About Opportunities

TPM

CREATING

Orient

Renew

Trust

Perform

Clarify

Implement

Commit

SUSTAINING

DECIDING

THESE CHAPTERS MATCH THE MODEL!

VI. New Technology Tools
A Revolution in Visual Collaboration

VII. Links, Tools, & Other Resources

Introduction
Imagining Better Results for Teams

This book is an outgrowth of 35 years of working with organizations and their teams, helping people cooperate to achieve results. I've worked all over the world with large and small, private, nonprofit, and government organizations. During that time the principles and practices that guide this work have become clearer and stronger, and it is time to share these widely. In the past ten years particularly, the interest in these tools has increased dramatically, specifically the Drexler/Sibbet Team Performance® Model (TPM) and a related system of tools that have been in development since 1980. Increasingly the system is a standard reference in schools of organizational development, and is the system of choice at leading companies such as Nike, Becton Dickinson, and Genentech/Roche. This book provides the often-requested introduction to the use of these tools.

My Inspiration

My work with teams is inspired by three things. First is the long-held conviction that if the communications and innovation strategies that successful design teams use were generally understood, then the whole field of team development would benefit. I've found that working like a designer broadens my repertoire of tools when it comes to starting, improving, or collaborating on work that requires shared commitment, innovation, and high performance. Simply put, a visual team is a team that works like designers.

My second inspiration is my work with the Theory of Process formulated by Arthur M. Young. I came across this work in the 1970s. It is the most comprehensive system I know of for integrating the findings of contemporary science with traditional wisdom about how nature works. It has provided an invaluable set of lenses for seeing the patterns of process that underlie any kind of workgroup or team.

My third inspiration is Allan Drexler. He inspired my professional work with teams in 1981

THIS TEAM PERFORMANCE MODEL LOOKS LIKE A BOUNCING BALL!

COOL. I WONDER HOW IT COMPARES?

WHO IS THIS BOOK FOR?

New team leaders

Team members wanting better results

Managers wanting to support team environments

Leaders wanting to support creativity and innovation

Young people learning about groups

People interested in collaboration

Coaches

Human resources managers

Human resources development professionals

Consultants who work with teams

Nonprofits working with volunteers

when I met him in a workshop I was leading on graphic facilitation. At the time Allan was (and still is) an organization development consultant working with companies such as General Mills and RR Donnelley. He was focusing on "matrix organizations" —the type of organization in which workers report to both functional managers in areas like manufacturing, human resources, and sales, and also to project managers of cross-cutting lines of business. The built-in conflicts these forms of organization generate are tough on teams. He was passionate about finding answers.

At the time I met Allan I was immersed in working visually with groups and facilitating meetings and organizational strategy sessions. My book *Visual Meetings: How Graphics, Sticky Notes, and Idea Mapping Can Transform Group Productivity*, is a summing up of this long experience. But I was also very interested in the larger problems of organization effectiveness. As I began working with Allan at General Mills, we began the exciting adventure of creating the Drexler/Sibbet/ Forrester Team Performance System (TPS), synthesizing his rich field research in teams and my deep explorations of group process. Our goal was to create a framework for teams as useful as the Meyers-Briggs Type Indicators (MBTI) is for individuals. This intention has carried on since, re-sulting in engagement in a wide variety of explicit team-development efforts at companies such as Nike, Mars, Procter & Gamble, Mentor Graphics, Otis Spunkmeyer, W. L. Gore, Hewlett Packard, Becton Dickinson, Chevron, Agilent Technologies, the San Francisco Foundation, and the National Park Service.

My Motivation

When Richard Narramore, my editor at John Wiley & Sons, broached the idea of writing a sec-ond book after *Visual Meetings*, I immediately thought of the need to show how visual meetings integrate over time to get real results. But writing about teams would be a different challenge. There are many, many resources on teamwork (a good number of the leading ones are listed in the back of this book). But I appreciated, being familiar with the field, that there still weren't many books touching on the application of new design and visualization tools to teams. I also knew that Allan and my work on the TPM had developed some fresh approaches to explaining team dynamics through the power of visual language. I'm not a researcher, but I believe that senior practitioners should share their experience as a contribution to the field. I agreed to write *Visual Teams*.

Since that commitment another deeper motivation has surfaced. I have been president of my own company, The Grove Consultants International, since 1977 (it's gone through a few name changes but is basically the same business). In that time I've been a team leader of our own and client projects many, many times. I've also trained a large number of people who have learned their facilitation and consulting craft at The Grove. I know that collaboration can result in amazing, creative results. But I also know that collaboration is a learned capability, and effective teamwork is increasingly challenged by 24/7 work environments, virtual work, ideological divisiveness, and lean, overworked organizations. I am also acutely aware that the scale and complexity of problems in our cities, states, country, and world are also increasing. I see young people in Eastern Europe, the Middle East, and in Asia calling for this in their own way. I see my own children and grandchildren heading into that same world. So my motivation has flowed well beyond my personal interest in teams. I feel a deep obligation to share what I've learned in a way that young people can benefit.

Why "Visual Teams"?

Visual work has always been a feature at The Grove and in my consulting with teams. It stems from a lifetime passion for design and visual language. The success of *Visual Meetings* in reaching a new audience of beginning consultants, teachers, facilitators, and human resources staff convinced me that teamwork needs the same contribution.

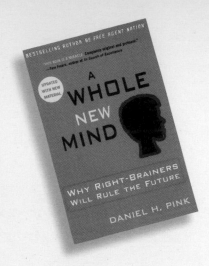

A WHOLE NEW MIND

Daniel Pink introduces his popular book with this clear stance:

"The last few decades have belonged to a certain kind of person with a certain kind of mind—computer programmers who could crank code, lawyers who could craft contracts, MBSs who could crunch numbers. But the keys to the kingdom are changing hands. The future belongs to a very different kind of person with a very different kind of mind—creators, empathizers, pattern recognizers and meaning makers. These people—artists, inventors, designers, storytellers, caregivers, counselors, big picture thinkers—will now reap society's richest rewards and share its greatest joys."

(A Whole New Mind, 1)

I'm using the term "visual teams" to point at three developments that in the last 20 years have significantly broadened the choices of how to work together visually to achieve results.

1. **The evolution of traditional design tools** such as white boards, markers, large paper, tape, cameras, sticky notes, and other tools. They are both higher quality and increasingly interactive digitally.

2. **The explosion of groupware and social media** since the early 1990s. Groupware includes all of the software tools designed for group collaboration, including the social networking tools. Most of these integrate text, graphics, and video, making it possible to work visually across a wide range of media.

3. **An accelerating interest in "design thinking" and innovation**. Competition from emerging economies increases every day and puts a premium on creativity. The popularity of Daniel Pink's book, *A Whole New Mind: Why Right-Brainers Will Rule the Future*, is the crest of a wave of research on cognitive psychology, neuroscience, and emotional intelligence, all pointing to reasons why working more like designers and artists is not only possible but desirable.

We live in a time in which graphics and text are dancing together continuously on our websites, smart phones, magazines, ads, and television. Was there ever a culture more visually stimulated and literate? There is no reason why teams cannot take advantage of all of this. Perhaps they do not realize how easy it is.

The "West Coast" School of Facilitation

The Grove is part of a West Coast (of the United States) school of facilitation and organizational work heavily influenced by the way designers and architects work. (It's spreading rapidly, so many of you wouldn't associate it just with the West Coast.) For several years after college I was determined to become an architect and even enrolled in school. But a job offer from the Coro Foundation turned me in a new direction toward leadership development in the public sector (I was a Coro Fellow in Los Angeles right after college). But my interest in design sustained itself as I took my passion for visualization into the realms of information architecture, graphic design, learning materials design, and process design. Initially I supported seminars with Coro Fellows as they learned from their field experiences, and then worked for years on strategy-consulting projects. I developed a strong practice helping architecture firms with their strategies, and have worked extensively in Silicon Valley with design teams at Apple, HP, Agilent Technologies, Juniper Network, and other high-tech firms. I know how interface designers, software designers, chip designers, and other people in "maker" cultures work.

As I explained in *Visual Meetings*, both David Straus and Michael Doyle, founders of Interaction Associates (IA), were trained architects. They pioneered facilitation as a profession in the 1970s, and one of their first projects was writing *Tools for Change* with a Carnegie Foundation grant. Its goal was showing teachers and others how to use the problem-solving approaches of architects and designers in the classroom!

Geoff Ball, who worked with Doug Englebart and was another pioneer in graphic facilitation, was trained as an electrical engineer. We all approached collaboration the way that architects approach design—playing with patterns and prototypes, visualizing contexts and visions, modeling proposals, and recording everything on paper. My work with Apple Computer during the 1980s convinced me that working like designers was a key to innovation.

The new technologies coming out of Silicon Valley have had a shaping influence. During the 1990s, I led The Grove side of a strategic partnership with the Institute for the Future (IFTF) in Palo Alto on the Groupware Users Project, one of the first efforts to research and map the

THE IMPORTANCE OF DESIGN THINKING

Tim Brown, CEO of IDEO is one of the leaders in the movement toward design thinking. He writes:

Design thinking taps into capacities we all have but that are overlooked by more conventional problem-solving practices. It is not only human-centered: it is deeply human in and of itself. Design thinking relies on our ability to be intuitive, to recognize patterns, to construct ideas that have emotional meaning as well as functionality, to express ourselves in media other than words and symbols. Nobody wants to run a business based on feeling, intuition, and inspiration, but an overreliance on the rational and the analytical can be just as dangerous. The integrated approach at the core of the design process suggests a "third way."

(Change by Design, 4)

Visual Teams pulls all these threads together in a book showing how your teams can work like designers, even if you can't draw or don't think of yourself that way.

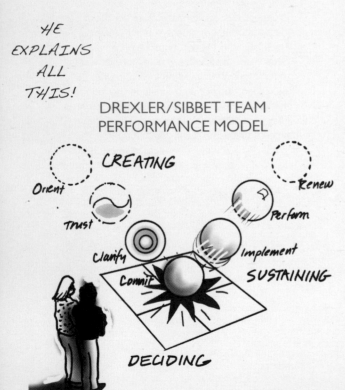

HE EXPLAINS ALL THIS!

DREXLER/SIBBET TEAM PERFORMANCE MODEL

CREATING

Orient

Trust

Clarify

Commit

Renew

Perform

Implement

SUSTAINING

DECIDING

growing amount of technology and software directly designed to support teams and collaboration. The IFTF and The Grove recruited what grew to be four dozen client organizations and agencies. They supported us in writing one of the first books on groupware, holding twice-a-year user exchanges, and conducting several focused research efforts and reports each year. These tools have evolved to define a huge suite of choices for teams that are empowering distributed work, applications of visualization and multimedia to meetings, and ever-expanding possibilities for innovation. The project continues to this day as the IFTF Technology Horizons work has pushed into the areas of social networking, crowd sourcing, games, and simulations.

As you will find in one of the chapters on the use of technology with teams, the TPM guided our work with IFTF and provided a structure for thinking about what-to-use-when across the full range of predictable stages of team development. We considered that and other methodological tools such as Group Graphics as forms of groupware.

What Is in This Book?

Visual Teams pulls all of these threads together in a book showing how your teams can work like designers even if you can't draw or don't think of yourself as visually inclined. The book is written in seven sections that each have several chapters. Each chapter is summarized on the section pages, so I will just provide a general overview here. If you find that a given chapter is already familiar to you, the book is designed so that you can skip ahead to the relevant sections. It's also designed for having as much fun scanning through and reading all the side stories as diving in for a full read.

Section I, "What Is a Visual Team?" provides an overview of visual teams and the Drexler/Sibbet Team Performance Model, the working language of the book. Its chapters elaborate on the case I'm making here that design professions, such as architecture, graphic design, information design, software design, website design, and even urban design, hold a storehouse of methods and practices for the rest of you who might not consider yourselves designers. It provides you with some initial tools to assess what kind of team you are leading and what the opportunities are for becoming a visual team. The chapter on the TPM will provide you with a panorama of all the key challenges and success factors for any kind of team, including visual teams, and indicates the specific opportunities for becoming more visual and where it provides benefits.

Section II, "Leading Visual Teams," directly addresses the situation in which a lead performer has been placed in charge of a team for the first time and wants to succeed at the job. If you are in this position, this section will describe tried-and-true principles and practices. It identifies the four big tasks of a team leader, and the inner work required to be an excellent one. It frames the challenge of leaders as one of integrating attention to purpose, energy, information, and operations in a smooth, ongoing flow of work. I also step back and reflect on how more senior leaders can work to support an environment of innovation, and use assessment tools to develop ongoing teams. As you will come to see, an effective team is a partnership between internal leadership and external organizational support. Managing this connection is a key leadership job.

Section III, "Visual Team Startup—Creating Trust, Focus, & Commitment," steps you through what the TPM calls the "creating" stages of teamwork. These chapters provide specific guidance on orientation to purpose, trust building, clarifying goals, and committing to a common direction. Workgroups that don't have to cooperate closely while actually doing the work will benefit a great deal from this section. You will also find that the more ambitious your goals are in terms of high performance, the more investment you will need to make in these early stages of teamwork. They are the foundation upon which later stages depend.

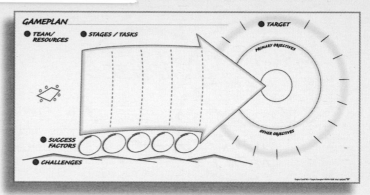

GRAPHIC GAMEPLAN FOR NEW TEAM STARTUPS

Section III will detail how to use this most popular of all The Grove's Graphic Guides. An earlier form was also the first graphic template I ever saw used—by Geoff Ball—and convinced me to jump into graphic recording years ago. It builds off of a deeply embedded metaphor—that planning is like a journey. A good action plan describes where you are, where you want to go, and how you plan to get there.

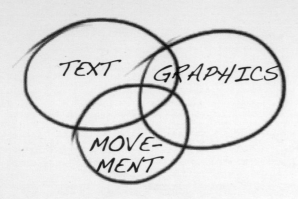

VISUAL LANGUAGE

Bob Horn is one of the first to write comprehensively about visual language. He says:

> We are just at the beginning of another communications revolution—the modern equivalent of the one that Gutenberg sparked (with the printing press). The visual language revolution is taking place alongside other communications revolutions—the World Wide Web, animation, three-dimensional virtual reality, and intelligent and interactive visual elements. The new mix of technologies and techniques will irreversibly alter communications in the 21st century.

(Visual Language, 240)

Section IV, "Sustaining Results—Innovating for High Performance," deals with the three stages of team performance after committing to be a true, interdependent team. I share tools for project management and tracking progress, making persuasive visual presentations, using graphic communications and rich metaphors to guide and inspire high performance, and ways of using visualization to support knowledge sharing and organizational improvement in the area of teaming. I also share the story of a high-performing team working to create a multistate environmental cleanup network.

Section V, "Growing a Visual Team Culture—Thinking BIG About Opportunities," specifically deals with how you can introduce the idea of visual meetings and visual teams to your manager and organization. It argues for ongoing learning and development in this area, and the importance of having robust shared language for teaming—especially if your organization is working globally and/or over multiple sites. The TPS, because it is based on the Theory of Process, functions like an operating system for groups. In those organizations where visual teams have flourished, the human resources development people who supported the trainings found the approach informed much of their other training work as well.

Section VI, "New Technology Tools—A Revolution in Visual Collaboration," directly addresses the opportunities for virtual teams with new visualization software. This section opens with the rich story of the Groupware Users Project team, a truly high-performing visual team. You can see through the lens of this story how the tools and methods described come to life in a real, ongoing team. Specific chapters on web and teleconferencing, tablets, team rooms, social networks, and mobility follow the IFTF story. I am not trying to write a comprehensive book here on virtual work, but to share the tried-and-true visualization methods we've explored and know work well. I do speculate on where this all seems to be heading.

Section VII, "Links, Tools, & Other Resources," suggests sources for developing a more general understanding of teams. The Grove engaged two Coro Fellows in civic affairs to help us research the area and document the leading tools other than those provided by The Grove. We've identified websites that have particularly useful information, as well as links to the many tools The Grove provides.

A Summary of Visual Meetings for Those Who Haven't Read It

Visual Teams builds on my book *Visual Meetings*. For those of you who haven't read it, the following summary should provide some context. As I said in the introduction to that book, I've written many books for professional graphic recorders, facilitators, and consultants that we've published through The Grove. *Visual Meetings* with John Wiley & Sons was written for the legions of people who are not artists or necessarily good at drawing but still want to get in on the visual revolution.

Visual Meetings describes how graphics and visual language can support group process through the entire cycle of learning, from IMAGINING through ENGAGEMENT through THINKING to ENACTMENT. With many examples and stories, I paint a picture of how the design environment of the West Coast of the United States gave rise to highly visual and design-oriented ways of working in meetings, far afield from the specific design professions of architecture, engineering, graphic design, and other fields. (This point of view will be expanded upon in this book.)

Visual Meetings to Spark Your Own Imagination

To begin with, I explore how visualization can be used to have meetings with yourself to stimulate your own imagination, through journaling, metaphoric thinking, diagramming, and other

VISUAL MEETINGS BOOK NOW IN FIVE LANGUAGES

This initial book on how to use interactive graphics, sticky notes, and idea mapping for group collaboration has been a best seller. It was published in August of 2010 by John Wiley & Sons and is now in Chinese, Brazilian Portuguese, Dutch, Korean, and German. *Visual Teams* shows how to apply these ideas across the full arc of a team process.

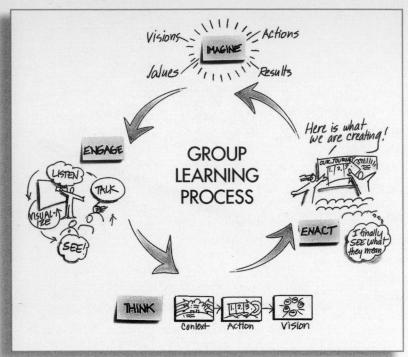

MODEL FROM *VISUAL MEETINGS*

Visual Meetings is organized around this group-learning model. It illustrates the ways visualization is used for all four stages in the insight-to-action process.

visualization strategies. "Paper is brain interface" as Paul Saffo, a forecaster member of the Groupware Users Project, liked to say. Drawing is the way we develop new perspective, especially in regard to thinking about systems. I suggested ways to used forced metaphors to expand your thinking about your own practices and business, by, for instance, comparing your business to a garden and identifying all the plants as different kinds of clients.

I recommended people read Dan Roam's excellent books, *Back of the Napkin: How to Use Graphics for Selling and Problem Solving* and *Unfolding the Napkin,* in addition to *Visual Meetings.*

Visual Meetings for Engagement

The second part of *Visual Meetings* deals with interactive graphic communication as a superior form of engagement for groups. I compress some of the rich information in a comprehensive book called *Graphic Facilitation: Tapping the Power of Groups Through Visual Listening* (available through The Grove) and demonstrate that anyone can create the simple frameworks and icons used in visual meetings. I provide a graphic overview of the way we train people to unlock their drawing capability by having them practice at large scale, and some of the more common ideographs and pictographs people use in graphic recording.

Chapters also detail how sticky notes, dot voting, group drawing, templates, and other strategies let people get their hands directly on information. I make the argument that having groups interact with partially completed frameworks and displays greatly increases involvement. I reflect on presentation software such as PowerPoint. While appreciating the extent to which it is an excellent, individual, prototyping environment, it many times results in a pushy kind of presentation that all too often isn't very involving. (If you want to learn to use PowerPoint well read Nancy Duarte's book, *Slideology*, and her companion book, *Resonance*.) In *Visual Meetings* the chapters on sticky notes go into great detail on how to use these extremely flexible tools.

Visual Meetings for Thinking Together

THINK

In the third section of *Visual Meetings* I cover the Group Graphics Keyboard, a framework for thinking about seven archetypal types of displays. This Keyboard is an application of the Theory of Process to visual work with groups, and looks at displays as a dual process of display creating and display perceiving. The simpler visualization processes become foundations for the more complex ones, just like in natural systems. There are detailed explanations of each Group Graphic format and examples. I follow this with a description of The Grove's Visual Planning templates (called Graphic Guides) with lots of examples. I will be describing the ones that are especially relevant for teams in this book in greater detail.

The chapters on visual thinking argue that all systems thinking is based on display making—distinguishing the parts so you can look at relationships. I cover the most common types such as Mind Mapping, causal loop diagrams, total quality management charts, and the like.

Visual Meetings for Enactment

ENACT

The final step in the learning cycle is to take ideas to action. The chapters in this part of *Visual Meetings* show how action plans, road maps, and Grove Storymaps support getting results from meetings. These tools are also critical ones for teams and will be treated in much more depth in this book. *Visual Meetings* describes how involving leaders in creating their own visual communications builds buy-in and ownership.

WORDS FOR TEAMS

At the conclusion of their internship with The Grove, Daniel Cheung and Victoria Bensen gave a presentation to staff on what they found about tools for teams. "The word *teams* seems to be used to cover the entire work of people in organizations," they said. "Some even said the word is so overused that it doesn't communicate anymore." They reported that one person said that "collaborative work" is becoming a more common designation. Another distinguished between "workgroups" and "teams." I began writing down all the words I'd heard used for groups that need to cooperate to get results. Here is my list. What's yours?

- Team
- Workgroup
- Task group
- Task force
- Partnership
- Duo
- Trio
- Foursome
- Party
- Band
- Family
- Council
- Committee
- Crew

- Function
- Unit
- Squad
- Gang
- Posse
- Pod
- Cell
- Troop
- Troupe
- Cohort
- Force
- Camp
- Community of practice

SCAN OR READ?

This book was designed to be scanned like a website, read like a book, or both. The items in these boxed margins contain stories, tips, and checklists relating to the content being addressed in the chapter.

You may notice that some boxes have dark blue heads with reversed type and numbered steps, such as the example here. These are intended to be exercises that you can do and are written in that spirit: as instructions.

EXERCISES

1. Read through the exercise once.

2. Dip into the book to get some of the context.

3. Take a break and do the exercise with your team.

All of the sample charts and tools included in this book have captions that explain them.

The graphic template designs included from The Grove are copyrighted and available for purchase at our online store: www.grove.com. Ideas, of course, can't be copyrighted. My hope is that the abundance of examples included in this book will encourage your own templates and charts.

The final chapters look at how visual meetings are being amplified by new technology. I touch on tablets, web conferences, object-oriented programming, and virtual worlds.

*Visual Meeting*s also has a good resource section for anyone wanting to put these ideas into practice.

Visual Meetings and Visual Teams

A visual team, in one sense, is any team that is adept at visual meetings! However, in actual practice, visualization works well beyond meetings to support the in-between communications, reporting out and evaluating results as well. Visuals provide a common language for teamwork across the entire spread of the organization. Katzenbach and Smith, the McKinsey & Company consultants who wrote the widely respected book, *The Wisdom of Teams,* point out that one of their "uncommon findings" was that "many of the highest performing teams … never actually thought of themselves as a team until we introduced the topic" (Katzenbach 1993, page 4). I think the same is true of visual teams.

You could think of this book as the summing up of a professional lifetime of developing strategies for collaborative work. Whether or not you think of yourself as a team, if you are interested in how people can work better together you will get a bushel full of good ideas. In a time of networks, multiple team assignments, virtual work, and even virtual organizations, the common idea about what a team is and isn't is evolving rapidly. I hope this book helps build your confidence so that you can become part of a bounty of innovation in how people can work more effectively together.

Acknowledgments

I would love to repeat all the acknowledgments I made in *Visual Meetings* about all the people at The Grove Consultants International, the International Forum of Visual Practitioners, the Organizational Development Network, the Pathwalkers, the Thought Leader Gathering, and Coro who have been so helpful in shaping my career as a visual practitioner, but the list is long. Here, I want to give special thanks to those who have supported my development as an organization consultant and team developer.

Allan Drexler was my mentor and teacher for most of the 1980s and into the 1990s. Our companies are still partnering successfully in the shared ownership of the Drexler/Sibbet Team Performance Model. We cocreated the National Training Labs five-day workshop on Creating and Sustaining High Performance Teams—conducted continuously since the early 1980s by Allan and Russ Forrester, who joined our training team in the early 1980s. Russ and Allan have evolved an assessment business built around the TPM, and authored the Forrester/Drexler Team Performance Indicator, a self-scoring assessment, and its companion field book. They live on the East Coast of the United States and have teamed on many projects.

It was my good fortune to meet Arthur M. Young, the developer of the Theory of Process, when he first published it in 1976. I was part of his Institute for the Study of Consciousness from 1976 through the early 1980s and continue a relationship with Young's primary students. The TPM is one of the most successful applications of this theory to organizations, and was recognized as such by the Anodos Foundation, which is carrying on Young's work. A colleague, Jack Saloma, now deceased, introduced me to Young and was an intellectual partner in developing some of The Grove's organizational applications. Frank Barr and Michael Buchele also contributed, as we wrestled through their application of the theory to bioprocess.

My experiences teaming with the Institute for the Future has been integral to understanding the TPM applied to new technologies and supported by tools for visualization. Thanks to Bob Johansen, distinguished fellow at IFTF, as the leader of our groupware team. We were joined by Paul Saffo, Andrea Saveri, Alexia Martin, Robert Mittman, and Stephanie Schacter from IFTF. Tomi Nagai-Rothe, Suzyn Benson, and Mary O'Hara-Devereaux participated from The Grove.

Mary O'Hara-Devereaux came to The Grove from collaborating on a project at the University of Hawaii's Medex program. With her help we applied the TPM to training nurses in Kenya and Costa Rica. Later we collaborated on writing the book *Global Work*. During that same time I was working with the training team at Mars, Inc. (led by Martin Prentice) to design a worldwide facilitation training centrally focused on the TPM. This team was instrumental in teaching us how to train with the TPM cross culturally. Albert Gibson, Mary Jane Eckart, Eileen Matthews, and Joan Scarrott all deserve special thanks. Eileen and Joan became masterful graphic facilitators in the process. Recently Mars supported a Russian translation of our *Team Leader's Guide*.

Joan McIntosh deserves special thanks. As The Grove's director of marketing during the early 1990s, she codeveloped with me an application of Team Performance at 3M, and became so extensively involved that she ended up moving to the Twin Cities, where 3M is located. She has been a steady advisor and friend. As founder of the Change Agent's Café, Joan made it possible for a network of us to work with these ideas for nearly 20 years. I owe special thanks to Lenny Lind, Sandra Florstedt, Meryem LeSaget, Jim Ewing, and John O'Connell, an early pioneer in new games. Meryem is a consultant and professional writer about new management ideas who included the TPM in her French book, *Manager Intuitif*. She has become a student of the Theory of Process and its other applications. Another Grove partner, Vaugn Strandgaard, led in bringing the TPS to Denmark and Europe. Jonas Kjellstrand and Roy Bartilson helped in bringing the system to Sweden.

The TPS as a system would not have developed without amazing client-partners and the help of my longtime colleague at The Grove, Ed Claassen, who worked with me on many of the client projects. At Agilent Technologies, our longtime partners Christine Landon, Leslie Camino-Markowitz, and Teresa Roche facilitated the TPS being included in a new first-line manager's training program in the late 1990s. Ed worked with myself and Bobby Pardini, and Linda Castillo at Agilent, in creating the first *Team Leader Guide*. Tony Jimenez at Chevron worked closely with Ed to develop a self-teaching team performance module for their manager trainings. Wendy Witterschien at Becton, Dickinson and Company worked with Bobby Pardini at The Grove to adapt these materials to a flash-based, self-learning program available system-wide in that company. Kathy O'Connell and Kathryn Santana Goldman were codevelopers at Genentech/Roche of a team refresher application of the TPM. Nancy Stern brought in Strategic Visioning templates. Jennifer Clonmell had the TPM translated into five langauages for use at Citicorp. At Nike, Inc., Hannah Greenfeld, Steve Bence, Jigna Desai, and Nate James were instrumental in testing The Grove's new Team Performance On-Line Survey and contributing to a greater understanding of the integration of the TPM and other team development models. Most recently, W. L. Gore supported worldwide team training. Ed and I traveled to Germany, New Jersey, Arizona, and China, learning a great deal about how widely practices vary within a common set of archetypal challenges. As a colleague, Ed's intellectual partnership has been invaluable.

I also owe a lot to those clients who have championed visual meetings applied to their teams. Thanks to Susan Copple and Jim Lyons of HP, who created an opportunity to work with the BLAST team. Thanks to Joel Birnbaum, former head of HP Labs, and Barbara Waugh and Srinivas Sukimar. John Schiavo, CEO of Otis Spunkmeyer, and his team have been champions, including Ahmad Hamade, Steve Ricks, and Robyn Meltzer in particular. Thanks to Scott Kriens, former CEO of Juniper ,who sponsored ambitious applications of visual meetings, and

Joceyn Kung, the consultant who introduced us. I learned about design organizations working with Bryce Pearsall and Dale Hallock, leaders of the DLR Group, and Jon Petit, Griff Davenport, and Steve McKay, DLRG partners with whom I've had many discussions about how design teams work. Thanks to Chris McGoff at The Clearing for collaborating on bringing this kind of work to government. My work with Tom Wujec and Autodesk have added immeasurably to my understanding of the role of design. In that regard I also owe thanks to Dave Gray of XPlane (now Dachis Group), Kristina Woolsey at the Exploratorium, Luke Hohmann of Innovation Games, and Bob Horn of MacroVU.

This book would not have been possible without The Grove team. Laurie Durnell, our director of consulting, and Tomi Nagai-Rothe, a senior consultant, teach the TPS and adapt its tools to ever widening groups. Donna Lafayette manages our team performance workshops. Tiffany Forner, our art director, and Bobby Pardini, director of design services, have jumped in repeatedly. Rachel Smith, director of The Grove's digital facilitation services, helped on the chapters on the new technology. Anne Merkelson and Julia Sibbet helped with insights into social media and marketing. Thom Sibbet, director of client services, has been a close link to our team performance customers. Our customer support team—Noel Snow, Andrew Underwood, and Ed Palmer (our IT manager)—has provided very practical feedback about how clients use the tools. Very little of my work life would be possible without the support of The Grove's chief administration officer and my assistant, Megan Hinchliffe. I also want to thank Daniel Chueng and Victoria Benson, the Coro Fellows who interned with The Grove and helped develop the bibliography. A special thanks goes to the John Wiley & Sons team—Richard Narramore, my editor, Deborah Shindlar, senior production editor, and Lydia Dimitriadis, editorial assistant.

A final note of thanks to my wife, Susan, a poetry teacher and writer herself. We share our San Francisco studio. Her unstinting support of my writing makes it a joy to undertake.

I: What Is a Visual Team?
Using Graphics Across the Whole Workflow

I: What Is a Visual Team?

Chapter 1: Working Like Designers The book begins with a link to *Visual Meetings* and the idea that the ways of working coming out of design teams in Silicon Valley and other centers of innovation are transforming the way teams work in general. Themes in the book are introduced through the story of the Boise LasterJet Advanced Sales Teams.

Chapter 2: Why Be a Visual Team? This chapter explores the difference between workgroups and teams, and shares a tool for assessing the difference. It introduces a graphic portrayal of the types of teams and some opportunities for visualization.

Chapter 3: A Graphic User Interface for Teams This chapter describes the TPM, its key success factors, and reviews my work with Allan Drexler in setting out to create a "Meyers-Briggs" of team building. It will review the assumptions we made in its design and provide pointers for deeper study. I explain the reasons for moving from a "building" to a "performance" metaphor and using a "bouncing ball" as a graphical user interface for thinking about team process. It will also show how this framework bridges to other popular visual frameworks for thinking about teams.

1: Working Like Designers
Why Visual Teams Get Results

Let us begin our exploration of visual teams with a story about a task group at Hewlett Packard (HP) that deeply shaped my thinking about what was possible when a team learns to use visualization to support its work. Then, in the following chapter, I'll describe the specific, practical ways visualization can help your team. Remember, this book is designed to be scanned as well as read, so if any chapter isn't relevant to your situation then just skip ahead!

Help Us Present to Management

When Susan Copple called and asked if I would help a team at HP's Boise Printer Division prepare a visual presentation for top management, I didn't suspect that we both were on the edge of a breakthrough assignment that would transform the work of my company, The Grove Consultants International, and many HP divisions that picked up on our success. I initially thought it was just an interesting communication design job.

"Our team is a cross-functional task group that has been assigned the job of finding our next billion dollar businesses," Susan said. "We've been at it for about two months, but are running into some challenges in figuring out how to present our findings. Can you help us design our presentation of findings to top management?"

Susan was the quality professional on the team and had worked with me before. She told the team that I was a designer who helped with presentations, even though most of my work at the time was as a strategy consultant, facilitating visual meetings and change processes. But several decades of visual work and design of many different reports and output media from meetings left me quite experienced in what is now thought of as "information design" or "presentation design." Susan knew this. She also knew the team wasn't looking for help with its work, but how it could communicate it.

We have been assigned the job of finding our next billion dollar businesses ... Can you help us design the presentation?

COULDN'T HE PICK A SMALLER EXAMPLE?

I THINK HE WANTS TO SHOW THE TRUE VALUE OF A VISUAL TEAM.

At that time in the mid-1990s, the Boise Printer Division was one of the most successful within HP, and had in fact set records as the company's first billion-dollar revenue division. Personal computers and LaserJet printers that often accompanied them had exploded in sales growth following the initial HP printer's introduction in 1984. Profits rolled in. But successes in high tech don't last forever. Top management picked Jim Lyons, one of its most creative marketing leaders known for new ideas, as well as some other promising staff at their Boise site to conduct a two-month research project and recommend where to look for the division's next big wins.

TELL ME YOUR HISTORY

At the beginning of any team consultation it makes sense to know how it came to be and what work has been accomplished so far. This is the way we began with the Boise LaserJet Advanced Sales Team as they began to consider how to design presentations to top management from their research finding the next big opportunities for the LaserJet division at HP. Mapping the story visually is a guaranteed way to get everyone talking.

What's the Challenge?

Jim, Susan, and some of the team met me in a conference room at the San Francisco airport on one of their trips to headquarters. I brought large paper and magic markers. I asked team members to introduce themselves and tell me the story of their project. I found out they were called the BLAST team, for Boise LaserJet Advanced Sales Team. They repeated the goal Susan had shared with me, which was to identify the next multi-billion dollar business opportunities for their division. Soon I had six-to-seven feet of graphics detailing out how they received the request, conducted internal research by phone and e-mail, held many meetings to begin making sense of their findings, and were now facing the job of figuring out how to report that to their management. They didn't want their report to be the end of it. They really liked their ideas and wanted to see the division move on them.

But I began to feel that something was amiss. It was a gut feeling, not anything anyone said really, but the team didn't feel at ease with its work. Jim was a very bright, somewhat tightly wound manager who had lots of ideas. Another engineer and a business-planning professional were pretty active in the conversation. Trusting my instinct, I asked if there was a problem.

"Yes," Jim said. He went on to explain that in the relatively recent history of the division, two prior teams had been assigned similar projects, and at the point of sharing their results ran right into a wall of resistance and even hostile response from upper management. "It was a career-limiting experience for many on the team," he said. This new team was scared stiff that it would come to the same end. So this was the underlying reason they wanted outside help. They simply weren't confident that their traditional strategies would work. This challenge gave them the courage to step into becoming a truly visual team, innovate, and surpass all their original thinking about what was possible in a situation like theirs.

Thinking Like a Designer

At this point in the meeting I was working like a designer. My mind was racing with possible "solutions" to their problem, even though I really didn't know enough yet to be confident of any. But this is what designers do—they let themselves play with ideas in various stages of realization. Let me depart from the story a bit, and take you inside some of the thoughts that at the time were flashing through my mind.

Even though there are many kinds of design, design teams have much in common across all disciplines. Design teams know that something needs to be produced to fulfill specific goals and objectives, often within specific constraints and criteria—budget limitations, specified materials, and the amount of time that can be spent on the project. The excitement of design is being creative within these constraints.

Design is also, in most cases, a collaboration among many different people who have a stake in the outcome. Anybody who has worked this way much, be it designing a meeting, designing a new organization, designing a presentation, or designing a product or piece of software, knows that early ideas will evolve as users give feedback. In software design in particular, a process called

Design teams know that something needs to be produced to fulfill specific goals and objectives, often within specific constraints and criteria.

"agile development" explicitly presents solutions that are just good enough to deliver some value, and then iterates and improves them at a rapid pace. Brainstorming many ideas, playing around with tests and what are sometimes called "prototypes," working quickly, and making improvements are all basic tools in a designer's tool kit.

If this sounds like a description of any productive project team, you are reading my mind. Many project teams are implicitly being asked to work like designers and come up with something specific. This is precisely what brought me to write this book. After years of working with visual meetings and applying many tools like the ones I just described, I've come to appreciate that design thinking is a generally useful way for any team to work that needs to both produce results and be creative.

I knew what the goal of the BLAST team was: multi-billion dollar businesses. I also appreciated another hidden goal, which was to have this experience be a career-building experience, not a career-limiting one for the team itself. And I appreciated the constraint of only having a few more months to pull everything together, and of having the report presented to one of the most successful management teams in the entire HP business—the vaunted LaserJet management!

Initial Assumptions

From the time of the first phone call, some initial assumptions about the BLAST team's challenge guided my work. These are products of many different experiences and study of organizations. It's the mental "software" of any consultant or designer. The key is to be aware of them.

- Successful people (and organizations) may think they are open to new ideas, but they have a lot of attachment to current success.

- For people to accept anything new, they need to experience and feel, not just think about it.

Brainstorming many ideas, playing around with tests and what are sometimes called "prototypes," working quickly, and making improvements are all basic tools in a designer's tool kit.

- Slide presentations are often one of the least-involving ways to engage people's feelings.

- I immediately assumed that the management group to which the BLAST team would report was very smart and very happy with its success, and needed to be fully involved in the excitement and potential of the new ideas if they were to have a prayer of coming true.

How Could We Get True Engagement?

I knew from long experience with visual meetings that using large murals is a very involving way to present. They allow the user to tell stories and hop around in response to questions in ways that a fixed presentation can't. Susan knew of The Grove's work in this area for other parts of HP and I assumed that was probably one of the reasons she thought I could help. The team immediately agreed to avoiding slides, but didn't have experience with being a visual team in a true sense. And I didn't think eye-catching murals would be involving enough.

I then reflected on what I know is true universally: that everyone LOVES to see drawings and sketches unfold in real time. But it didn't seem possible to use graphic facilitation or live recording as a way to present about this subject. Management was looking for answers, not a facilitation experience.

Like many designers, I've found that holding two seemingly unrelated ideas together and seeing if I can make a connection can often spark some original thinking. In this case it did. My one idea was to use murals. The other was that live drawing is engaging.

Breakthrough Idea!

"Is there a conference room anywhere near the management team's offices?" I asked. The BLAST team looked puzzled. "Yes," someone said. "Why do you think I find this interesting?" I asked. They were still puzzled.

WHAT ABOUT A THEATER OF IDEAS WITH MURALS!

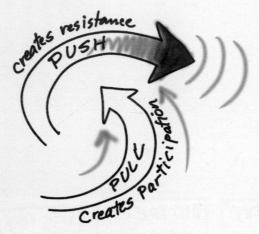

"PUSHING" INCLUDES

- Dense slide content
- Fully formed ideas
- Direct instructions
- No interaction

creates resistance
PUSH

PULL
Creates Participation

"PULLING" INCLUDES

- Simple, open frameworks
- Incomplete ideas
- Questions
- Invitations
- Interactive visualization

"I have an idea," I said. "What if I flew out to Boise a couple of days before your presentation, and we, as a team, created the big murals in the conference room during those days?"

A huge smile spread across several faces. Of course! Management would not be able to stay away, and like camels poking their nose under the tent, would come in and get to see all the ideas emerging in real time, with real drawing, and lots of engagement! And if they didn't come, we knew we could get them to! This would ensure that the ideas weren't experienced as a big PUSH in the face of the successful managers, but would PULL them in.

For those of you who are familiar with facilitation or have read *Visual Meetings*, you will recognize the push/pull idea—a very useful way to think about group dynamics. Pushing—which is presenting content, requests, answers, or anything already worked out—usually creates resistance and "push back." Pulling—which involves asking real questions, having blanks and open spaces, using silence, waiting—creates participation. Nature abhors vacuums and so do people.

Creating True Engagement

So our team now had a working idea, but the challenge was to identify which murals we would create in this workshop setting as part of the presentation. Again, as a facilitator of many planning sessions in organizations, I had more assumptions.

- People's understanding of new ideas is filtered through past experience.
- People's assumptions about context are as critical as responses to the new idea.
- If new ideas can find a basis in past success, they have a better chance of being adopted.

"Context" is a word for everything that surrounds an idea. In the case of the BLAST team it included the division's relationship with its own larger group within HP and the company as a whole, and it included its assumptions about how long the printer market would hold, workforce capability, and so forth. To get their new business ideas to take root the team needed to describe the soil and environment.

I began asking the team questions about the history of its division. I was actually looking for something very specific. I wanted to discover where in the past this particular management team had succeeded by being rebels and risk takers. I knew if the team could connect top management with its own risk-taking experiences early in the presentation, it would be more receptive to the BLAST team ideas.

It didn't take long. A clean sheet of paper went up. On it I drew a simple time line and led a fast, half-hour review of the recent history of the division. In 1992 the Printer Division had experienced several failed projects that cost a lot of money and put the division in the crosshairs within the company. Everyone was on edge. They had to get a "win."

Laser printing had been a new technology in the marketplace ten years prior, when the original LaserJet came along. Apple Computer had a competitive model introduced somewhat later, and delivered the concept of "Desktop Publishing" to the market. Boise LaserJet's offering was strong and as an "everyman's" solution sold like crazy. The LaserJet management, led by Dick Hackborn (who went on to become a very influential board-of-director member of HP in the 2000s), went against corporate policy and brought out a laser printer that would hook up to any PC, and eventually Macs as well (see side story). It rocketed to success. At the time of the BLAST team's work the division was a highly profitable and still growing multi-billion dollar hardware and toner business. So current management success was rooted in being rebels!! What luck. "We should make one of the murals be a summary of this history and you should lead with that story," I suggested. Everyone loved the idea.

HP LASERJET 4

The HP LaserJet was the first in a series of laser printers, launched in 1984 and continuing on in many versions (the 1992-vintage LaserJet 4 is shown here). Over the years numerous models have been designed for home, small business, and corporate use, incorporating other functions such as scanning, copying, and faxing, and offered in color as well as the original monochromatic (black and white) printing capability. It was without question one of the most successful printers of all time, and spawned many of the HP printer lines we see today. Attesting to its popularity and longevity, an extensive and ever-growing history of the LaserJet can be found on Wikipedia at http://en.wikipedia.org/wiki/Hp_laserjet. Laser printers are one of the technologies responsible for the revolution in visualization in business communications.

MURAL IDEAS
Here are some of the concept sketches
for the BLAST team murals.

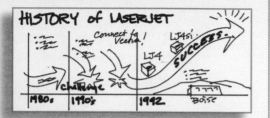

The other murals took shape. By that time I had already begun to develop standard frameworks for visual meetings. These graphic templates weren't actual preprinted tools as they are today, but were developed in our practice.

We decided on the following murals:

1. **History of the team**—showing all their interviews and research (to build credibility)

2. **History of the division**—to anchor the presentation in past success of being risk takers

3. **Context map of the current printing environment**—to frame the proposals

4. **Team visions of the opportunities**—outlining their big ideas in a general overview

5. **Three game plans**—one for each of the big ideas; two clearly defined and named initiatives, and a third, more general, process-oriented opportunity.

This made seven in all. The BLAST team would wrap the management in a theater of thinking!

Solving a Prioritization Problem

I touched in with the team once before the big event to help it review its content and sharpen the big ideas. This was a standard visual meeting in which I was graphically recording the conversations of the team, and using all the tools described in *Visual Meetings* to help the group come to a good conclusion about what it would do.

This meeting surfaced another design challenge arising from the team's struggle with all the juicy additional ideas beyond their two big ones. They simply couldn't agree on which to present. Because my role was that of a presentation designer, they didn't mind my chiming in with some thoughts. My mind began to apply another type of design thinking, which is to turn problems on their heads and look at them as assets and features.

In this case I thought, "what a bounty, to have so many ideas." If an organization wants to have ongoing innovation, wouldn't they want to have a kind of greenhouse operation or set of projects that could test and prototype new things on an ongoing basis? I began to think about where in other areas this is true. I could imagine a farmer having two main crops, and then a side field with lots of other crops. We decided to illustrate the third recommendation as a tractor pulling what looked like a plow with all the additional ideas as little arrows attached to a big frame. We had a working plan.

Using Subteams and a Shared Workroom

I flew to Boise three days before the big presentation with a big role of paper, magic markers, and dry pastel chalks. (I've found that dry pastels can create effects that look like an airbrush if you rub the colors in with tissue paper.) I knew that if the team was to work like designers and help cooperate on the murals, it needed a structure in which to work. I'd already seen that the team could flounder a bit with completely open conversation. I also knew that to draw these murals, I needed agreement on the wording.

The way we set up the workshop was a new experience for me, and really worked. Jim, as leader of the team, had the most knowledge related to which recommendations the team should actually advance. He and a couple of others needed to make some final decisions. Others were good at internal communications. I was the lead creating the actual murals, but wanted someone familiar with the team's recommendations to watch over me and answer any immediate questions about wording. We came to a design that broke the BLAST team into three parts.

Because my role was that of a presentation designer, they didn't mind my chiming in with some thoughts. My mind began to apply another type of design thinking, which is to turn problems on their heads and look at them as assets and features.

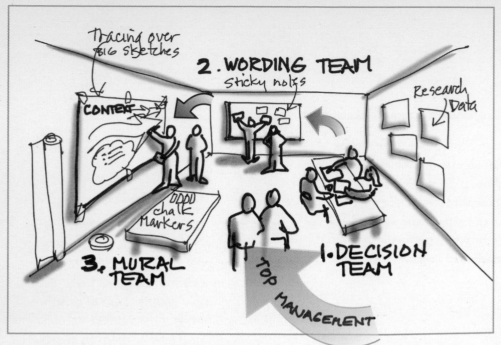

Tracing over BIG sketches

2. WORDING TEAM
Sticky notes

CONTEXT

Research Data

chalk Markers

3. MURAL TEAM

1. DECISION TEAM

TOP MANAGEMENT

1. **Decision Team**: Jim and two of the most knowledgeable members would settle all remaining issues having to do with the content of what they would present—such as deciding on the names of the big ideas and the main features.

2. **Wording Team**: A second team of two would take the information BLAST wanted to present and determine the precise words that needed to go on the chart, using sticky notes and a rough sketch of the mural.

3. **Mural Creation Team**: I would draw the mural, working with one other person to answer any questions I had and make sure I was accurate.

Ground Rules Helped

As a team, we all agreed on some ground rules that helped make the process possible. I knew we would have to work productively, use the power of both hierarchy, as reflected by the three teams, and group consensus, working as a whole team. Bringing in an idea from the teams I'd seen work at Saturn Corporation, General Motor's new car company that was completely team-based, I suggested that if anyone ran into a problem or question on their team that they could not handle, they could "stop the line" and call a quick meeting of the whole. I asked if I could do the same, functioning as the outsider representing the uninformed audience. By this time the team's trust was high, and they liked the idea. We were soon off and running!

And what fun it was. The conference room was fairly small, and got steamy pretty quickly. Sure enough, top management couldn't stay away. They were very apologetic about peeking in, but were fascinated.

THE BLAST TEAM WORKROOM

In a conference room near top managements' offices, the BLAST team created an assembly line of three subteams to create the Big Ideas presentation. Top management couldn't resist coming to get a preview, and became fully engaged. The visual environment made it possible.

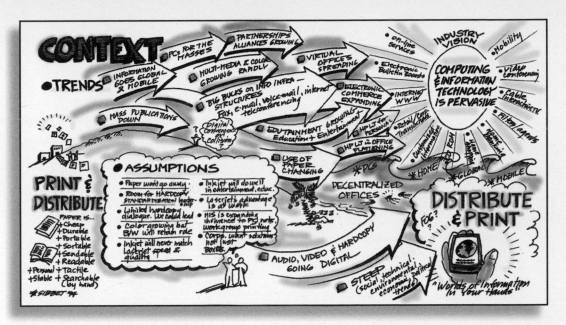

I worked out a way of doing a fast sketch for the mural designs to get spacing and visual ideas, and then putting a large piece of paper over the top. The poster-maker bond that I was using was transparent enough that I could see through, essentially tracing and improving the work underneath. This business of doing versions of drawings is a standard method architects and designers use to think through ideas. Three, four, or five versions result in a design that comes alive.

Success on Success

The actual content of the BLAST team's presentation is and was proprietary, and not essential to understanding the power of this story. I flew home after the murals were done, and the team went into its presentation, creating a theater of ideas for their managers, each taking a part in the presentation. Because the managers had already seen the murals in the making, the presentation became a celebration. Not only was the BLAST team roundly thanked, but also the top managers decided to use the murals as the springboard for their annual strategic planning meeting, which they invited me to facilitate, and the group-level managers decided to do the same thing at their strategic meeting.

I heard later that indeed Boise LaserJet did create some new businesses around the ideas, and that members of the BLAST team in several cases were tapped for the new work. Their assessment of the industry moving to a "distribute and print" paradigm was far-sighted and became a generally understood vision within the printing groups of HP, including the InkJet side of the house,

BLAST TEAM CONTEXT MAP

The Boise LaserJet team chose to assemble all the assumptions it was making about the printing environment on one large mural to set the stage for their presentation of the next billion-dollar businesses to pursue. This is a black-and-white version of what was a very effective, full-color final version.

and even beyond to the industry at large. So the BLAST team achieved both of its goals—the primary one of identifying new large business for the division, and conducting a "career enhancing" process. Jim Lyons' note in on this page tells that story.

Let's turn from this specific example to look more generally at why visual teams are better positioned to get results than ones that don't use visual meeting and planning methods.

2: Why Be a Visual Team?
The Case for Collaboration

If you are on teams in your organization there are no doubt expectations of what you will achieve. Like HP, your managers probably want you to meet your goals. I would guess that they would be pleased if you were creative in addition. They would be thrilled if you were paying attention to costs and return on investment, as well.

We can do all this, you might think—*if* we have clear goals, plenty of resources, time to work, people we like, and leaders we trust! You can guess what I'm going to say next. The way forward isn't that simple. Even though most researchers agree that humans are deeply social, cooperating in results-oriented teams within the time frames and expectations of our contemporary, fast-paced lives is not necessarily second nature. It takes training and practice to be a high performance team, and as Katzenbach and Smith emphasize in *The Wisdom of Teams*, high performance doesn't happen all that often.

I would also guess that no one is asking you to be a "visual" team.

Start with Why YOU are Interested in Visual Teams

This book will share a visual framework for thinking about teams and well-tested tools and methods for working graphically that will greatly increase your chances of being effective. But before we delve into these in the next chapters, let's orient to *your* purpose and intention in even picking up this book. Something must have sparked your interest! Was it an inkling that maybe being able to have fun while getting results is possible? Was it a memory of what it was like to be a kid without fear of creating and drawing? Was it having read *Visual Meetings* and wanting to apply these ideas to bigger challenges than just one meeting? Or maybe you are really floundering and don't know where to start and are willing to reach for something different? It doesn't matter, really. What does matter is that you have a seed of hope and an intention to water it and try something new. You'll need persistence. Group skills take practice. Look at any high-performing

HOW DO WE START ON THIS?

WE NEED TO START WITH PURPOSE

HOW MUCH DO WE REALLY HAVE TO COOPERATE?

Check the ones that apply to your team.

Orientation and mission

❑ *Setting clear purpose and scope*

Trust and competency

❑ *Working across generations, cultures, and time zones*

❑ Great individual performers that don't understand how to lead a team or have the correct skills

Clarity and communications

❑ *Increasing complexity of information and data*

❑ *Finding a common language for talking about team issues*

Commitment and resources

❑ *Picking the right communication technology*

❑ Getting organizational support

❑ Resource limitations

❑ *Membership on multiple teams*

Implementation and timing

❑ Coping with a 24/7 work environment

❑ *Cross-functional alignment and collaboration*

❑ *Managers pushing lean teams to innovate*

Performance and improvement

❑ Increasing demands for speed

❑ *Tracking and evaluating progress*

❑ *Getting timely help from other team members*

Renewal and change

❑ System-wide disruptions from reorganizations

❑ *Finding time to learn and debrief*

(Italics indicate advantage for visual teams)

sports or performing arts team. They practice! And they play!

So you need to be motivated. Look at the two lists on this and the next page. The one on the left lists all the challenges teams face in today's work environment. The one on the right holds out some possibility of meeting these challenges. A part of your success in learning the tools and methods in this book will be having enough discontent with the current situation and enough pull toward a vision of something being possible that you are willing to change. (If you look at the list of team challenges again, I made all the items where visualization is directly helpful in italics!)

The Advantage of Visual Teams

There are several key arguments for working visually as a team that flow from the list of challenges on the left. I've grouped them as the four "Fs":

1. **Focus**: An effective team converges on a common purpose and set of goals, and shares common assumptions about what it's doing. Visual work focuses a group, because everyone is looking at one display, not the many different versions inside their own imaginations.

2. **Fellowship**: I make the case in *Visual Meetings* that the interactive, engaging qualities of working with graphics, sticky notes, and idea mapping is much more effective at supporting relationship building, trust, and participation than pushy presentations. On the delivery end, cocreating communications to the larger organization can be very energizing, as I described in the story of the HP team.

3. **Fragmentation**: The explosion of types of information, channels of communication, and global use of English means that finding patterns and making sense out of the avalanche is increasingly difficult. Visualization is a direct support to pattern finding, and

allows the aggregation and analysis parts of teamwork to be a group activity. Most of the progress that scientists are making in understanding dynamic systems comes from visualizing and literally seeing patterns. Work teams can tap the same advantage.

4. **Follow-through**: Connecting everyone's activity over time is essential to producing anything. The difference between relying on everyone's individual perception and having a shared schedule and road map everyone agrees upon is night and day. Graphic records allow teams to brief stakeholders and sponsors, support after-action reviews, and document best practices for future teams.

Hindsight, Foresight, and Insight for Action

At an even deeper level there are reasons for making visualization central in teamwork. It's a key to our imagination of possibilities. In the 1990s, when The Grove formulated our Strategic Visioning process for supporting planning with graphic templates, we concluded that the reason managers wanted to do strategy was to bring their best hindsight from the past and foresight about the future together to create insights for action in the present. Think about these words. They all have "sight" in them! When we think backwards our understanding is embedded in narratives about how this or that happened and we literally "see" patterns of connection and flow. The same is true when imagining the future. We *imagine* it. We form pictures. We *see* possibilities. And the same is true when we bring our future thinking back into the present and determine action plans. We want to see them clearly laid out.

From a cognitive science point of view it is common knowledge that humans cannot hold more than about four to seven data points in their attention at one time without resorting to displays. I think this is why Geoff Ball, in writing about explicit group memory when he was working with Doug Englebart at SRI, claimed that a shared working display is the single most productive tool any group can use to support its activities.

OPPORTUNITIES FOR VISUAL TEAMS

Check the ones you can imagine.

❑ Using graphic visions to energize everyone's sense of purpose

❑ Recording meetings graphically to honor everyone's input, build trust, and foster mutual respect

❑ Transforming virtual meetings

❑ Mapping and display-making to pull information together and find patterns

❑ Getting everyone's commitments to action on one sheet of paper (imagine that!)

❑ Visually sharing plans with sponsors and potential supporters

❑ Having decision making be fun and interactive

❑ Seeing the big picture while working on the details

❑ Collaborating on making videos, multimedia presentations, murals, and other visualizations as a direct way to have fun and be productive at the same time

❑ Drawing attention to team outputs and results

Are You a Workgroup or Team?

If you are convinced about visualization, the next question is how much you need to invest in being a team. The word "team" is used very broadly inside organizations. One way to start thinking about how much effort you want to put into team development is to distinguish between those workgroups that essentially work individually, perhaps coordinated by a manager and aligned with common goals, but are working most of time on an individual basis, and those teams that require cooperation. The first kind might include teams that work in accounting, or call centers, particular crafts, or some professional services. In this book I'm calling these kinds of teams

TEAMS and TASKS	Can be completed relatively independently			
I. EXECUTIVE TEAM	Read Reports	Hire Personal Staff	Talk to a Customer	Meet with Staff
II. HR TEAM		Conduct a Survey	Serve Individual Clients	Conduct a Training
III. DESIGN TEAM	Do E-mail			Research Options
IV. OPERATIONS TEAM	Fill Out Time Sheets		Operate Station	Fix Broken Machinery
Low interdependence	0 1	2	3	4

"workgroups." There are many ways that visualization can support this kind of work. But there are many cases where work cannot get completed without people closely cooperating. The BLAST team is a good example. A management team, production team, design team, sports or performing arts team, or organization change team are all examples of teams where tasks require coordination and cooperation all the way along. It's helpful to call these groups "teams."

How much effort you personally or as a team invest in learning to work together should be a direct result of your answer to the exercise described on this page. If you need to cooperate to complete your work, then investment in the methods and tools in this book will be well worth it.

One way to start thinking about how much effort you want to put into team development is to distinguish between those workgroups that essentially work individually ... and those teams that require cooperation.

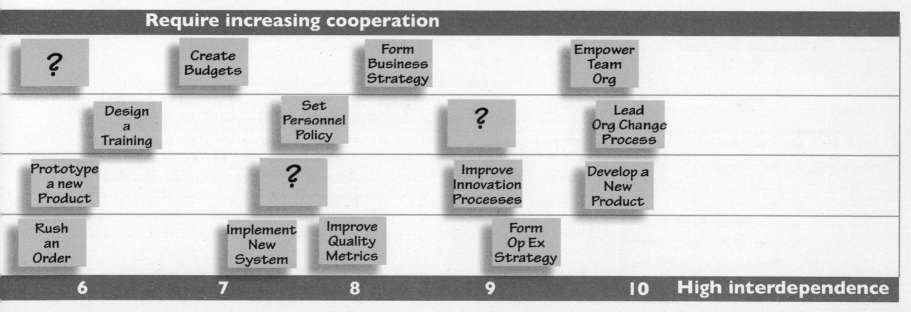

If you don't need to cooperate so much, but would benefit from more camaraderie, goal clarity, and such, then skip to those parts that share best practices in these areas.

Appreciating New Groupware Tools for Teams

Let's assume you appreciate the value of being visual and do want to be more of a team. The next question is "what kind of tools are available?" I remember Jim Whittaker, the climber and founder of REI, saying at the Apple Leadership Expeditions in the 1980s, that most climbers when they first join up as a team talk about tools. It's a way of calibrating competency and imagining what will need to happen on the climb. So let's pretend we are going on an expedition of learning about visual teams. Here will be your chance to check out what you are familiar with and not, and what you might have imagined using to support your team. I'll go into more depth in later chapters.

In Chapter 17 I will share the story of the Groupware Users Project that The Grove and the Institute for the Future conducted during the 1990s, when group-oriented software was being developed at a rapid pace parallel with the growth of the Internet. The term "groupware" refers to software specifically designed for collaboration. It included in our initial research video conferences Lotus Notes, decision-support tools, graphic recording software, and interactive whiteboards. I argued then that Group Graphic and visual-meeting methods were also a kind of nonelectronic groupware. As the Internet exploded in 1993 with the advent of the Mosaic browser (the first widely used graphical user interface), these tools accelerated in their development. Now in the 2000s social networking, smart phones, and tablets are pushing the boundaries of what is possible even further. I appreciated early on that most groupware tools worked because they provided a common, visual working display for groups. All the features and benefits aside, they allowed people to see what they were doing over time and space.

One of the first things we did in the Groupware project was map this phenomenon. Our first report to clients, called *Leading Business Teams*, was one of the first books published about this. (See side story on next page.)

Visual Thinking Applied to Groupware Tools

Visualization works at two levels for teams. One involves the communication tools and methods the teams use to actually manage work and make sense of things. The other is using visual concepts and models as a new kind of language for thinking about team dynamics and organizational process itself.

We wanted to describe choices of tools, so we developed the Four Square Map of Groupware, explaining our intention in *Leading Business Teams*:

> An early goal of the Groupware Users' Project was to create a single-page map that could be placed in front of someone who had never heard about the emerging technology (in this case groupware) and be used to explain the subject at a general level within five minutes. Within ten minutes, a newcomer should be able to talk through the map as he or she asks questions and makes comments about the groupware concept. When frameworks are this clear, then the focus can be on the territory and finding the new patterns with it. (Johansen 1991, 14)

This is about as clear an argument for the power of visual language that I know. Let's use it now to look at the kinds of visualization tools I'll talk about in this book and that you can think about learning to use. In order to map anything, a designer needs a "map base." For geographic maps this is a given—it's the north-south-east-west grid. For conceptual maps one needs to think about the natural ways people understand things and find a map base that is intuitively clear. Four-square maps are quite common because they cross two dimensions to create four categories. This is a

I appreciated early on that most groupware tools worked because they provided a common, visual working display for groups. All the features and benefits aside, they allowed people to see what they were doing over time and space.

LEADING BUSINESS TEAMS

One of the first things we did in the Institute for the Future/Grove Groupware project was map the explosive growth of group-oriented software in the late 1980s and 1990s. Our first report to clients, called *Leading Business Teams*, was one of the first books published about this new development by Addison Wesley in 1991. It is called *Leading Business Teams: How Teams Can Use Technology and Group Process Tools to Enhance Performance*. It contains maps to this territory of new tools that are still very relevant today.

perfect balance of simplicity and complexity. The art is choosing the two dimensions and having them be relevant. This groupware map has held up, and provides a perfect base map for looking at all the choices for visual tools for teams by comparing time and place. I've upgraded the mapping for this book to include all the new tools that have come into being since we wrote the original book back in 1989.

Same Time/Same Place—Face-to-Face Meetings

The traditional, and historically most familiar way to work as a team, is face-to-face at the same time and in the same place. This is the space of face-to-face meetings and was the focus for *Visual Meetings*. Many kinds of work groups are still located in the same geographic area or building and can meet together this way. The tools we'll look at in this team mode are:

- Graphic recording on large paper
- Static and interactive whiteboards and multitouch screens (and walls)
- Computer projection of idea mapping, flow charting, and other software
- Predesigned presentation murals and charts
- Wall and tabletop graphic templates
- Workbooks, worksheets, and handouts
- Sticky-note displays
- Decision-support software for electronic brainstorming, voting, and ranking
- Tablet computers for active graphic recording that is projected

Same Time/Different Place —Virtual Meetings

Increasingly teams aren't in the same location, and are distributed in different locations, many times all over the world. But they still want to meet every now and again at the same time, hearing each other's voices and perhaps seeing themselves on video and looking at shared drawings. Many face-to-face meeting involve a virtual component with several people calling in. This is the same time/different place way of working. Its tools are:

- Teleconferences with target documents
- Web conferences with shared whiteboards and interactive presentations
- Web conferences with active recording on tablets
- Video conferences with telepresence and interactive whiteboards integrated
- Interactive whiteboards and telephones
- Live chat with or without video
- Browser-based decision-support software

Different Time/Different Place—Internet Connection

A third, and you will realize, very common way of working in today's technical environment, is at different times and different places. This is the world of e-mail, team websites, and social media. Tools used here include:

- E-mail and texting
- Shared databases in "the cloud"
- Electronic bulletin boards
- Social media, such as LinkedIn, Facebook, Google+ and Twitter
- Fax and overnight mail
- Team-oriented project-management software

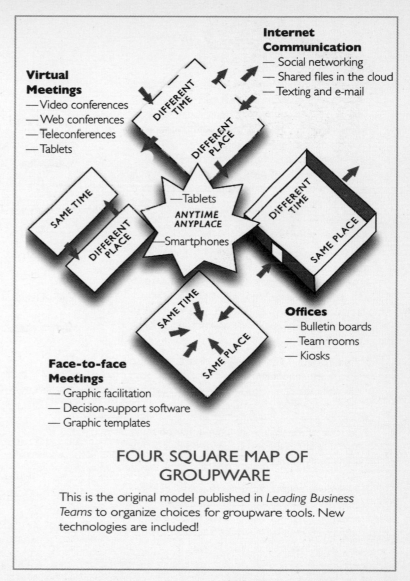

Virtual Meetings
— Video conferences
— Web conferences
— Teleconferences
— Tablets

Internet Communication
— Social networking
— Shared files in the cloud
— Texting and e-mail

ANYTIME ANYPLACE
— Tablets
— Smartphones

Offices
— Bulletin boards
— Team rooms
— Kiosks

Face-to-face Meetings
— Graphic facilitation
— Decision-support software
— Graphic templates

FOUR SQUARE MAP OF GROUPWARE

This is the original model published in *Leading Business Teams* to organize choices for groupware tools. New technologies are included!

SOME HYPOTHESES ABOUT VIRTUAL WORK

In the late 1990s I was invited to be one of the keynote presenters on the first ever computer conference hosted by the Organization Development Network, called Collaborate 98. Hundreds participated over a three-week period, with each one of us who agreed to be "keynoters" taking one of the weeks. I agreed to check into the conference two or three times a day and respond to the comments and questions that were posted following my five-page introductory "address"— actually an essay I wrote for the occasion.

I had three hypotheses at the time that are even more relevant today when it comes to working in team situations that involve virtual elements, and are quite relevant to thinking about how to use this book and all its ideas. I took a stand that three things were going to shape online collaboration.

1. **Face-to-face meetings will become less frequent and more important** in that they will need to be well-facilitated since virtual teams depend on them to develop personal relations.

2. **In spite of the variety of communication platforms, teams will need to agree on one or two basic ones** to connect.

3. **Narrower communication channels** (i.e., texting, phone vs. face-to-face) **will require more robust meta-language** for talking about talking and thinking about thinking. The visual models in this book are good examples of what I mean.

Different Time—Same Place Meetings

This brings us back to a physical office or workspace. When teams are collocated they can communicate visually through the physical environment in ways that allow coworkers to see what is going on at different times. These tools include:

- Physical bulletin boards and project-management walls
- Posters
- Posted action plans and road maps
- Team rooms with displays
- Kiosks—physical and electronic

Anytime/Anyplace—Social Media and Cloud Computing

Our Groupware Project foresaw the blooming of mobile media and the possibility of virtual communication almost anywhere. With cameras on smartphones and tablets, wifi and other Internet connects becoming universal, and data access from the cloud expanding exponentially, the "anytime/anyplace" possibility is becoming reality. Some of the tools that specifically make this possible are:

- Texting
- Video and photo sharing
- Teleconferencing on smartphones
- All the above plus drawings on smart tablets
- Coordinating through cloud computing services
- Mobile appliances of increasing variety

This last category isn't different from the basic four, but integrates and blends them. People are texting and tweeting in face-to-face meetings now. Virtual meetings dip into the cloud to reference documents. Apps allow linkages across e-mail, social networks, and websites. Where this integration and cross communication will move is the open question of our time.

Thinking About Teams Over Time

Thinking about all of these tools without a specific team in mind is like going into a sports recreation store without an idea for what sport you want to play. It is overwhelming how many choices there are. So the next step in working with a team is to understand how things move over time. The good news is that there are some very predictable stages to team process, when reviewed at a high level. There are definite steps involved in creating the team in the first place, and then there are phases when you are trying to sustain performance. That is what the next chapter will provide—a detailed, step-by-step look at team process through the lenses of the Drexler/Sibbet Team Performance Model.

But before getting into that level of detail, let's look at teams more metaphorically, staying within the adventure metaphor. The next two pages illustrate a team process as though it is a river journey, and names some of the common, repeating meetings and activities you will no doubt engage. Thinking this way will also help you make choices about the best sort of tools.

The chapters after the explanation of the TPM focus in more specifically on how to make tools choices as a leader and how to set your team up for success. Then chapters will step through each of the seven stages of team performance, elaborating on best practices and describing specific teams that have come to represent what truly visual teams can accomplish when they become fluid with the tools.

THIS IS CONFUSING—TOO MANY CHOICES!

THAT'S WHY YOU HAVE TO THINK ABOUT TEAMS OVER TIME. THE NEXT PART EXPLAINS.

Lessons from River Guides

My favorite metaphor for the process of teaming is the experience of rafting down a river. Like a river, team process is usually bounded on one side by high hopes on the part of sponsors, team leaders, and other people in your organization who depend on you, and on the other by real-world constraints. If these boundaries are tight, and the goals are very practical and focused, the river will run faster. If the hopes are very high and lofty, the process may meander, and have more variety.

In between these constraints is the life of the team. My niece is a river guide on the American and Sacramento rivers in California. She's convinced me that no matter how much you know about the river, it is always different and special. That's true of teams. But she also knows there are predicable challenges. In river guide terms they are (as illustrated):

1. **Forming the Team**: It always involves discussion about outcomes, the raft, roles, rules, safety, and rest options.

2. **Building Trust and Alignment**: Getting everyone in the raft to pull together.

THINKING OF TEAMING AS A RAFTING ADVENTURE

The next chapter will translate this imaginative picture into a formal model for thinking about teamwork. You will find that the four channels illustrated here are pointers to the Four Flows that underlie all group process—the flows of attention, energy, information, and operations. The different stages in the process are the recurring challenges, such as rapids, holes, waterfalls, and slow water are for rafters. The river boundaries in real life are hopes and aspirations on the top line and real world constraints on the bottom.

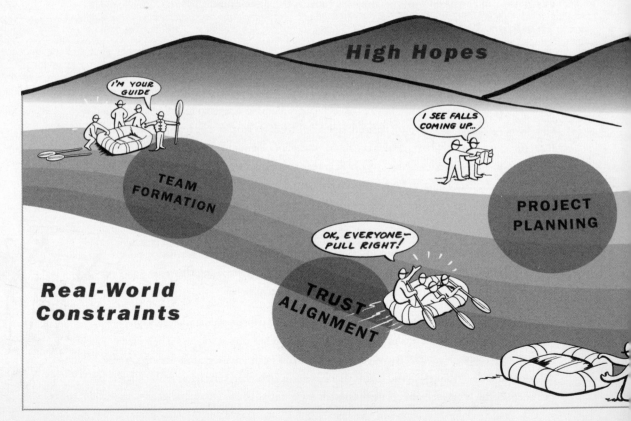

MAP YOUR OWN RIVER

1. Put up a big piece of paper and explain this river metaphor.

2. Get everyone on the team to identify on sticky notes the predictable challenges that you will face.

3. See if you can organize them in a sequence that has a high probability of happening.

4. Create your own names for these kinds of predictable stages.

3. **Planning the Big Run**: Before going into tough waters rafters usually pull out and form a strategy.

4. **Decision Making**: All along the guides have to make decisions, the rafters make small decisions, and everyone needs to be clear on how that is done because lives are at risk.

5. **Progress Reviews**: On longer trips pull-outs and surveillance downstream is required, to make sure assumptions about water levels are correct.

6. **Creative Problem Solving**: When big obstacles appear (waterfalls, huge snags, deep holes) everyone needs to flex and adapt, maybe even porting overland for a while.

7. **Learning from Action**: Good guides think through their runs and tuck away best practices and learning for the next one. Improvising in action is a repertoire problem. Having good choices makes for a better guide.

You may call these kinds of predictable challenges different names, but they should feel familiar. Having a deep sense of teams and processes over time is the key to determining what to do when and what tools are best to choose and learn.

Visual Teams Work Panoramically

As we move into chapters describing the TPM as a framework for thinking about team process, imagine having the tools and practices of using rich visualization throughout. The Groupware Project team at the Institute for the Future, which I will describe in Chapter 17, worked with charts like those on this page as a regular part of its work. Large murals helped the team communicate more integrated results and ideas later on, as a wider audience became engaged. Iterations of these large images served like a kind of thinking-software for the group mind. Version 1.0 would get things going, and by versions 2.0 and 3.5 assumptions and assertions would become clear and compelling.

PANORAMIC PRESENTATION

A Badlands metaphor serves as a framework for a team at the Institute for the Future portraying its forecasts about the future forces that will shape the economy in the early twenty-first century. By this time graphic recording and facilitation has become a standard way of making sense out of the complex patterns IFTF studies and reports.

3. A Graphic User Interface for Teams
The Drexler/Sibbet Team Performance Model

I met Allan Drexler at a graphic facilitation workshop I was conducting on the East Coast in the early 1980s. Allan was an expert on teams, working to help large companies like General Mills deal with the inherent tensions and conflicts in the matrix-model of organization. He had developed a team-building model called the Gibb, Drexler, Weisbord Team-Building Model with the help of some other pioneers in organization development, Jack Gibb and Marvin Weisbord. Allan drew it out in that initial workshop (see illustration here). He also shared a much more complex consulting model that would follow once the team agreed on how it was going to work.

The Gibb, Drexler, Weisbord Team-Building Model

The beauty of the Gibb, Drexler, Weisbord model, and the widely popular Tuckman model (Forming, Storming, Norming, and Performing) that is similar in its stages, is its simplicity and focus on how you start a team. It describes the progression of what people care about as they enter into any group process, and especially teams. First you will want to know why you are a team, then who you are working with, then what you are doing, and finally, how you are going to work.

In the workshop I was reviewing Arthur M. Young's Theory of Process. I immediately recognized the first four stages of Allan's model as reflecting the first four stages of Young's theory, but felt that the mapping of the stages was "upside down" graphically and that the model only dealt satisfactorily with the initial phases of teaming. I imagined that the implementation and performance stages could be shown as a process of overcoming the constraints taken on during the creating stages—with one model that dealt with both creating and sustaining aspects of teaming.

Our conversation in this workshop initiated a two-year collaboration that became one of the most exciting in our professional careers, and a great example of how a team can use visualization in practice. Let me share the story of how we developed our thinking, and then provide a more formal overview of the model itself and the seven key challenges it articulates.

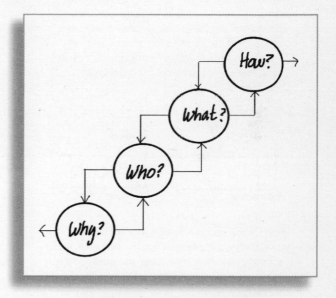

GIBB, DREXLER, WEISBORD TEAM-BUILDING MODEL

This was the drawing Allan Drexler made to explain his team-building model. It suggests that these four concerns are the most basic ones of teams. Without good answers team members go back to prior questions.

USING METAPHORS TO THINK

Much of our intuitive thinking is guided by comparing what we know to what we don't know. This is metaphoric thinking. Drawing and illustrating invites teams to be conscious about what metaphors they are using and to pick ones that are most appropriate for the task at hand. The "building/construction" metaphor did not feel as accurate for teams as did the "performance/bouncing ball" image.

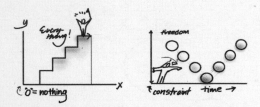

Rene Descartes developed a way of mapping numeric data that places "0" at the center of an "x" and "y" axis, with increasing quantities moving up and out from there. This kind of imaginary, mathematical space has become a standard way of making bar charts, line charts, scattergrams, and other data maps. A curious property of this way of mapping is that quantities are mapped higher on the page the larger they are. This is the reverse of people's natural orientation to having heavy things lower and immaterial things higher. Arthur M. Young reversed this convention and had the "0" point indicate "no freedom," the "y" axis move up toward more freedom, and the "x" axis indicate more time. We chose this base map for our model.

Developing a New Model for Team Development

Mental models aren't easy to change once they are established. It is even harder when they are distributed widely in an organization. If our brains were a type of computer, then mental models function like software. Allan wasn't about to abandon his model quickly. It had a lot of credibility in practice. We had to work out the details over many meetings—and our decision to cocreate a strong visual model integrating words and graphics assisted our thinking a great deal. What emerged was a synthesis of our two perspectives and a remarkably useful way to think about team process. (If you want to read more about Gibb and Young's work that underlies the TPM, check the appendix.)

From my work with visual thinking I appreciated that the name of Allan's model was drawing from one of the most common metaphors of the industrial age—"building." The implication is that each step of creating a team is like constructing a building, with each step providing a foundation for the next one. The illustration even suggested this, moving up and to the right like stair steps. But my work with Young had led me to see movement and process as more fundamental than structure, and I didn't think that implying that people are like building blocks made sense as a contemporary way to think. We ended up agreeing that working teams were much more like performing artists, actors, musicians, and athletes. We began thinking of our creative work together as developing a team *performance* model.

I had, from my work with the Group Graphics system, developed the habit of mapping information on charts in a way that resonated with the normal orientation of human beings to having the ground and "concrete reality" being down toward the bottom of the chart, and the cosmos and intuitive realities being "up" toward the top. I'd developed the habit of listening to what people say in meetings and tuning into what level of reality they were talking about, and recording appropriately. Do the little exercise suggested on this page to see what I mean about this. (For a much more developed description of these kinds of concerns see my book, *Visual Meetings*.)

Young made a very persuasive argument that these four distinctions are archetypes flowing from how humans make sense of anything. He called the framework the "four-fold operator" and had us students use the distinctions like lenses to analyze a wide range of subject matter. He saw Carl Jung's modalities of intuition, feeling, thinking, and sensing, as reflected in the Meyers-Briggs Type Indicators, as one example of this.

This kind of mapping made sense to Allan. He wanted our new model to work with all kinds of teams and be both comprehensive and accessible. I suggested that if his model was flipped upside down it would have the "why" question at the intuitive level, inside the consciousness of the new team members, and the "how" at the bottom where material plane decisions are key. Allan liked the new graphic orientation and the reasons.

Words Are Just as Important as the Graphics

Both Allan and I were concerned about the names for each stage. We agreed that what's important is that the words for the stages call up the most appropriate conversation among team members. We knew we could list more detail in the key success factors, but we wanted the top-level words to be the most useful. We decided that this first stage should be called "ORIENTATION," with the *"Why am I here?"* question as an additional reminder about the concerns at that stage.

I saw the "who" questions about trust, competency, and motivation being resonant with emotional realities. Allan argued that in all the teams he'd worked with trust was the most important element to get right. He didn't like the bias built into the Tuckman Model that called this second phase "storming." This stage isn't always a conflict, but it is always about trust. We did

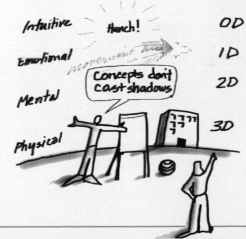

MAPPING
LEVELS OF REALITY

Listen visually to your team at different levels.

1. When you record people who are talking about tangible, physical things, draw pictures of those things in 3-D and map them toward the bottom.

2. If they are talking about concepts and ideas, using words, numbers, or images, map those in 2-D, using talk balloons, charts, and flat graphics.

3. If they talk about emotional, experiential realities—feelings and movement—use color and the movement of the lines on the chart.

4. Map intuitive realities—purpose, intention, attitude, awareness—toward the top of the chart. Point at these words with lines suggesting auras..

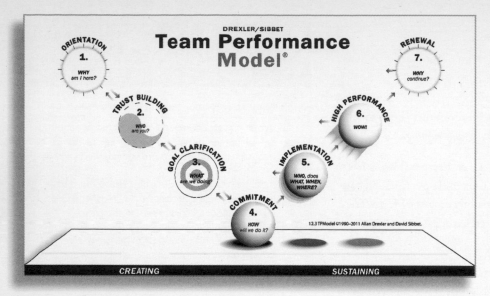

DREXLER/SIBBET

Team Performance
Model®

1. **ORIENTATION**
   WHY am I here?

2. **TRUST BUILDING**
   WHO are you?

3. **GOAL CLARIFICATION**
   WHAT are we doing?

4. **COMMITMENT**
   HOW will we do it?

5. **IMPLEMENTATION**
   WHO, does WHAT, WHEN, WHERE?

6. **HIGH PERFORMANCE**
   WOW!

7. **RENEWAL**
   WHY continue?

12.3 TPModel ©1990–2011 Allan Drexler and David Sibbet.

CREATING   SUSTAINING

DREXLER/SIBBET TEAM PERFORMANCE MODEL

The TPM shows the integration of the key questions from the Gibb, Drexler, Weisbord Team-Building Model and mine and Allan's work finding stage names that would stimulate the right conversations in teams. It has gone through 12 versions and is now widely accepted. As you can read in Chapter 17, it was also the integrating framework for making sense out of groupware (collaboration software for teams) in the Institute for the Future Groupware Users Project. The full model with keys to success follows in a few pages.

decide to name the stage "TRUST BUILDING" since that term is so widespread, and has taken on a life well beyond the metaphor of construction.

The third phase, the "what" phase, was clearly about making intellectual sense out of things and articulating clear goals and assumptions. We knew that next to having a purpose and trusting each other and your team leader, being clear about goals was the most critical step in team development. We called it "GOAL/ROLE CLARIFICATION." Later we decided the role agreements were really part of the commitment level.

The bottom-line phase was clearly the "how" phase, which involves agreeing on all the practical aspects of time, money, and resources. Mapped this way, we could literally see the journey from freedom of initial ideas to the constraint of agreeing on how to do things bottom line. We felt the central question at this moment was "COMMITMENT." In choosing the word "commitment" we realized that this word is sometimes used to mean emotional buy-in and not bottom-line agreement. But achieving bottom-line agreement is a true turning point. It is when team members become truly interdependent. Commitment, not just from the team, but from the organization that supports the team, needs to be front and center in everyone's awareness. We put a big platform representing the organization under the model to make this point clear.

Creating and Sustaining in One Framework

Our most engaged discussions were around what happens once you have created a team. Young's observation of evolutionary process in nature was that light takes on constraints as it evolves—initially a positive or negative charge at the level of forces, then an identity at the atomic level, and finally a formed substance as a molecule. Some of these molecules with branching structures—DNA and cellulose—combine to grow and reproduce themselves as plants by throwing off seeds, regaining a degree of freedom.

Young noted that in nature, this process of taking on constraints only to master them and regain freedom is a fundamental pattern. I saw the parallel with teams right away. The most constraining part of any team process is getting the approval to spend money and bring on staff and pull in other resources. Things only begin to get productive when the group makes a schedule and begins to follow it, sequencing actions over time in a direction and "throwing off" results.

We chose the word "IMPLEMENTATION" for this stage. This is when, like plants, the team learns how to sequence its work. The key question becomes *who is doing what when and where?* It is also the point at which things get a little less predicable, especially around timing. Think about any workshop or training you might have designed and led. Once you "go live" and begin to implement, the uncertainties begin, especially around how long things take.

In evolutionary process, animals learn to overcome the constraints of space through movement. We saw that this is what teams do when they master their processes and learn to adapt them over geographies and functions. We called this stage "HIGH PERFORMANCE." We saw the team as transcending the thinking level at this point and learning to be truly synergetic and improvisational. It's the *"WOW!"* stage.

Mapping these stages on the arc, we could see the team taking on constraints and then overcoming them, leading to high performance. But this involves less certainty and more degrees of freedom as new members and changes shift conditions. We saw the need for a final, reflective stage we named "RENEWAL" and believed the key question to be *Why continue?*

Achieving bottom line agreement is a true turning point. It is when team members become truly interdependent. Commitment, not just from the team, but from the organization that supports the team, needs to be front and center in everyone's awareness.

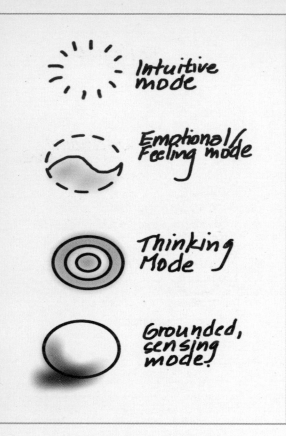

EMBEDDED GRAPHIC LANGUAGE

These are the base graphic conventions used in the TPM for the first four stages.

Designing Graphic Language Into the Model

This process of working through the model and developing all the language took several years and a great deal of testing with our clients. We worked out three keys to success for each of the seven stages based on our experience (see the spreads that follow), and developed a team performance inventory of nine questions per stage that would allow an organization or team to assess how resolved each of the team issues were for any given team. At the same time, I was working to embed the distinctions we were making about teams into the way in which the model was illustrated. We wanted both the words and the graphics to dance together in tight integration, and for the graphics to be a reminder to anyone using the model about what to look for in teams.

Why Number the Stages?

One of our key discussions was whether or not to number the stages and imply that there was a sequence to the development. I knew from working with Young's study group that all the processes we looked at had many variations in the beginning until rules and constraints were understood. Only then could it use mastery of theses constraints to regain freedom. This means that in real time a team might actually begin work by getting its goals clear and *then* spending some time on trust-building, and then argue over resources, and then maybe tune into what its real purpose is in a trial-and-error sort of way, going backwards and forwards through the stages.

So why have numbers? We decided that for a new team, the sequence indicated was the most natural way to go about addressing each concern. It also indicated which of the stages are more fundamental than others, meaning that the handling of one stage, like IMPLEMENTATION, depends on having a certain amount of clarity around the prior stage of COMMITMENT. This means, then, that the first stage, ORIENTATION to the purpose of the team and determining if you are an appropriate member, is the most fundamental concern. Then comes TRUST. Then comes CLARIFICATION. In a developed team, all seven concerns are at play. But problems in the more inclusive aspects, like IMPLEMENTATION and HIGH PERFORMANCE, are usually stemming from insufficiency in one of the earlier stages. We kept the numbers and added arrows to suggest the back and forth movement that was also possible.

Graphics in the "Bouncing Balls"

I wanted to illustrate the differences among the intuitive, feeling, thinking, and sensing levels in the TPM in subtle but clear ways, overcoming a common irony that very different kinds of phenomenon are illustrated with the same kinds of graphic symbols on a lot of conceptual models.

- A light burst indicates an intuitive mode.
- A wave icon somewhat like the yin-yang symbol points at the emotional, energetic aspect of that level.
- A target felt appropriate for the thinking mode.
- The ball becomes tangible and physical at the bottom level, when it contacts the organization itself, represented by a long platform. Having this meeting of the two commitments as a prominent feature felt very important.
- Stage five, IMPLEMENTATION, is all about sequencing, so now the balls are shown in sequence.
- HIGH PERFORMANCE is vulnerable to change, so it becomes a bubble that might burst.
- RENEWAL returns to an intuitive, reflective mode. The shadows indicate that all these latter stages are productive and "real" in that they combine the physical, mental, emotional, and intuitive in action. Before commitments are added, teaming is just talk.

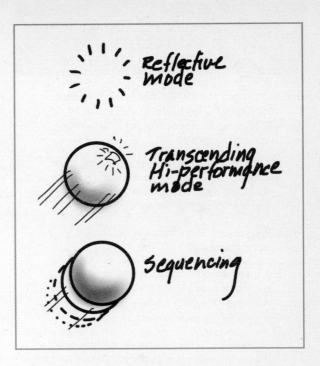

EMBEDDED GRAPHIC LANGUAGE

These are the base graphic conventions used in the TPM for the last three stages. At these stages teams have substance, symbolized by the shadow.

As you study the full TPM it will help if you pick a team that you work with as a reference. Begin with the graphic overview of the Drexler/Sibbet Team Performance Model on the next page.

1. Think of the stages as being like "lenses" of attention. Think about where different members of your team seem to have their focus. Make a pencil tick by that stage or just remember.

2. Ask yourself where the center of focus is for the team as a whole.

3. Read over the keys and see which ones your group seems to embody. This will allow you to get deeper insight into where you might have opportunities for improvement.

4. Continue on to the full spreads that describe each stage and success factors in detail and refine your perceptions.

5. Read through Sections III and IV in this book to find best practices related to the stages where you think you are stuck.

The Grove provides this model in many different sizes and formats, including a puzzle (see Appendix for ways to obtain these tools).

Keys to Success

Our final work with the model was refining the 21 "keys," included in the image of the full TPM on the next page. The following pages describe these indicators in detail—how much your team has resolved the challenges of a given stage, and what the indicators are of that set of concerns being unresolved. These words point at behaviors you can observe in most cases. In the initial stage, of course, individuals are imagining the purpose of the team and their fit with it within the freedom of their own minds, so detecting signs of how resolved these are isn't quite so obvious. But the other stages all have observable indicators. The stage names and keys provide enough information for teams to begin having a very rich discussion about team performance right away.

How to Use the TPM

The image on the next page was designed to help a team leader or team member orient to what needs to be attended to in a high-performing team. We have found people like to use just this image in the following ways.

1. **Hand out an A3 or 11x17 version** and have groups conduct the intuitive assessment as described on this page.

2. **Post a large version of the model** and have groups put sticky notes where they believe the focus of attention of the group lies. Then discuss.

3. **Have a group speculate on what the graphics and words are telling them** about team performance—noting how much development has gone into making sure that all the words and images indicate something important about team performance.

4. **Lead a team discussion about different practices** being used to respond to the challenges identified in each stage. Map these with sticky notes.

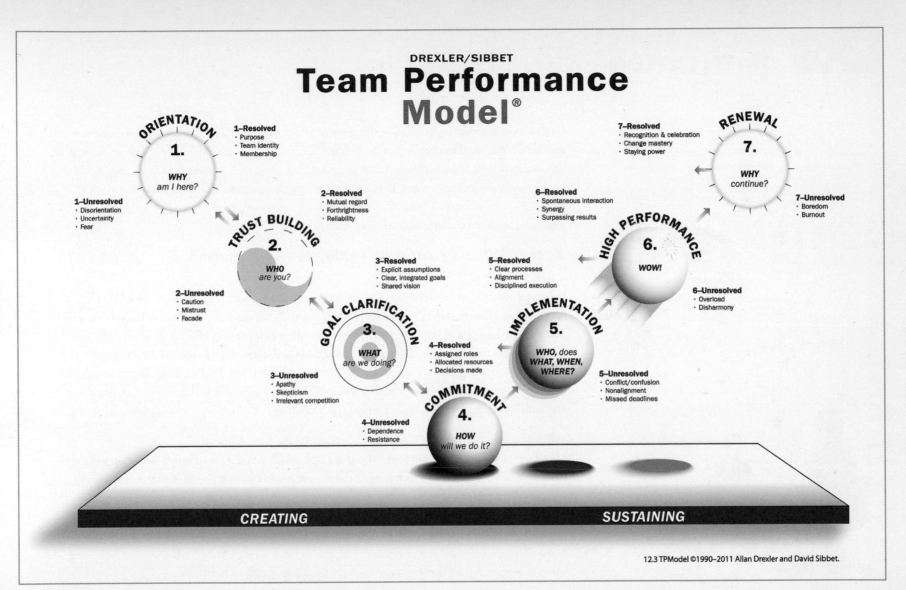

DREXLER/SIBBET

Team Performance
Model®

ORIENTATION

1.

WHY
am I here?

1–Resolved
· Purpose
· Team identity
· Membership

1–Unresolved
· Disorientation
· Uncertainty
· Fear

TRUST BUILDING

2.

WHO
are you?

2–Resolved
· Mutual regard
· Forthrightness
· Reliability

2–Unresolved
· Caution
· Mistrust
· Facade

GOAL CLARIFICATION

3.

WHAT
are we doing?

3–Resolved
· Explicit assumptions
· Clear, integrated goals
· Shared vision

3–Unresolved
· Apathy
· Skepticism
· Irrelevant competition

COMMITMENT

4.

HOW
will we do it?

4–Resolved
· Assigned roles
· Allocated resources
· Decisions made

4–Unresolved
· Dependence
· Resistance

IMPLEMENTATION

5.

WHO, does
WHAT, WHEN,
WHERE?

5–Resolved
· Clear processes
· Alignment
· Disciplined execution

5–Unresolved
· Conflict/confusion
· Nonalignment
· Missed deadlines

HIGH PERFORMANCE

6.

WOW!

6–Resolved
· Spontaneous interaction
· Synergy
· Surpassing results

6–Unresolved
· Overload
· Disharmony

RENEWAL

7.

WHY
continue?

7–Resolved
· Recognition & celebration
· Change mastery
· Staying power

7–Unresolved
· Boredom
· Burnout

CREATING

SUSTAINING

12.3 TPModel ©1990–2011 Allan Drexler and David Sibbet.

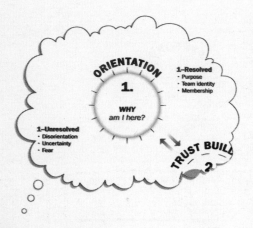

Stage 1:

ORIENTATION—*WHY Am I Here?*

Orientation is about understanding the purpose of a team and assessing what it will mean to be a member. You need to understand the reason the team exists, what will be expected of you, and how you will benefit from membership. In a new team, these are individual concerns, because the group is only potentially a team. That is why these concerns are illustrated as occurring in your imagination at an intuitive level. As a team leader it is important to provide time and space for people to answer these internal questions themselves.

Keys to When Orientation Challenges Are Resolved

• Team Purpose

Everyone on an effective team needs an answer to the key orientation question, "**WHY** *am I here?*" If you are invited to be on a team you will assuredly form a story of why the team exists and what is expected of it. If you can't you probably won't participate very effectively. This is why setting direction and clarifying charters is so central to team leadership. To the extent you personally embrace the stated purposes, you begin to identify with the team. To the extent that the purpose is vague or at odds with what the members care about, you may well withhold your allegiance and feel disorientation, uncertainty, and maybe even fear. A team's purpose is its reason for being.

• Team Identity

Members of well-functioning teams also share a personal connection to its work and are willing to identify with it. This involves having conviction that you can make a difference to the team and that the work of the team will be relevant to your personal interests. The emphasis in the key question shifts to "*Why am I here?*" This sense may be undeveloped at the beginning of a new team with no history, but should get stronger as it becomes clearer to you that the team is important and needed. A team leader needs to keep his or her eye on members who seem to be having trouble connecting and feeling good about being associated with the team.

• Membership

The orientation stage also concerns the social dynamics of the team as a whole. The focal question shifts to, *"Why are WE here?"* If you know who you are as a team, what you stand for, and what you are about, then you will form a strong sense of yourselves as one group. In the beginning, if you are a new participant you will probably be concerned about whether or not you will be accepted as a full member in the group. If this concern is well handled everyone can focus more fully on the work. When you feel isolated and not accepted, it will definitely affect your performance.

As a team leader, taking responsibility for orientation at the beginning of a team's life, and sustaining attention to it throughout its work, is one of the primary jobs of a leader. People need to be able to see how their individual work links with the overall purpose of the team. This is what "providing direction" means on a personal level.

When a Team Is Blocked at Stage 1, Members May Show . . .

• Uncertainty

Often a team's purpose is not clear in the beginning, or some members know the purpose while others do not. If you are uncertain about why the team has been formed, you will more than likely resist moving forward.

• Disorientation/Fear

Disorientation may trigger anxiety or even fear. Deep inside all of us is a survival instinct to run away from or fight things that feel threatening. In the void of not knowing a team's purpose, or having no information about personal fit or membership, you may be fearful of what team membership offers.

WHAT VISUAL TEAMS DO TO ORIENT

Here are some of the best practices of visual teams at this stage. Many of these will be elaborated in the following chapters.

❏ Take time to **imagine success** and even draw out some pictures of what it might look like.

❏ Create a **graphic purpose and mission poster** that each team member can keep for reference.

❏ Create a **graphic charter** for the team, listing out all the expectations and reasons for being a team.

❏ Record a **visual history** of the story of how the team came to be, inviting in some of the sponsors (like I did with the HP BLAST team described in Chapter 1).

❏ Hold a **team leader meeting** with each member to share why he or she was invited on the team and inviting him or her to imagine the contribution he or she can make.

❏ Have an important stakeholder attend your first meeting or web conference as a **visible symbol** of the importance of the team to the large organization.

TRUST BUILDING—*WHO* Are You?

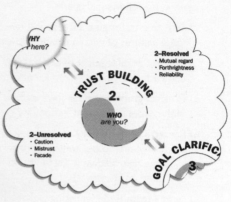

Trust is a measure of your willingness to work together with others for something important. Because team members have to depend on each other to be successful, trust is essential in direct relation to how much cooperation is needed to get the job done. In the beginning of a new team's life, trust involves some risk and uncertainty about dealing with strangers. This is why the key question is *"Who are you?"* An unstated aspect of this question is wondering, *"What will you expect from me?"* For a team to work well, you need to accept that you can depend on team members to work together to accomplish the team's purpose.

Keys to When Trust Challenges Are Resolved

• Mutual Regard

For trust to sustain itself among team members, people need to open up to each other's talents and contributions, and empathize with each other's personal challenges. Mutual regard is one result of this kind of trust, and is built over time through knowledge and experience. Trust is foundational to all subsequent stages and builds as the team grows. Mutual regard should grow stronger as a team successfully resolves its different challenges and concerns.

• Forthrightness

When trust is strong, information flows among team members. You are forthright with one another, willing to share your expertise and tell the truth. You have confidence in one another, enough to air your views and come to grips with differences of opinion. This quality differs a bit across cultures. Americans expect to be forthright early on. Other cultures may be more reserved initially and open up later, say during implementation or high performance.

• Reliability

To trust other team members you also have to know enough about them to believe that they have the competency necessary to fulfill their roles and will act in the best interests of the team.

This quality may not be assessable at first, but can surface as a trust issue during later implementation issues. If you are joining a team and know someone who has a reputation for unreliability, this will affect your participation. This is another quality that will grow as the team develops. If a sense of reliability doesn't appear, then perhaps understanding of the purpose and importance of the team needs to improve. New team members may need more oversight and guidance from the leader if they don't understand what being interdependent means.

As team leader, investing in trust building early pays off later on. It is especially important to pay attention to this set of concerns if your team is culturally diverse, dispersed, and cross boundary. Facilitating relationships is primarily about building trust among members. The higher the trust level among team members, the less work there will be for you in handling relationship issues.

When a Team Is Blocked at Stage 2, Members May Show . . .

• Caution/Façade

Skepticism, passivity, silence, and mask-like exteriors among team members are signs that they feel cautious or may mistrust each other. The failure to share critical information and address important issues undercuts team effectiveness. Again, bear in mind that for some cultures this would be quite normal at early stages of the team's life.

• Mistrust

Manipulation and deceit quickly undermine team spirit. Simple withholding of information, hidden agendas, or failing to meet promises can do the same. The failure to address these issues will erode trust still further. Cultural differences play a strong role in trust building. Some cultures are what is called "high context," where people expect to know each other personally, know about families, laugh, and play together. Other cultures are "low context" and expect to focus on tasks.

<aside>

WHAT VISUAL TEAMS DO TO BUILD TRUST

Some of the best visual practices for trust building are the following:

❑ Create a **team portrait** listing the skills and resources each person is bringing to the team.

❑ **Share photos** before a web conference and record a round of personal information at the beginning of a meeting on a composite group portrait.

❑ **Use templates** for breakout groups that allow everyone a chance to contribute. Mapping the larger context, team challenges, history, and benefits of working together all lend themselves to this kind of graphic work.

❑ Create a **stakeholder map** with sticky notes and share observations about different stakeholder interests.

❑ **Review the TPM** and talk about what you can expect from the process of working together through the different stages.

❑ **Record some ground rules** for working together.

❑ Have everyone make a **poster of the best team experience** they have ever had and share these in small groups (or as a whole group if you are a small team).

</aside>

GOAL CLARIFICATION—*WHAT Are We Doing?*

Sometimes teams have precise charters that specify what they are responsible for accomplishing. More often, they are given a broad mandate and need to make choices about how they will pursue that mandate and translate it into goals. *"What Are We Doing?"* is a more specific question than the larger question of purpose asked during Orientation. During this stage of a new team's life, it will need to do research and develop clear understanding of the job that is required, as well as generate agreements about goals and specific deliverables.

Keys to When Goal Clarification Challenges Are Resolved

• Explicit Assumptions

If your team is new, there is information that you must exchange to develop mutual understanding of the work involved. Working through the interdependency analysis suggested in Chapter 2 is a good way to surface assumptions about what parts of the work need close cooperation. When problem solving, it helps to describe problems before trying to solve them. Being explicit means listening past positions to underlying interests and assumptions, developing a foundation of mutual understanding in service of more creative solutions. Strategy teams need to spend time examining the relevant environment and organizational capabilities to feel confident in whatever priorities end up being agreed upon. It's safe to assume that assumptions are explicit if you can write them down and visualize them! This is one of the clear and consistent advantages of working as a visual team.

• Clear Integrated Goals

The central task in Stage 3 is to specifically clarify what your team is to do. This means integrating the long-term goals expressed in your overall mission with short-term objectives concerning deliverables and immediate results you must produce. Objectives serve as progress markers that are as measurable or testable as possible. This phase also involves you setting your own goals in alignment with the team goals, especially if you are in a workgroup where people work somewhat independently. Goals are clear when you can write them down and create a version that people can post in their work space.

• Shared Vision

Implicit in high performance is the idea that team members are inspired to excel. Extensive research on sports performance shows that high performers can imagine success, and see it vividly. This is what it means to have a vision. As a team leader, if you can lead your group to articulate a real vision of what success looks like if you accomplish your goals, your chances of reaching them are greater. A vision provides the focus and energy that brings objectives to life and brings meaning to hard work. The process of creating a graphic version of your vision is a great way to make sure it is a shared vision.

When a Team Is Blocked at Stage 3, Members May Show . . .

• Apathy and Skepticism

People respond differently to unclear goals. Quiet, sensitive people may find themselves retreating from argumentative discussions. Analytical people may find themselves skeptically questioning the team's readiness to move on.

• Irrelevant Competition

Take-charge people might aggressively challenge ideas and people even on minor points. Recognizing that nonconstructive activity is taking place can help your team focus on the concerns underlying the actions.

WHAT VISUAL TEAMS DO TO CLARIFY GOALS

This is a stage where being visual makes a huge difference regarding clarity and efficiency. Some of the best practices are:

❑ Develop **"Voice of Your Customers" maps** that illustrate real field research.

❑ Cocreate **Drivers-of-Change maps**.

❑ Create **graphic case studies** of past successes.

❑ **Brainstorm problems visually** using graphic recording, sticky notes, and idea maps.

❑ Do **force-field analysis** of what is supporting and resisting your work.

❑ Use **sticky notes and affinity diagrams**.

❑ Create **goal alignment charts** showing the connection with larger organizational goals.

❑ Create **SMART objectives** that are specific, measurable, actionable, relevant, and timely.

❑ Create **graphic visions** of the team project.

❑ Share **videos from interviews** about customer and stakeholder interests.

❑ Post team info in an **online team room**.

❑ Use **tablets to record web** conferences.

❑ Use **target visuals for teleconference**—sending out proposals, plans, or sets of goals—gathering input, then publishing a second version with changes.

COMMITMENT—*HOW* Will We Do It?

When goals are clear and options are identified, your team is probably eager to act. Attention moves to the question, *"How will we do it?"* This stage occurs at the bottom of the "V" in the TPM, the point of greatest constraint. This means commiting to a specific course of action, making decisions about resources, and being clear about roles. These are also the indicators of having addressed the "turn." Remember that the initial stages of team performance involve a good bit of trial-and-error. Embracing these questions might require backtracking to goals, investing more in trust development, and revisiting initial purpose before you can fully resolve commitment issues.

Keys to When Commitment Challenges Are Resolved

• Assigned Roles

As your team turns toward implementation everyone will want to be clear about roles and responsibilities. You may have considered these during stage three planning, but now need to commit to what your function, authority, and responsibilities will be in practice. Role definitions have to be complete enough to cover all the tasks that must be done to accomplish your team goals while minimizing overlaps and role conflicts. A big part of your job if you are the team leader is to help match goals to competencies, and help people step into roles that will develop their abilities and improve results for the team.

• Allocated Resources

In addition to role clarity, your team must deal with another constraint—how to provide for and deploy its limited resources, including time, money, and so forth. These hard choices usually involve setting aside some useful tasks because the resources are not available to support them. Indecision in this area breeds confusion and stalls work. For virtual teams, decisions about tools and communication platforms are essential at this stage. Teams may have to negotiate with the larger organization to get the kind of tools and support they need. This is why the TPM intersects the organization "platform" at this stage.

• Decisions Made

Finally, a team needs to get clear about how members will handle decision making. Will authority be shared? How will you stay in touch with one another? Who can spend what funds? In a dynamic work environment where plans can change frequently, decisions about course corrections are common. Thinking through in advance how these will be handled moves the team's focus more productively toward implementation and high performance.

When your team commits to roles, resources, and decision making and sets its course, you will probably feel a real release of energy—a "bounce" in the metaphor of the TPM. Work begins to progress. Actions begin to sequence over time. This is what Young describes as a "turn"—in this case toward high performance.

When a Team Is Blocked at Stage 4, Members May Show . . .

• Dependence/Resistance

You can tell when your team is not committed when you see members acting in one of two ways:

1. **Dependent**—They do not feel they really understand how the work should proceed and what commitments have been made. They keep looking to the leader or another strong group member for guidance.

2. **Resistant**—They act annoyed. They actively resist whoever is providing direction or passively resist by failing to give their commitments priority. These behaviors occur because the call to make the turn to implementation was premature and the team lacks the commitments it needs to work effectively.

Commemorating agreements visually grounds commitments in visible reference documents. Here are some of the best practices.

❏ Create **graphic action plans** with clear role assignments.

❏ Have individuals make **responsibilities posters** and have everyone review each other's lists for accuracy and agreement.

❏ Use **graphic metaphors** of comparable kinds of teams to sort out roles and suggest ways of working together.

❏ Use a **Sow, Grow, Harvest, Plow four-box template** of where you are spending the team's resources and on what.

❏ **Map infrastructure requirements** illustrating all tools, supplies, software, licenses, and other materials you need to work effectively.

❏ Review the **chart of decision styles** in this book and develop a common language.

❏ Create **decision funnels** that cycle through proposals, dot voting, discussion, high-low sorting, and commitment checks—recording each step visually.

❏ Set up so you can work visually in distributed meetings—**purchase tablets for recording.**

IMPLEMENTATION—*WHO* Does *WHAT, WHEN,* and *WHERE?*

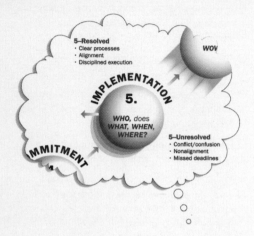

Implementation involves scheduling and sequencing work over time. The key question is *"Who does what, when, and where?"* A visible schedule, strategy, and/or process liberates the team to move into action confidently. Conflicts and confusion arise when there is commitment but no clear way forward.

Keys to When Implementation Challenges Are Resolved

• Clear Processes

Confusion over how to schedule and sequence work ties up a great deal of energy and attention on a team. When the sequence of work is understood, you can devote yourself to the work itself. If you are the team leader you may be expected to be the one who drives for results and helps resolve issues dealing with process. Cross-boundary and culturally diverse teams have more challenges agreeing on common processes. Time zones and travel schedules complicate people getting together. But any kind of team appreciates knowing who does what when. Describing the way visual teams use charting to get clear on processes will be a big part of the chapters in Section IV.

• Alignment

It is not enough to have clear processes. They need to be aligned with the purpose and goals you set earlier. Sometimes the processes need to adapt, like a sailboat tacking in the wind. Collaborative drawing up and revising schedules directly grows alignment in self-managed teams. If your job is team leader, reinforcing the directions in which the team is moving is a big part of the job. Alignment also involves working horizontally with associated teams and vertically with other parts of the organization that need to support your work. On large, cross-functional task forces and project teams, creating large process murals of strategies and roadmaps serves as a framework for getting agreement and alignment.

• Disciplined Execution

People on effective teams need to keep their commitments and pay attention to timing and delivery of what they promise. This is essential if separate tasks are to integrate into a smooth operation that delivers results. Coordinating sequence and timing, meshing activities, and keeping the whole system in balance is what project management and disciplined execution means in practice. Parts must integrate with the whole if your team is to experience full benefit from everyone's individual contributions.

When a Team Is Blocked at Stage 5, Members May Show . . .

• Conflict, Nonalignment, and Missed Deadlines

If you missed your fourth deadline and find yourself blaming team members, you have implementation problems. Other signs might be disagreements about quality standards and cost factors. These are signs that processes are not clear. Reflect on the earlier stages of team process and see if you can spot areas you rushed by or neglected. Suggest a team meeting to resolve misunderstandings and strengthen commitments.

One of the insights Young's work on process brings forward is the way in which processes in nature nest inside each other and repeat. During implementation your team will reexperience all the stages of the TPM, but now operating within a set of commitments to collaborative action. You will revisit orientation, trust, goal clarity, and commitments as you move through implementation, but with much more traction and focus. This is why a little arrow from the IMPLEMENTATION stage points back toward the four foundational elements of the creating stages.

If you've worked as a visual team, then bringing out key charts and target documents allows your team to do this looping back quite easily.

HOW VISUAL TEAMS IMPLEMENT

Visual teams have a real advantage when it comes to working across time and space. Here are some of the practices:

❑ **Graphic road maps and schedules** allow everyone to see the streams of activity and major milestones.

❑ **Review process maps** and diagrams are for understanding of structure and timing.

❑ **Gantt charts** are used to track activity.

❑ **Gather key metrics** and use **data visualization** to stay on top of quality issues—using the visual tools of Total Quality Management.

❑ Use **graphically facilitated problem-solving sessions** face-to-face and online to brainstorm ideas and solutions.

❑ Make **graphic proposals** for what deliverables should look like.

❑ Share **online documents** through networks and "the cloud."

❑ Use **scheduling walls** in studios and facilities.

❑ Use **online screen sharing** to share visual documents, actively record in web conferences, and connect with video.

❑ Use smartphones to **share snapshots and video reports** from the field.

❑ Keep **visible logs of progress** and activity.

HIGH PERFORMANCE—*WOW!*

High performance is a *"WOW"* state, as a team masters its processes and begins to experience the ability to change goals as well as achieve them. You can feel when it happens and observe its effects, but not necessarily control it. Teams achieve a flow state when trust is high and people have mastered their roles. In a state of high performance, boundaries and individual limits soften, everything moves together, and everyone responds as if they are part of a whole. The indicators of that having happened are spontaneous interaction, synergy, and a team that is surpassing their expectations on results. *"WOW"* symbolizes how high performance teams transcend rational processes by working with all the human faculties—spirit, soul, mind, and body.

Keys to When High Performance Challenges Are Resolved

• Spontaneous Interaction
When trust and acceptance of one another supports a lively give and take, and mutual knowledge of one another enables everyone to communicate clearly and efficiently, anticipating one another's needs, and becoming more spontaneous, high-performing teams are spirited and creative in ways that set them apart. Since flexibility and adaptability is one of the features of high-performing teams, being able to improvise is essential.

• Synergy
"Synergy" is the phenomenon of a whole manifesting characteristics not present in the separate parts. In high performance, it seems as if something bigger is happening than anything that could be achieved from individual efforts. This is what emerges when people bring out the best in one another, pushing beyond what any of them are able to accomplish individually.

• Surpassing Results
High-performing teams get results above and beyond initial expectations. A crisis may release bursts of cooperation and energy that allow people to rise to an occasion. A team can experience a

breakthrough by working hard to solve problems and creating a foundation for high trust and flexibility. Sometimes the "chemistry" is just right and teams find themselves experiencing what some call "flow states" and the "zone." Sports teams and performers know this feeling, and know that it is not a steady state, but dependent on many factors. Hard work, practice, mastery of tools, and an openness to high performance being possible all optimize the chance that true high performance will manifest.

It is important to distinguish the kinds of high performance resulting from overwork and wasteful expenditure of resources from ones that reflect mastery of constraints and processes.

When a Team Is Blocked at Stage 6, Members May Show . . .

• Overload and Disharmony

High performance is not stable. Successful teams can become hyperactive, accept too much work, or become workaholics. You may be high-performing for a while and then have team members assigned to other teams and find that the energy has begun to disperse. Another common challenge is having to bring on new team members who haven't gone through the earlier processes and aren't fully aligned and aware of all the operating agreements. Symptoms may include increases in grumbling and expressed discontent, or in extreme cases, sickness and stress conditions.

Being on too many teams or being too distributed also gets in the way of teams experiencing high performance. This kind of overload can't be handled by the team alone, but needs to be addressed by the organization as a whole.

HOW DO VISUAL TEAMS SUPPORT HIGH PERFORMANCE?

Superior performance results from mastering team communications and learning to adapt quickly to changes. The practices visual teams use are the following:

❑ **Debrief meetings** by recording what works and what could improve.

❑ Hold **"pop-up sessions"** to share observations, conclusions, and new ideas about how to improve work.

❑ Readjust with **graphically facilitated problem-solving sessions.**

❑ Use the **TPS assessments** to review performance and identify areas for improvement.

❑ **Analyze workflows** with sticky note diagrams to find efficiencies.

❑ Find **powerful metaphors and analogies** that allow team members to communicate about complicated matters effectively.

❑ Learn to use **audio-graphics and web conferences** to do problem solving and coordination at a distance.

❑ Create **video conferences and shared whiteboard** capability for remote teams.

Stage 7:
RENEWAL—WHY *Continue?*

Over time the conditions that initially set your team in motion will change. High performance is demanding. Don't be surprised if people ask, *"Why continue?"* This key question reminds us that team performance is an ongoing process, and must be renewed by returning to Stage 1 and reassessing if the work is still needed, worthwhile, and has some personal value and meaning. Spending time on renewal puts your team back in touch with meaning and purpose and refreshes everyone's commitment to keep going. It also includes learning from what you have accomplished, and building a repertoire of best practices for the next journey on this or other teams.

If your team's work is completed, RENEWAL is the time to wrap things up, freeing members to move on to new challenges.

Keys to When Renewal Challenges Are Resolved

• Recognition and Celebration

Whether you are recharging to continue or are completing your team's work, acknowledging people and celebrating their contributions is important. It helps complete key cycles and allows everyone to move on with good feeling. Recognition is one of the strongest forces in creating great places to work. If you've been working as a visual team you will have lots of displays and props you can bring out on these occasions, and tangible ways to tracking back and comparing how performance matches with plans.

• Managing Change

In today's dynamic environment, teams need to learn to invest directly in change management and transition. This may involve integrating new people, working out leadership transitions, or realigning team roles so that members are working with motivation and competence. If you are the team leader then consciously taking time for this kind of activity will allow team members the chance to reinvest in each other and new team members or new managers.

• Staying Power

Teams are always in transition. Renewal means examining what has been learned, so that it carries forward to the next challenge. Ideas, discoveries, and new practices emerge out of team experiences that are worth capturing and sharing. One of the advantages of visual teams is having the skills and tools for creating useful communications to other parts of the organization and future team members. Some organizations actually require contribution to general knowledge bases at the end of projects to increase their competitiveness and staying power.

When a Team Is Blocked at Stage 7, Members May Show . . .

• Boredom and Burnout

If your team takes no time for renewal you and your fellow teammates will inevitably burn out. Working nights and weekends may be necessary on occasion, but it is generally an indication that a team is not practicing renewal. Are members of your team complaining a lot or counting the hours until breaks? Are members feeling underappreciated or disengaged? It may be time to take a long look at your team effectiveness and start over.

In your own reflections while reading the rest of this book, remember that the TPM is consciously designed to support understanding a full range of possibilities across many kinds of workgroups and teams. It functions like a piano keyboard functions for a musician, in having an ordered set of "notes" that are organized in a logical progression, in this case from fundamental and basic to more inclusive and complex. But the life of teams has as many variations in how these "notes" are played as real music. It makes a big difference to have a shared language about all this—just as having the eight-tone scale empowers music.

HOW VISUAL TEAMS SUPPORT RENEWAL

At this stage, if a team has been working visually there are lots of ways of revisiting key agreements and processes. Here are some of the best practices.

❏ **Visually review accomplishments** with a large display that looks at different phases of your project.

❏ Visualize the **story of your team journey** by creating a graphic storyboard.

❏ **Revisit the vision and action plans** and see where they need to be changed.

❏ Use **rituals and celebrations** to visibly mark endings and transitions.

❏ **Write up best practices** and add them to your team repository.

❏ Create **special environments** for recognition events.

❏ Hold a **"Back-on-Board" session** inviting people to express needs on sticky notes.

❏ Create a **celebratory video** that reviews the work and results of the team.

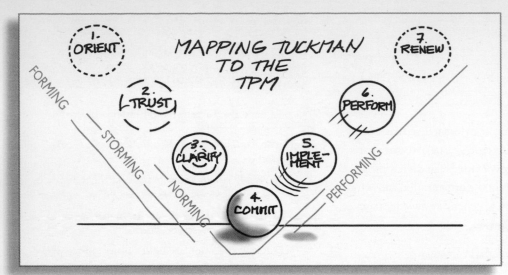

MAPPING TUCKMAN TO THE TPM

Relating TPM to Tuckman

I suggested at the start of this chapter that mental models are a bit like software, and once "installed" are hard to change. If you are in an organization using the Tuckman model (shown here) you will want to be able to explain how it relates. It is one of the most popular simple models for teamwork, formulated by Bruce Tuckman in 1966. Its four stages are memorable, describing the process that teams go through as Forming, Storming, Norming, and Performing.

TUCKMAN MODEL

Here is a graphic mapping of the Tuckman model onto the TPM. The way Tuckman describes the stages, they are combinations of the TPM stages and reflect the way teams cycle through primary concerns as they progress.

This progress is reflecting the same pattern in process illustrated in the TPM, with different names. There are two ways of understanding the connection. One would be to see the four stages as substituting for the first four stages of the TPM. A more accurate way would be to see them overlapping. I've come to appreciate that the trial and error process of orienting, trust-building, and clarifying goals is the "Forming" stage. "Storming" clearly points to the trust-building stage of the TPM, but also includes struggles to get clear on goals and potential conflicts over bottom-line commitments. The reason the Tuckman model seems to resonate with teams stems from the well-researched fact that people in groups need to sort out their social relationships before they can work effectively together. The illustration shown here seems to be the most appropriate way to connect them.

Five Dysfunctions of a Team

Many organizations love Patrick Lencioni's fable, *Five Dysfunctions of a Team,* and related materials from his Table Group. He models the five, shown here mapped on the TPM, in a pyramid, with "absence of trust" as the foundation. This is a classic application of a simple framework model to

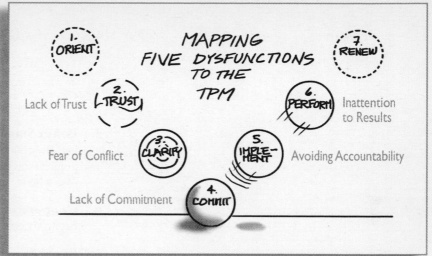

something that is inherently dynamic. When working with several clients who use this system, Laurie Durnell, director of consulting for The Grove, had the insight that the TPM is really a set of preventions related to these dysfunctions. The "lack of trust" is rooted in fear of vulnerability. Gibb's research on people's need for membership and acceptance early on supports this insight. The "fear of conflict" is characterized as unwillingness to have productive, ideological engagement, an obstacle to getting clear about assumptions and goals. "Lack of commitment" as a third dysfunction is completely harmonic with the TPM.

If you understand "avoiding accountability" as being unwilling to have your actions align with agreements, the whole idea makes little sense apart from implementation concerns. Accountability is one of the keys to disciplined execution.

Lencioni's fifth dysfunction, "inattention to results," describes a state of unwillingness to be aware of the impact and implications of implementation. This kind of unconsciousness stands directly in the way of high performance as Allan and I characterize it.

Cog's Ladder

Another popular team model is Cog's Ladder, outlined by George Charrier at Procter & Gamble in 1972. It outlines five stages in group development that map to Tuckman and TPM.

1. **Polite Stage**: An introductory phase where members get acquainted with one another and set the basis for group structure. It is characterized by polite social interaction and is characteristic of Stage 1 of the TPM.

2. **Why We're Here Stage**: This stage in Cog's also maps to Stage 1 of the TPM and

FIVE DYSFUNCTIONS OF A TEAM

Patrick Lencioni's fable about the ways teams get in trouble has been a perennial best seller since it was published in 2002. It mirrors the TPM almost one for one, includes forming social cliques.

3. **Power Stage**: Cog's model, like Tuckman's, emphasizes the struggle aspect of trust building. The counter-dependent and resistant behaviors characterized in Stage 4 of the TPM point to this possibility if commitment issues are left to drift, or contests develop in Stage 3 over who is "right."

4. **Cooperation Stage**: This describes the turn to implementation in the TPM, and what it begins to feel like as work gets under way.

5. **Esprit Stage**: This is Cog's term for the High Performance stage in the TPM, and is described as dependent on the prior stages for manifestation.

It is interesting that this model evokes a "ladder" and "end state" metaphor, and ignores the cyclical aspect of group process that underlies the need to invest in renewal.

II. Leading Visual Teams
Seeing the BIG Picture

II: Leading Visual Teams

Chapter 4: So You've Just Been Promoted A team needs to know how you think about your team leader role. What is the importance of having purpose and intention? How do you facilitate relationship building and trust? How do you support communication and learning? What does it mean to drive for results? This chapter describes these key leadership tasks.

Chapter 5: Managing Four Flows of Activity There are four levels of leadership that need attention on any team. What are the best practices for managing these as a leader?

Chapter 6: Supporting Innovation How do you move from working on problems directly to creating an environment where the whole team can work on problems together? How do you introduce visual problem solving? How do you use assessments to support dialogues for improvement?

4: So You've Just Been Promoted
Understanding Team Leadership

This next section is written to those of you who have just been promoted to team leadership, or want to rethink your role. If you are not a team leader, and aren't interested in this part of the book, you can move right to Section III and the chapters that describe the tools and approaches for creating a team from the beginning, and then in Section IV about how to sustain it over time.

What Are the Basics of Team Leadership?

In the early 2000s, following the crash in the dot-com industry, companies in Silicon Valley were focused on recovering their momentum. The cry with my clients was "back to basics." Agilent Technologies, the company that spun off the original instrumentation businesses from Hewlett Packard, decided to launch a new front-line manager training program with "back-to-basics" as the theme. Leadership within the company thought the training should focus on three areas that I still believe are the basics that any new team leader needs to understand. They chose the TPM as an integrating framework and then emphasized some top and bottom-line skills regarding management by objectives (MBO), and Situation Leadership. To support the course they engaged The Grove to create a *Team Leader's Guide* that integrated best practices for new team leaders with the TPM. This book elaborates on many of the core ideas in that guide (available in a public version through The Grove).

Team Performance

The TPM provides a reliable checklist of things to attend to, not only for teams but for first-line managers. For instance, it underlines the importance of beginning with a clear purpose, and then focusing on building trust and clarity around goals as foundation elements in the team. The first four stages of the TPM are divided into four tasks that were expressed in leadership terms and visualize a model that illustrated these four as a "frame" that a leader can hold onto to direct the different flows of activity on the team.

HOW AM I THINKING ABOUT THIS CHALLENGE?

Imagine the TPM flowing in repeating patterns like music, and the team leader providing a "frame" around these activities that guides the flow.

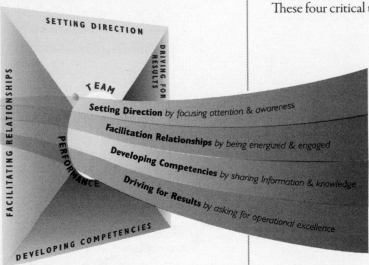

SETTING DIRECTION

DRIVING FOR RESULTS

FACILITATING RELATIONSHIPS

TEAM

Setting Direction *by focusing attention & awareness*

Facilitation Relationships *by being energized & engaged*

Developing Competencies *by sharing Information & knowledge*

Driving for Results *by asking for operational excellence*

PERFORMANCE

DEVELOPING COMPETENCIES

Here is how you might visualize it. Each of these critical tasks of a leader persists all the way through each of the seven stages of team performance.

Critical Leadership Tasks

These four critical tasks are called:

1. **Setting direction**

2. **Facilitating relationships**

3. **Building competencies**

4. **Driving for results**

By focusing on these four tasks you as a team leader can manage the four flows of activity that are true for any team. In the next chapter we will explore practices for doing each of these.

Task 1:
Setting Direction and Creating Clear Charters

Let's return to the first of the leadership jobs—setting direction. What does it mean to have purpose and intention, and how does this mesh with "managing by objectives"? Managing by objectives (MBO) was first popularized in the 1950s after World War II. Organizational thinking was still heavily influenced by what was called scientific management. This school of thought held that organizations and teams would work best if you matched the right person with the right job, and were very clear about defining and measuring competencies, and defining and measuring tasks, and analytically matching everything up. In extreme cases you might think that people using scientific management believed that organizations were like machines, and just needed to be tuned and adjusted.

If you are in an organization that determines pay and promotions based on performance, wouldn't you want to have your objectives be as clear as possible? Many businesses are very oriented to creating financial results, and are constantly working to have teams focus on specific things that will make a difference in the bottom line. When you read Chapter 9 on Clarifying Goals, I will explain some specific best practices for generating SMART objectives.

Going Beyond Goals to Purpose and Intention

The TPM is suggesting that before goals and objectives can be clear, your team needs to be oriented to its purpose, members need to feel that their participation is a good fit, and everyone needs to trust each other enough to be able to focus on the work at hand. Helping direct this process and set a good direction is one of the key tasks for leadership.

Let's examine what this entails. The word "purpose" or "mission" is often defined as a "reason for being." When people enter into a new team, everyone is telling themselves a story about why the team got started, and it usually doesn't appear as SMART goals. Jack Gibb's research, Arthur M. Young's thoughts on process, and my own experience all suggest that in one's own imagination these appear more often as something that feels like a story, and may be laced with feelings, impressions, and hunches about the eventual outcome.

If you've just been promoted to being a team leader, there are some predictable questions your team members are probably asking themselves privately.

- Why are YOU our team leader?
- What's in it for you?
- Why am I being asked to be on another team? I'm too busy!

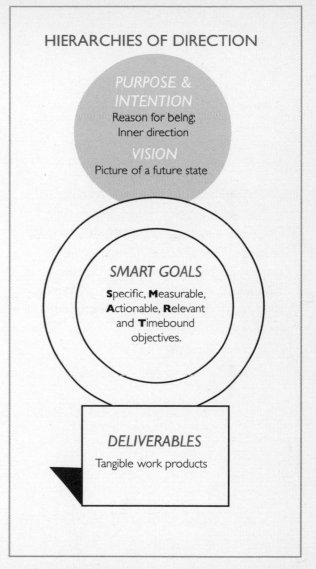

HIERARCHIES OF DIRECTION

PURPOSE & INTENTION
Reason for being;
Inner direction
VISION
Picture of a future state

SMART GOALS
Specific, **M**easurable, **A**ctionable, **R**elevant and **T**imebound objectives.

DELIVERABLES
Tangible work products

- I'm new here. Will you (as our team leader) appreciate me?
- Is this assignment going help me in my own career?
- Are we going to be able to do this?

These kinds of questions are not going to be satisfied by having SMART objectives alone. They need to be addressed by you connecting with and sharing your own answers to these questions and embodying a sense of purpose in your very being. Purpose and mission tell this kind of story and point at why the team was formed.

A second quality, your "intention," is what you personally determined to accomplish given your mission. "In-tension" means just that—having and holding a vision that is "in tension" with current realities. If you are holding a steady idea of what you are trying to accomplish right in the midst of the realities that stand in your way, you will experience psychic tension!!! And in asking your team to step up they will experience tension.

But this kind of tension is exactly what catalyzes high performance if you are willing to embrace it and not let it resolve too quickly. Communicating about all this is the starting point in leadership.

Leadership and Mastery

Early in my consulting I was able to attend a workshop called Leadership and Mastery that Innovation Associates, Peter Senge's original consulting firm, conducted here in the San Francisco Bay area. Peter is now well-known for having written the *Fifth Discipline: The Art & Practice of the Learning Organization*. He also helped create the Society on Organizational Learning, and has done more to bring systems thinking and environmental consciousness into the realm of actionable tools than almost anyone in the organizational development field. Embedded in the training was a principle that has come to shape my own thinking about intention and what it means. It

Your "intention" is what you are determined to accomplish given your mission. "In-tension" means just that—having and holding a vision that is "in tension" with current realities . . . this kind of tension is exactly what catalyzes high performance if you are willing to embrace it and not let it resolve too quickly.

was a set of insights that Peter gained from Robert Fritz, author of *Path of Least Resistance: Learning to Become the Creative Force in Your Own Life*.

The workshop leaders passed out rubber bands and had all of us stretch these and feel the tension embodied in the stretched rubber. "Imagine that this rubber band is you," they said. "If your upper finger on the rubber band represents your vision, and the lower one represents current reality, when you stretch it you will experience what structural tension feels like. This is not a stable system!" Robert Fritz believed that this kind of systemic tension is the driver in human creativity and problem solving. Engineers know that in physical systems, structural tension always seeks resolution. This is why suspension bridges stay up and why cantilevered decks don't fall down. Fritz took the jump to psychological systems and suggests that humans are the same, in that psychological tensions between vision and reality also work to resolve, one way or another.

Imagine doing this exercise yourself and compare the rubber band you are stretching to your team. Now imagine all the ways this "creative tension" might resolve. Here are some of your choices.

1. You could lower expectations and get your vision closer to current realities (this is traditional problem solving).

2. You could break the rubber band and not connect the two (this would be like generating a team vision but never measuring progress).

3. You could hold the vision and convince yourself reality is changing (this is being the team leader and convincing yourself everything is working in spite of evidence).

4. You could persistently hang on to the vision and get reality to move closer to the vision (this is the path of the effective visionary leaders).

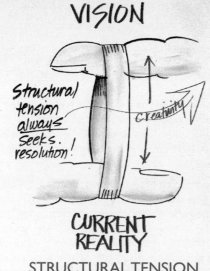

STRUCTURAL TENSION DRIVES CREATIVITY

I drew this poster to explain to participants in the Greater Baltimore Committee's Leadership program why we were structuring the two days the way we did, and why being willing to hold a vision for yourself that does not match current reality is important for driving innovation and creativity. The leadership program involves 50 people who work together for more than nine months. It's a different kind of team than a production team, but this metaphor and common language about visioning helped them stay oriented to its importance. The leader of the retreat, Jan Houbolt, and I reinforced the concept with the poster and by handing out actual rubber bands and having everyone experience what structural tension feels like.

❏ **Interview sponsors**: Sit down with whoever promoted you or sponsored your team and interview them about why they want you to lead and what they hope you will accomplish. Take notes and create a visual image.

❏ **Importance Mandala**: Use a Grove Mandala Graphic Guide and put the team's stated charter in the middle of the circle of smaller circles. Then in the surrounding balls brainstorm with yourself about all the reasons why this team is important. Perhaps split the chart into what's important to you and what's important to the organization.

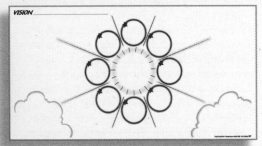

❏ **Elevator speech**: Write out an "elevator speech" about the reasons why it is important for your team to succeed. An elevator speech is something concise enough that you could tell it to someone in the time it takes to ride an elevator between several floors in a building.

How Much Performance Do You Want and Need?

The rubber band metaphor is a good example of how a story can inspire. Most of the people in the workshop wanted to be the type of leader who could get extraordinary results, high performance, and all the creative results that come from this. Most of us wanted to be that person who can hold a strong vision in the face of daunting challenges and persist. Peter embellished the story by stating that his experience and research showed that truly creative people are those who have a strong appetite for creative tension, and have the ability to hold it for long periods of time. These are the people who can make change. We came to see the rubber in the band as the value being placed on connecting the two ends.

If you imagine the top and bottom line in the TPM as having a rubber band between them, then the amount of stretch you have between your sense of purpose and vision and the everyday operation realities is the amount of creative tension, or "intention," you are bringing to your role.

No one can decide this for you. This comes from within. And it precedes and enlivens SMART objectives. This is about your own inner story of what you are "up to" in common language.

Let's go back to the first four choices you have as a team leader. There is a parallel set of choices your team has to make about how much everyone wants to achieve together. These different levels of effort may be clear in whatever assignment you received when the team was formed, or they may be vague and you have to determine how ambitious you are as a team. The assumption is that as the challenge increases, so does the strength of what you need to bring to the task in regard to orientation, trust, clarity, and commitment.

In describing the choices of how high to bounce, shown on the next page, I was imagining moving up the right side of the TPM, initially dealing with operational, physical plane issues of systems and how they work. Then I imagined working on the technical level (Level III) with clear processes for producing something at the level of implementation. Then I was imagining being at the level where the experience of working together evolves (Level II)—the level at which "high performance" is an accurate descriptor. And finally at the level of overall awareness (Level I), renewal activity, learning, and consciousness are the principle results.

If Robert Fritz is right, and Arthur M. Young is right, the higher you want to "bounce" the more momentum you need from the early stages. In other words, if you want to be involved in culture change you will need much more team trust and resilience than if you are merely fixing something that is broken—where competency about the problem may be the most important factor.

Take Ownership for Your Own Intentions

How you answer the question of your own purpose as a leader will shape how much motivation and involvement you will be able to generate from others. Leaders with strong intentions that they are capable of sharing are going to be more effective than leaders with weak intentions and confusion about purposes.

On the last and the next page are some of the practices that you can use to get clear about your own purpose and intentions. Surprise, surprise! Visualization turns out to be a real power tool.

IS MY TEAM UP FOR A BIG BOUNCE?

HOW HIGH SHOULD WE BOUNCE?

In terms of the TPM "bouncing ball" metaphor, you can ask, "How high do we need to bounce?" The choices map to the four levels of the TPM.

I. **Transform the organization?** Ignite a movement, open up a whole new field of work and opportunity, or create a brand new organization. We'll have to "be the change" and live the vision of a new possibility.

II. **Change a culture?** We need to change our current organization—redefining behaviors, motivations, and a different kind of culture. We'll have to be persistent, and go above and beyond, enrolling others at an emotional as well as the rational level.

III. **Produce something?** We could produce a new product. It will involve design, budgeting, recruiting, training, testing, manufacturing, fulfilling—all the implementation functions. It will most likely require planning, group decision making, involvement of other parts of the organization, and coordinating multiple streams of activity.

IV. **Fix something?** We just need to fix an operational problem and get on with other work. This will require bottom line, operational know-how, and resources.

☐ **Collage About Intent**: Create a collage for yourself with images that speak to you about why this team assignment is important. Let your intuition pick the images while holding the question "what do I care about in relationship to this team?"

☐ **Journal Work**: Take a journal and interview yourself. Write a question and then immediately write the answer, without editing. Then look back over everything and pick out the answers that speak most deeply about your reasons for wanting to lead this team.

☐ **Share Your Leadership Vision**: At an initial team meeting share in your own words the reasons why this team is important and what you hope to achieve with everyone. Have some record of what you are saying on a chart. Ask the team to then share what spoke to them most deeply and what calls them to the task.

Task 2:
Facilitating Relationships

If you successfully provide a time and space for everyone to get oriented to the purpose of the team, and have some time to imagine how they will fit in, then you can move your attention to getting people to know each other and being comfortable working together.

One of the pioneers in applying modern psychology to teams was William Schutz, a transpersonal psychologist and PhD, who developed the FIRO B assessment (see Bibliography for links). The letters stand for Fundamental Interpersonal Relations Orientation. It was created in the late 1950s to aid in the understanding and predicting of how high-performance military teams would work together and is widely used to see into the needs people have interpersonally when they join groups.

Schutz began with the premise that "people need people," using the term "interpersonal" to indicate any interaction—real or imagined—occurring between people. He used the term "need" to describe a psychological condition that, if not satisfied, leads to a state of discomfort or anxiety.

The FIRO B Model
Schutz suggested that interpersonal needs could be grouped into three categories: Inclusion, Control, and Affection.

- **Inclusion** is the need to feel accepted by a group. Jack Gibb agrees in his research as well, pointing to the concerns people have about membership and fitting in with the group as being primary.

- **Control** involves sorting out power relationships. Some people have very low needs in this area. Some are quite concerned about having power in the group. One reason Bruce Tuckman calls the second stage of teaming in his model "Storming" (see page 52) is that sorting out control issues can often be bumpy. It might occur over who is right, or who can be involved in decisions, or over who gets to work with whom.

- **Affection** is a need that follows the other two, and involves wanting to be liked by other teammates. This also has a spectrum of need depending on the person. Some people need a great deal of attention in this area. Others don't.

There aren't clear formulas for handling this part of teaming. But there are some principles you can follow. (If you want to learn more about this look in the resources section for good links to FIRO B, see Tuckman and other literature.)

Over the years I've come to believe that unclear purposes and distrust in leadership are the two biggest reasons teams become ineffective. It pays to really work on how you are received by the other people you work with!

How Do You Lead Relationship Development?

Visualization can support you in facilitating relationship building in many ways. All these strategies rely on the fact that when people are working together to create something they are actually experiencing working together, not just talking about it. The active nature of visual meetings, virtual or face-to-face, provides a very productive setting for working out inclusion, control, and affection issues in spaces that are safe and not directly affecting the work.

In addition, drawing is a physical act that engages more of our full sensibility than just engaging in a discussion. Preceding important conversations with some reflective drawing brings out deeper insights and participation.

In the side box are some principles you can use.

PRINCIPLES FOR HAVING GREAT RELATIONSHIPS

- Respect everyone's right to be themselves.

- Accept differences and look for how they can be strengths.

- Look for time, informally and in meetings, where people can work with interpersonal concerns.

- Show up authentically yourself.

- Connect with your team members individually.

- Accept interpersonal needs as legitimate and important.

- Be truthful and keep your word.

As a new team leader it's important to know what your intentions are in regard to how much emphasis you put on building competencies in others versus doing things yourself. There are four classic choices. Which of these describes yours?

1. Working directly on the task your team has been given or taken on

2. Working to support your team members to work on the tasks

3. Working to support a number of other teams and their leaders working on tasks

4. Working on creating an environment that allows team leaders to flourish working on tasks

The last choice in this list is called working at the "C" level in an organization. This is usually the level of the "Chiefs" in a large organization. But it might also be a leader in a rapidly growing political campaign, or the leadership role in a nonprofit organization. If your new role is heading up a top management team this very well might be your choice. But if you are a team leader of a production team it might be between 1 or 2.

Task 3:
Developing Competencies

After orienting to direction and building some trust in each other, teams naturally want to focus on preparing for whatever task they have taken on. This will put technical competencies to the test. In many cases, like with the HP BLAST team, the research and learning phase is a key part of the project, and necessarily precedes making recommendations. For problem-solving teams, exploration and analysis is critical to getting good solutions. As a leader, your job is to focus on the team and whether or not they have the skills and are prepared to handle the upcoming team performance challenges.

Scan the choices in the box on this page and reflect on your initial move from being a good individual contributor to the job of being a team leader of a single team. What was important when you were an individual contributor? It was probably things like getting the job done on time, doing it well, and using your best skills to tackle problems. You probably had some attachment and pride in being effective. Being one of the better people at your job may well be why you got promoted. So working directly on the task and getting it done seems like the obvious choice—right?

Maybe it is in the very beginning. But longer term your best results will come from choice 2—supporting others to work on the task. Having this intention is the big challenge for a brand new leader. The team leader who gets this right will probably be the one getting additional promotions! The TPM suggests that getting clear on assumptions, developing clear goals, and clarifying the vision are all parts of your job in creating the team, often happening in that order. But you as leader need to determine if you are going to just dictate these things, or collaborate in having the team take some ownership for handling these themselves.

Visual practice is hugely important here, and will help you create environments that both get the clarity you need and develop more understanding and competency in the team in general. Mapping out information on displays, as I explain at length in *Visual Meetings*, is how humans think about systems. Diagramming and drawing out ideas is also the way to develop more complete and accurate mental models, and increases your ability to perceive what is going on around you in the larger organization and marketplace.

Building Competency in Communication

A story about how you can go about this will be helpful here. A consulting firm working in high tech specialized in helping its clients develop all the specifications they would need to find and purchase large computer systems. They were at the beginning point of work with a large European bank that needed to upgrade its back office operations. Seven consultants were assigned to the team working on the project, and they needed to organize themselves before flying over and having initial meetings with the client.

One of the members, George, was a visual practitioner trained by The Grove who often facilitated client engagements with graphics on his projects. By the time they called me the entire team was sold on the approach and wanted to upgrade their skills for use on this project.

"We want to learn facilitation, and get some help on team building," George said. "And we need to get ready for our project." Here was a team leader who was focusing on development *and* getting the work done in the early phases of the project. We came up with the idea of spending a week organizing the project by having different team members facilitate different pieces of the work, stopping after each piece for feedback and critique from the others. I would provide coaching and tips all the way along, so they would learn graphic facilitation while getting the work done.

Stage 4 of the TPM, at the turn in your group process, your team will agree on roles and get clear about responsibilities heading into implementation. At the relationship-building stage, however, everyone is still working to figure out where they will contribute, and you as a team leader are making assessments. The little diagram here illustrates four roles that crop up in any group. These arise from the fact that we are living on an arrow of time, looking forward and backward. Some of your teammates are more able to look forward and propose new ideas, visions, and the like. Others will be much more comfortable looking to the past and things they can analyze and be clear about with references and data. Others will be in the present moment concerned about relationships and whether or not the group is having fun or dealing with conflict. Others will want to get the task completed. As a leader you should from the start work to understand the different capabilities of your teammates, and help people move toward roles where they will be most effective.

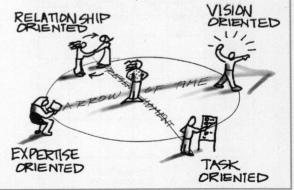

1. Create a grid on a large sheet of paper or web conference whiteboard and list team names on the left.

2. List potential areas of team experience along the top.

3. Ask each person to identify the "formative" experiences they have in each area—meaning where they spent enough time to deeply understand the patterns (perhaps years).

4. Discuss choices and look for common ground.

5. Encourage people to bring up secondary experiences that might relate to a promising set of connections.

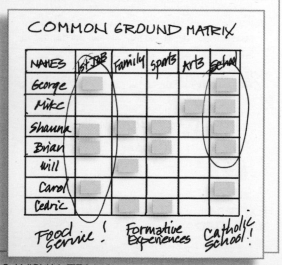

George also wanted the team to spend some time improving their communication and trust of each other, but we couldn't find enough time to conduct something elaborate. There was too much prep work to do. But I knew that one of the challenges of any new team is learning how to understand each other in spite of differences in experience. Sure enough, our vision of doing some team building and the reality of having little time created some "creative tension" that pushed us to an inventive approach that I later dubbed the "Common Ground Matrix."

One of the assumptions I make is that all human perception is filtered through our past experience, and when it comes to working on teams that is no exception. Our early experiences with groups and teams create understandings that guide our work later on—sometimes at a subconscious level. If this consulting team could find out where they shared similar experiences, it would help them communicate better through that shared experience.

So we conducted the activity described here on this page. Up went a large sheet of paper. On the left went seven names. Across the top we identified some categories—first jobs, family, sports, arts, and school. Then with sticky notes everyone thought about where they received their formative experiences in each area. It didn't take long to fill out the matrix—only about 20 minutes. Then we went hunting for common ground. Four of the people put something about food service in their "first jobs" category. As we discussed it, everyone had worked at one time or another in food service, not necessarily his or her first job. This provided our first area of common ground. Many things can be understood by looking at it as a food services system problem.

The next one was interesting. Several of the women identified Catholic school as formative. In the discussion we discovered that each of the men was also married to someone who was raised in Catholic school. So we found a second area of common ground.

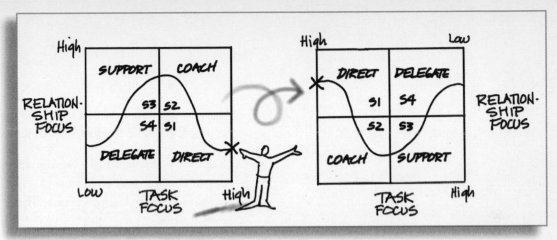

All during this discussion everyone was learning a lot about each other that would come into play during times of misunderstanding and fast-breaking work meetings on the client site. This activity, by the way, is a great example of combining both left and right brain ways of working. The grid is very analytical. But the stories and metaphoric thinking taps into the right brain. If you are working with engineers this kind of integrated approach works very well.

Situational Leadership

Another aspect of developing competency is how you relate to different needs on the team outside of meetings when people are working on individual tasks. The Agilent program focused on Situational Leadership as a set of skills that applied to the different aspects of team leadership.

Agilent used Blanchard's version of the Situational Leadership model and brought in some certified trainers from his organization to teach everyone how this worked. Their approach is proprietary, and very well tested, with many training courses and materials available. It supports the need to deal with people in different ways depending on the amount of directive help they need versus supportive work. It is interesting is to map Blanchard's ideas onto the TPM. They meshed perfectly.

The TPM added to my appreciation for Situational Leadership by appreciating the parallel between what individuals need and what the team as a whole needs. If you consider the team as a whole being like a person, when it is new to a task and unsure of itself, a lot of focus will be on learning the task, even though trust issues are more fundamental. You may need to be more

SITUATIONAL LEADERSHIP

Paul Hershey and Ken Blanchard developed a model in 1969 that contends that leadership cannot be one way for all people and be effective. Team members, and as a result leaders, are balancing two factors—one is focus on the task and the other is focus on the relationship. Workers new to their task need a lot of guidance. As they get more proficient they need more relationship support. Overlaying a quadrant scheme creates four "situations" where different leadership styles are suggested. Blanchard advises that an S1 "Directive" style is needed when people are new to a task. With a little experience an S2 "Coaching" style is appropriate. With some mastery an S3 "Supporting" style works. Finally, with very experienced people an S4 "Delegating" style is best. If you take this model (mapped on Cartesian coordinates) and turn it upside down, you can see how the four styles mirror the TPM.

directive and start there with basics, and then cycle back to working on relationship development as people get more comfortable with the work.

Remember that the TPM is organized from fundamental to comprehensive, and does not require that the specific sequence of activity follow that pattern. It simply means if you skip one of the fundamental elements you will have to return to it later to make progress toward high performance.

Getting Everyone Involved in Making Sense Out of Things

If as a team leader you want to encourage everyone to get involved and participate in the clarification stages of your work, then you need to suggest formats that support this. Interactive visualizing is a real power tool in this regard. Some of these techniques include:

❑ **Affinity diagrams**: Take a topic, hand out sticky notes, and have everyone generate examples of what you want to consider. The group then clusters, labels, and discusses, working bottom up from what can be entire walls full of information.

❑ **Small group sketching**: Have two or three people meeting in a small group and draw out a picture of what they would like to suggest related to whatever topic is being discussed.

❑ **Go-Arounds**: In virtual meetings have everyone respond to a question and write all the answers on the screen using a tablet computer.

❑ **Graphic Templates**: Graphic Guides like The Grove's Context Map are terrific at the early stages of teamwork for getting everyone to contribute something to one drawing. In this case it's a map of the environment that surrounds the team's operations.

When we get to the chapters on how to start a team and prepare an action plan I will walk you through some of these in much more detail.

Task 4:
Driving for Results

The bottom line in our Agilent model of leadership was to inspire new team leaders to be the drivers for results. Setting direction is primary. Getting people to relate well is the next most important. Being clear on goals and background information is also critical. But getting results means having all this work funnel into agreements and actions that actually manifest in the work being completed.

We'll focus on this a great deal in the chapters relating to sustaining your team in Section IV. Let's focus in on what a leader needs to do as a new team leader in this regard.

"Driving" implies keeping a constant movement in a direction. It implies a little pushing. It's active. Working groups that work individually need to be reminded of the group's goals and standards. Feedback on progress is helpful.

Highly interdependent teams that have to cooperate closely need to come to very clear agreements about direction, resources allocation, decision processes, and such. In the beginning stages of team performance, it helps to be directive. If you think back on the Situational Leadership model mentioned previously, a team that is new to its task will probably need more directive leadership. This is where the TPM is so useful, for it helps a great deal to direct the team to deal with orientation, trust, and clarification issues early and well. They are the foundation for everything else.

Once a team is truly committed and clear about its decision making, overall direction, and

USE VISUALIZATION TO DRIVE RESULTS

❑ Use graphic recording in web and face-to-face meetings to **validate contributions** and create a tangible output document right away.

❑ Use graphic templates to lead teams to **see relationships** and precipitate understandings more quickly and productively.

❑ Create visual diagrams and displays to **deepen problem analysis** and improve the chance of coming up with lasting solutions.

❑ Rate, rank, and decide on options with graphic displays to yield decisions that **foster more buy-in.**

❑ Use graphically oriented decision-support software with large, distributed teams to **share and analyze information** at levels not possible otherwise.

❑ Employ visual, public note-taking about roles and commitments to **anchor agreements**.

❑ Visually track progress with project-management tools to make it possible to **literally see progress**.

❑ Visually document meetings to **bridge time gaps** and reduce productivity losses due to poor group memory.

❑ **Support learning**, debriefing, and knowledge creation at the end of projects with visual meetings.

resources, the job of the leader shifts to being more of a coach, or being more supportive if the team is really functioning well. If you connect this idea with the 90 percent angle in the TPM, it will help you remember to change the direction of your leadership. When the team takes the turn *you* need to take the turn as well, to a more supportive style of leadership.

Driving for results doesn't mean being heavy handed. It means staying focused, and guiding the attention of the team to what everyone agreed they wanted to accomplish.

5. Managing Four Flows of Activity
Attention, Energy, Information, & Operations

The last chapter focused on the external work of the team and the four key roles of a team leader. This one focuses on the internal work you need to do to become a high-performance team leader. It will take us into some of the thinking underlying the TPM and how you can embrace a more holistic view of what you are doing.

In the late 1980s Martin, the head of leadership and education for a large consumer goods company, came to The Grove and presented the possibility of working together to craft a worldwide facilitation training program for their new Leadership & Education (L&E) group, recently centralized. Martin foresaw many challenges heading toward his company, not the least of which was expansion into Eastern Europe. They were also applying new technologies, and were challenged making corporate-wide programs work across formerly very independent businesses.

Thinking About Meetings, Teams, and Organization Change

"We want a flagship program that will teach our personnel people how to run meetings, lead teams, and facilitate organization change," Martin said. If you are a new team leader you can probably identify with this need to understand all three of these things—meetings, teams, and organization. You will have to lead your team, yes, but the meetings also need to be managed, *and* your interface with the larger organization is also important. But thinking about these all together is one thing and creating a training that integrates them is another!

The team Martin assembled was composed of a talented trainer from the United Kingdom, an HR manager from Southern California, and a top trainer from the East Coast of the United States. Martin was from Bristol, England. They all had long histories with the company. In order to have this project fly, we needed to enroll the top HR people in both North America and Europe by conducting two pilot programs. We worked hard to develop an approach that worked across regions and provided the basic skills workshop participants would need.

We want a flagship program that will teach our personnel people how to run meetings, lead teams, and facilitate organization change.

I took on the challenge because my work with Young's Theory of Process convinced me that similar process dynamics appear on all three levels of meetings, teams, and organization. But we needed an organizing framework. It was clear to all of us that how people handle teams was central. Meetings provide settings for check-ins and turning points for the more central team processes. On the other hand, organization change is to a great extent about creating an environment where teams can thrive.

But how would we train people when the situational differences are huge, and as we've pointed out, there are many different kinds of teams? How can you decide what to focus on as a team leader? We chose to focus the entire facilitation training around the TPM, but we built in an additional layer of understanding about the four flows of activity that underlie it. We called this the AEIOU model, where the "U" playfully points at "you" and the fact that the way you manage will be shaped by your own personality and style. It represented the unspoken, inner work of the facilitator and team leader. The drawing on this page illustrates this concept.

Managing Your Attention

Let's start with the least objective flow—attention. In fact, attention isn't objective at all. It's where your awareness is focused. I like to use the metaphor of a flashlight to think about this. If your attention is a flashlight, then you might have the following choices about where to guide both your and the team's attention.

1. **Inner focus**, on your own performance and process.

2. **Outward focus**, on seeing what is "out there."

3. **Narrow focus** on a specific problem or person.
4. **Broad beamed**, keeping it open and shining across everything you need to work on.

In truth, there is no way to characterize all the things you could be paying attention to, since our imagination and consciousness are quite vast. What is important is to be aware of whatever it is you are focusing on, and appreciate that it is always specific to you and does not represent general truth, but merely what you are paying attention to. A heightened awareness of this leads to better listening and more acceptance of why many different points of view are needed to innovate and find breakthroughs on tough problems.

General Principles for Managing Attention

In spite of the variety of choices, there are some principles that I believe apply to anyone in a role of leadership with other people.

1. **Leaders Are "Cursors" for Team Attention**: I assume that what I'm paying attention to will usually get more attention from my team, and my presence is like a "cursor" for the group's attention. Whether I attend meetings or not, listen to certain individuals or not, travel or not, or insist on firsthand experience or not all have an impact on attention.

2. **There Is Power in Paying FULL Attention**: I believe my full attention is different from partial attention. I don't believe that multitasking is paying full attention, and research is beginning to make this clear. If I am the leader this kind of thing is noticed, especially in face-to-face meetings or in personal talks with team members.

3. **Humans Generate Fields**: Attention may operate at the "field" level of human awareness. I assume that my attitudes and attention will "leak." If I have a negative attitude toward one of my teammates I believe it will directly affect his or her performance, even if they aren't explicitly aware of my attitude. The same goes for respect. The more sensitive people

---

FOUR FLOWS EXERCISE

Conduct this little exercise to think through what you understand about the different aspects of teamwork that underlie team performance. You can do this with your team as well.

1. Create four channels on a large piece of paper.

2. Take sticky notes and identify all the different things you work on in regard to your team.

3. Place them on the chart where they seem to be centered.

4. Are the items operational elements—tangible tools and mechanisms?

5. Do they represent working on communication and the different ways information is organized?

6. Is it phenomena arising from interactions of people and their feelings and behavior?

7. Are you working to focus the group's attention in different ways? What are the different choices of where your own attention could be directed?

are the more this is true. Systematically disadvantaged people can be extraordinarily sensitive to nuances in a leader's attitude.

4. **Frequency Carries Signal**: Attention operates a bit like a lighthouse. Repeated "touch-ins" create a pattern of attention that builds over time and becomes a trustworthy beacon for the group. How often a team meets, how fast you respond to inquiries, and how frequently you show interest are all patterns that carry a message.

5. **Spirit Matters**: I believe that if in my core being I am inspired and hold others in a good light at some level this directly impacts them. Having a personal spiritual practice that keeps me in touch with my own sources of "light" have proved important to my leadership work. I know this is true of many of my colleagues and effective leaders that I know. In common language terms, "being spirited" means your interest and attention beams out, and you are willing to spontaneously respond to your inner guidance. There are many choices and disciplines that work to help people develop their inner lives. It's not so important which one you pick as it is that you have one that matters to you. How alive and inspired you are will probably be a factor in how spirited your team can be.

In recent years a growing amount of research is being focused on the intangible effects of consciousness and awareness on everything else humans do. Young believed that reaccepting the role of consciousness in science was essential to its evolution as a field. I believe it's a factor that is crucial to high performance teams and organizations.

Managing Energy and Emotions

It's increasingly acceptable to talk about the importance of emotions and emotional intelligence in the workplace. Daniel Goleman's book, *Emotional Intelligence: Why It Can Matter More Than IQ*, broke open the subject in the mid-1990s by pulling together the increasingly persuasive evidence from neuroscience and psychology that emotions are integral to our thinking and work.

In regard to team leadership this aspect is at the heart of what is involved in gaining and fostering trust on your team. Trust is a feeling at core. Even though thinking goes along with it, it's the visceral reactions we have to each other that count. Managing this part of the team means looking after the team's heart and soul, starting with your own.

Jack Gibb, Bruce Tuckman, William Shutz, and many others agree on this issue. Leaders in team development work, Dennis and Michelle Reina, have focused their latest work squarely on this issue. Their book is *Trust & Betrayal in the Workplace: Building Effective Relationships in Your Organization*. It's interesting that they identify four kinds of trust that map very closely to the four flows we are talking about here. They describe contractual trust at the bottom line, communications trust, competency trust, and finally, transformational trust.

The kinds of trust that the Reinas write about are explicit. The energetic and emotional side of your leadership is more implicit. It has to do with the pacing, passion, and persistence of your involvement with others on the team, and the extent of your ability to both be aware of your own emotional states and be perceptive about others. While I am not trying to write a book on the interpersonal aspects of team leadership, there is a relationship between how you handle your own energy and the team dynamics. Think about the following aspects of team leadership that are all about managing the energy:

- **Pacing**: How fast and how slow you interact with people creates a "pace" for work. How much notice do you provide about changes and requests? How quickly do you jump into a conversation with your ideas? How much time do you allocate for online and face-to-face meetings? I've found that a key to managing energy is setting a pace you can sustain reliably, so that everyone else can get used to it. You must also be aware of the pace that your team members can actually manage. If you outstrip their ability to keep up it can be demotivating. Some people are sprinters. Some run marathons. Does your team have a drummer?

THE MASTER APTITUDE

Daniel Goleman calls our emotions the "master aptitude." He writes:

When emotions overwhelm concentration, what is being swamped is the mental capacity cognitive scientists call "working memory," the ability to hold in the mind all information relevant to the task at hand … working memory is an executive function par excellence in mental life, making possible all other intellectual efforts, from speaking a sentence to tackling a knotty logical proposition … when the limbic circuitry that converges on the prefrontal cortex is in the thrall of emotional distress, one cost is in the effectiveness of working memory: we can't think straight ….

On the other hand, consider the role of positive motivation—the marshalling of feelings of enthusiasm, zeal, and confidence—in achievement. Studies of Olympic athletes, world-class musicians, and chess grand masters find their unifying trait is the ability to motivate themselves to pursue relentless training routines ….

To the degree that our emotions get in the way of or enhance our ability to think and plan, to pursue training for a distant goals, to solve problems and the like, they define the limits of our capacity to use our innate mental ability, and so determine how we do in life. It is in this sense that emotional intelligence is a master aptitude, a capacity that profoundly affects all other aptitudes, either facilitating or interfering with them.

(Emotional Intelligence, 79).

A visual way to draw out the different energetic and emotional preferences of your team is to do some kinesthetic graphing.

1. Pick some of the choices below and write them on large sticky notes and put them up on opposite sides of the room.

2. Ask people to pick a spot along this spectrum of possibilities where they like to work, and then move there physically.

3. While standing at his or her chosen spot, have each person explain why they chose that position.

Some fun choices are:

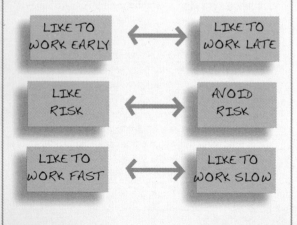

- **Participation**: How much contribution you invite and accept are a function of your own self-management. If you are hurried and rushed, and don't have time for input, you will subtly train people to avoid it. It may seem easier to pop together a slide presentation and "tell" everyone what they should know than to draw it out of everyone in an interactive session, but you will pay in terms of lower participation and ownership. How you gauge this kind of thing needs to flow from the level of involvement and interdependence your team requires.

- **Persistence**: An aspect of the energy flow of a group is how often you keep coming at issues and challenges. Different teams' tasks will require different levels of persistence. Leading with a long view takes a certain amount of confidence that you and the team can come up with relevant strategies.

Kinesthetic graphing is a way to draw out of your group how different people like to work in regards to the energetic, emotional aspects of the work. The exercise on this page explains how to do it. Have your team members line up by when they think they do their best work—early in the morning, later in the afternoon, or late at night? There is a wide range, it turns out. A recent conference hosted by the Institute for the Future cited research that shows there is a direct correlation between people having control over their time and health and well-being indices. It's a bit analogous to being the driver or the passenger on a winding mountain road. It's not the driver who generally gets nauseous! When your people can't anticipate the turns and starts and stops it is very upsetting.

Another visual way to think about working with the energy flow of a group is to imagine you are an orchestra conductor, conducting a symphony with many different kinds of movements. Let yourself be conscious of the pacing of work as an energetic flow that has shape and form. For projects that rely on careful timing and key deadlines, setting out a rhythm that people can follow is like providing your band with a good drummer. If you can't, enroll someone to help you.

The emotional, energetic aspect of a team's life operates like the heartbeat in a human being. A strong, positive, reliable one helps the whole team be healthy.

Managing Information and Communications

If the energy flow is the heart, the information level is the "mind" of your team. Much of what we think of as the real work of teams is in this realm, especially in any organization that is primarily dealing with information. Kenneth Boulding in his seminal book, *The Image*, points out that while the majority of jobs in North America are now service jobs, the majority of these do not involve working with people directly, but working with symbols!

Teachers, writers, market researchers, software designers, planners, facilitators, consultants, service bureau workers, lawyers, accountants, and trainers live in a sea of information and communications. If you are a publications or marketing team the primary focus of your work might be making sense out of the words, images, and numbers that appear in ads and go-to-market materials and brochures. If you are a planning team like BLAST, your product is a set of recommendations. If you are interface designers your results will be designs, wire frames, and icons. Some of this information relates to physical things, but a lot of it relates to knowledge and ideas that are purely conceptual. But even if you work with your hands and make physical products you rely on lots of information to do your job. Manufacturing teams depend on measurement tools for quality, processes and logs, standards, and inventory assessments. Builders rely on plans and maps. Increasingly all of us are immersed in screen-based information on our smartphones, tablets, portable computers, and visual media.

As a leader you need to pay attention to the languages and mediums that you are asking your team to use to communicate. Astute choices in this regard make a big difference in performance.

As a leader you need to pay attention to the languages and mediums that you are asking your team to use to communicate. Astute choices in this regard make a big difference in performance.

This is especially true for distributed teams. These choices extend to which mental models you support, which company policies you link to, and what interpretations you place on events that happen.

Warren Bennis has been a pioneering researcher in the field of leadership. I heard him speak at the Commonwealth Club of San Francisco one time shortly after finishing research with 90 known leaders in government and business. He distilled out four characteristics that ran across all 90 people, he said. The first, obvious one was they all had vision. A second was that they all had high personal self-regard and regard for others. "Not a one of them talked badly about any of the people on their teams," I remember him saying.

The third generalization stuck with me in regard to communications. All of his interviewees focused not on communicating information, but on interpreting information. They were focused on what events meant and how everyone should think about them. In organizational life all kinds of things happen all the time. But it isn't the event itself that is the most powerful influence, it is the interpretation that people put on the event. This goes for financial results, ups and down with clients, reductions in force, and all the other challenges.

One of the most powerful things about being a visual thinker as well as a writer in my case, has been to work out dilemmas in language through visualization. Two things that seem at odds in language can both find a common place on a single piece of paper. I believe it is one of the reasons that every consultant I know has a full portfolio of models and templates to stretch thinking and allow room for new interpretations.

Managing Operations

The bottom line concern you need to have as a team leader is to manage the flow of operations—

the "body" of the team. Operations include all the mechanical, controllable elements of your work, including all the physical tools and resources, the team rooms and platforms, the communication infrastructure, the budgets and procedures, and the processes by which you and your team will make a decision about all these things.

In the TPM a very large platform graphic underlies the entire model. This represents the organization that must meet your team at the point it is committing real resources to its work. Without organizational support the work of a team can falter. As important as working with your team directly is working with the larger organization to make sure it supports your team. Timing can be everything in this regard.

I've seen too many teams with high hopes experience delays in getting very basic resources deployed so they can do their work well. With virtual teams getting the infrastructure right early is essential, but many organizations are really stretched in their information technology functions and experience delays. Jumping in on these kind of problems and removing them for the team can be critical.

The point I made earlier about task 4, driving for results, is that it is hugely about keeping operations in a position where it supports and channels the other levels of work. Of course, as with a good musical conductor, all the elements need to come together and integrate. Whatever flow is having problems will take up energy and attention. If your team needs to focus on implementation, then work to eliminate infrastructure issues and provide proper organizational support.

Taking the Turn to Implementation

This chapter is meant to raise your awareness of all the things that need your attention as a team leader. But remember back to the choices about what level you want to work. Once a team has

In the TPM a very large platform graphic underlies the entire model. This represents the organization that must meet your team at the point it is committing real resources to its work. Without organizational support the work of a team can falter. As important as working with your team directly is working with the larger organization to make sure it supports your team.

I HOPE I'M ON TIME

reached a level of agreement about how it will handle all the challenges of the creating stages of team performance, it can begin working much more on its own.

In summarizing their research on teams, Katzenbach and Smith in the *Wisdom of Teams* state, "In high performance teams, the role of the team leader is less important and more difficult to identify because all members lead the team at different times (*Page 4*)." In some senses once a team has turned the corner, so must the leader. Learning to direct and coach in the beginning, and support and delegate as the team gains momentum, is key to masterful team leadership.

6. Supporting Innovation
Providing Visual Tools

Visualization is a key to the creative process in many, many endeavors. This chapter focuses in on the specific things you can, as a team leader, help your team be innovative by getting visual. But to get this result you need to know what's required.

One of the early insights our Groupware Users Project team had about the application of all the tools described with the Four-Square Map of Groupware, was how the different approaches mapped to the TPM. On this page is the graphic that we included in *Leading Business Teams*.

Face-to-Face for Orientation and Trust Building

Most people I talk with believe that teams benefit from meeting each other face-to-face early in a team process. Our social orientation is very deep, and conditioned for this kind of encounter. I talked with a sales manager from HP on a plane flight several years ago and he said his rhythm was to have one face-to-face meeting a year that was focused on relationship building, and all the rest of the year the team could work virtually. An HR team at Otis Spunkmeyer follows the same pattern.

It is possible that this bias is changing with the increase in virtual tools. In the OD Network's Collaboration 98 Web Conference I mentioned earlier, I had a long exchange with one participant who insisted that *not* meeting people but getting to know them online was actually a superior way to communicate. His argument was that humans make a lot of assumptions about each other based on appearance and social behavior that may have little to do with the work of the team, and people can be more focused without the distractions. I have another colleague at HP who works on many teams where she has never met the people face-to-face and believes that the work is going very well.

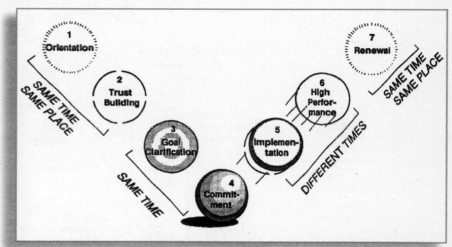

GROUPWARE MAPPED
TO TEAM PERFORMANCE

This is the way in which our Groupware Team at the Institute for the Future associated the choices in the Four-Square Map of Groupware with the TPM (see Chapter 2, page 23 for an explanation of the Four-Square Map).

FULLY EQUIPPED TEAM ROOM

A team that works visually will use many different kinds of tools. I've illustrated them all in one room in this picture. The opportunities provided by the many different tools for visual work bring along with them the need to learn and master the tools in order to have team energies focus on the work itself. Many organizations now provide most of these tools if you look for them.

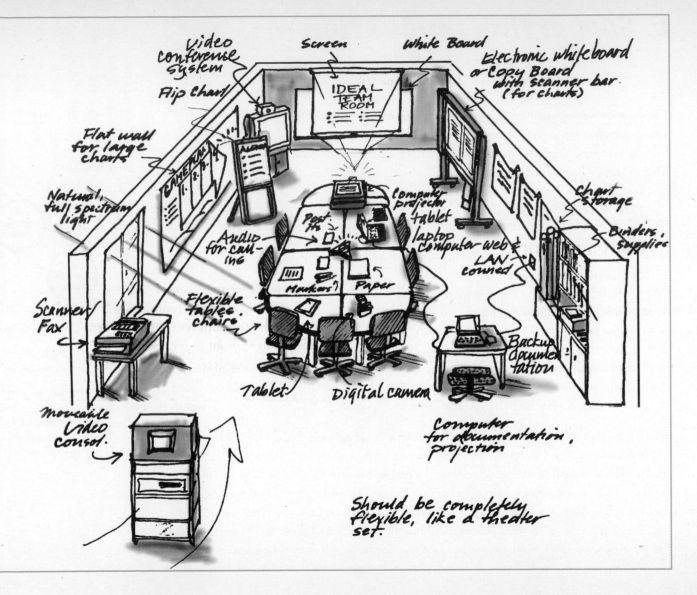

Video conference system

Screen

White Board

Electronic whiteboard or Copy Board with scanner bar (for charts)

Flip Chart

Flat wall for large charts

IDEAL TEAM ROOM

CAMERA

Natural, full spectrum light

Computer projector

tablet

laptop

Computer web & LAN connect

Chart storage

Binders, supplies

Post-its

Audio for calling

Markers

Paper

Scanner/ Fax

Flexible tables, chairs

Tablet

Digital camera

Backup documentation

Moveable video console.

Computer for documentation, projection

Should be completely flexible, like a theater set.

I still contend that having a richer rather than a narrower sense about people you are working with eventually helps. This may be more dependent on the type of work involved than we originally thought in the Groupware project. You will have to judge for your team.

I went back to our Groupware Report and found a picture I created of an ideal team room, which I have updated with contemporary tools. I was surprised how few things have changed regarding what truly supports teams. This kind of room is quite common now in high-tech companies. Nonprofits and government agencies more than likely will have fewer options.

As team leader you will have to work to help your team get the kind of tools indicated here. Unless they are available organization-wide, your team won't have much practice with visual meetings. The least expensive way to begin, of course, is to use whiteboards and flip charts. Adding big paper and sticky notes isn't too difficult. Getting special interactive whiteboards, video, and good projection is more challenging and costly. If budgets are a factor I'd invest in the paper and a good digital camera, relying on e-mail to send images around. Tablets are also quite inexpensive and open up web conferences for the one or two people who might be remote and want to see what you are working on.

In the later section on high tech I will describe where these kinds of tools are heading, with integrated whiteboards, tablets, and PCs allowing for distributed drawing and idea-mapping. Multitouch screens will make it possible to start getting hands-on digital information on a big scale!

Same Time/Different Place for Clarification and Commitment

Teams that know and trust each other can accomplish quite a bit without meeting directly, but still benefit in the early stages from the rapid give and take possible in same time meetings via web and telephone. At The Grove many of the meetings where we design agendas and processes

TOOLS THAT SUPPORT FACE-TO-FACE VISUALIZATION

- ❑ Smooth walls for graphic recording on large paper
- ❑ Portable walls for recording (large foam core on easels works best)
- ❑ Large plotter paper (3' or 4' wide and 25–50 yards long)
- ❑ Sticky notes of various sizes and artist's tape
- ❑ Water-based markers that don't bleed
- ❑ Wall and tabletop templates
- ❑ Blank journals, workbooks, and handouts
- ❑ Flip charts
- ❑ Whiteboards and whiteboard markers
- ❑ Digital cameras for documentation
- ❑ Computer projectors using various software (more on this later)
- ❑ Tablets for electronic recording
- ❑ Decision-support software (allowing electronic brainstorming, rating, ranking, and grouping)
- ❑ Electronic whiteboards
- ❑ Overhead projectors (still used for some purposes)

TABLET RECORDING

Inexpensive tablets for computers make it easy to do graphics on a web conference. The setup below is a Wacom Bamboo connected by USB to my MacBook Pro. I'm using Autodesk's Sketchbook Pro software to capture what I'm talking about with a colleague in preparation for a meeting about corporate communications.

for key strategy sessions and off-sites are accomplished by web or teleconference. To manage these you would need a new set of tools.

❑ **Target documents for teleconferences**: Send out word processor agendas, Excel spreadsheet of tasks, or slide presentations one participant modifies in advance.

❑ **Web conferences with shared whiteboards and presentations**: Most web conference platforms have a whiteboard capability that allows participants to type and draw on one surface. As a leader you need to make sure such a platform is available and used enough that the team isn't fumbling over technicalities.

❑ **Web conference with active recording on tablets**: Most web conference software allows for "desktop sharing," which means everyone can see whatever program you have running. Drawing programs allow a graphic facilitator to record everyone's ideas on a tablet. If some people are meeting face-to-face this can be projected and function like a virtual wall.

❑ **Video conferences**: These are helpful if your team needs to see each other while working. The various teleconferencing services are all working to integrate graphic communication but still make it somewhat awkward. If you have a teleconference setup that includes a moveable camera, it is possible to aim it at large wall charts and have remote participants follow along.

❑ **Browser-based decision-support software**: Some web-based systems such as CoVision's Council or Conexus polling keypads software allow for electronic brainstorming, rating, and ranking where everyone can see everyone else's entries. These systems need special setup and technological support.

❑ **Networked electronic whiteboards and telephones**: Smart Technology, a leader in electronic whiteboards, can link board, tablets, and computers up to 64 nodes.

Everyone sees the same thing, and can interact on shared working displays. (I'll describe more about this later.)

❑ **Live chat and voice-over Internet software**: An alternative to web conferences is live chat and teleconferencing over free voice-over Internet protocols (VOIP). This is an increasing choice for teams that work globally in the not-for-profit sector.

As a team leader, you will still probably have to work face-to-face to get the organizational agreements you need to obtain resources, budgets, and go-ahead decisions in a timely way. Personal relationships still keep things running in most parts of business.

Different Time/Different Place for Implementation Work

Once a team has made the turn and is fully into implementation you may want to consider supporting everyone with communication platforms that don't require same time work. These include the following kinds of tools:

❑ **Dedicated team rooms and special websites**: A growing number of solutions exist where teams can post work, create profiles, share forums and conversations, and have all their information in one place. Large enterprises often provide these spaces inside the firewall of their companies. Designing these from scratch is tough, and not advised unless you are willing to live through the several versions required to "get it right."

❑ **Shared databases in "the cloud"**: I'm writing this book using a database in "the cloud" that can handle large files so that my team can access and download the files at any point they need to work on different chapters. The cloud is "billowing" right now.

❑ **Social media pages**: It is so easy now to set up pages in social networking sites that many teams I know just use those platforms for communication. As a leader you need to work out which of these choices will actually be used. It can take as much work to get

---

TOOLS THAT SUPPORT VIRTUAL WORK

❑ **Web conference services** for enterprises—like Cisco's WebEx—or a lower end cross platform service like Go To Meeting, all allow for chat, shared whiteboards, shared presentation, sharing desktops, and usually some survey and polling capability.

❑ **Video conferencing software** covers a full spectrum of quality, from the large "telepresence" systems HP, Cisco, and Siemens offer to simply using the cameras built into portable computers, or small video cams. I think teams that know each other need to look at their work more than each other, so overinvesting in high-end equipment probably isn't necessary for most project teams. For management teams that is another story.

❑ **Interactive whiteboards**. Smartboards from Smart Technology have been leading the way in providing multitouch capability that works interactively across as many as six-dozen connections. Any engineering or design team would love to have this capability if they are virtual.

POSTED STORYMAPS REMIND TEAMS OF WHY THEY ARE WORKING TOGETHER

The Grove's vision is an example of a mural created by leadership to keep the teams in our organization remembering our purpose.

people on the same platform as the team's actual work itself.

❑ **Project management platforms**: There are many choices of programs that allow project managers to create Gantt charts showing task, milestones, and time lines; create calendars; store key files; post budgets; and generate diagrams, tables, and other reports analyzing progress from different angles. These programs all require some training and adaptation if your team is to benefit from using them as a common platform.

❑ **Fax, overnight mail, and e-mail**: A widely used lower tech way of coordinating is to send documents back and forth using regular mail and e-mail. When visualization is used adeptly it can greatly facilitate making sense out of complicated information. Contract work still uses hard-copy mediums in many cases. If you plan to use digital signatures and e-mail you need to make sure your team gets the training to be able to use them appropriately.

Different Time/Same Place Meetings

This brings us back to a physical office or workspace. When teams are collocated they communicate visually through the physical environment in ways that allow coworkers to see what is going on at different times. This is a mode of communication that is common during implementation of projects that extend over time. As a leader you can encourage people to use this environment in ways that keep everyone oriented. Your choices include:

❑ **Physical bulletin boards and project management walls**: I was interested to hear that Industrial Light & Magic, George Lucas' special effects company, kept its physical project management wall after moving from San Rafael to new offices in the Presidio. It is a large wall with colored cards that graphically show the status of all studios and projects to anyone who looks. The Grove has a board in one stairwell that allows anyone to post an acknowledgment of someone else on the team.

- ❑ **Posted action plans and road maps**: Many people who use Grove Graphic Guides like to post them in their physical offices. One architectural firm posts its annual priorities in large posters in each of several dozen offices. In a cubical environment, a team implementing a large systems integration project posted their action plan high up so anyone could see it over their cubicle walls.

- ❑ **Physical team rooms with standing displays**: When architect Bill Mc-Donough worked on Ford Motor Company's River Rouge Plant, making it one of the first truly green manufacturing plants in the industry, an entire room was dedicated to tracking and visualizing the project. The room was used by implementation teams and by communications teams orienting outsiders to the project. If a team is lucky enough to have a dedicated team room, then all kinds of working displays can remain up, allowing members to communicate back and forth both during and between meetings.

- ❑ **Kiosks—physical and electronic**: Manufacturers increasingly use special electronic displays to post announcements and provide access to information for teams on the floor. The kinds that you see in lobbies orient visitors to the company and recent activities. The same kinds of displays can be used in team environment to communicate important information in between meetings.

Managing the Decisions About Tools

You can see from the length of these checklists that working visually does come with some responsibility for helping a team sort out what to use when. The paradox of contemporary technology is that while there are more and more choices across a wide range of media, for a team to work together they need to *all* agree on common tools and platforms in order to connect. Of course, subgroups working on different facets of a problem aren't under that constriction, but the team as a whole is if it wants to have team-wide communications. Settling these issues inside the team and working to get support from outside the team is one of the big jobs for the leader of

When teams are collocated they communicate visually through the physical environment in ways that allow coworkers to see what is going on at different times.

Daniel Pink makes the argument for the rising influence of design thinking very persuasively:

> Design—that is, utility enhanced by significance, has become an essential aptitude for personal fulfillment and professional success for at least three reasons. First, thanks to rising prosperity and advancing technology, good design is now more accessible than ever, which allows more people to partake in its pleasures and become connoisseurs of what was once specialized knowledge. Second, in an age of material abundance, design has become crucial for most modern businesses—as a means of differentiation and as a way to create new markets. Third, as more people develop a design sensibility, we'll increasingly be able to deeply design for its ultimate purpose: changing the world.
>
> (*A Whole New Mind*, 70)

any distributed team in today's communication environment.

In mapping the applicability of different tools to the TPM, we on the Groupware Users team felt that high performing teams and ones investing in renewal and learning would benefit from face-to-face interactions. High performance usually involves being able to adapt to new conditions. This requires revisiting agreements and staying tuned in.

Supporting Innovation

You may have noticed, if you have studied any of the literature on innovation, that visualization is a central element, from imagining possibilities all the way to prototyping through enactment. When you change the media you use and represent ideas in new ways, such as drawing pictures, it breaks up the idea fixation that gets rutted into people's mind when they think the same way with the same kind of language all the time. And it encourages design thinking.

Daniel Pink calls out design as the first of six, new "conceptual age" senses needed to succeed in our times. These are *design, story, symphony, empathy, play*, and *meaning*. Design thinking is the doorway to innovation.

A point I'll make again and again is that teams need to "play around" to be creative, and that active visualization is a directly productive way to do this. A mantra in Silicon Valley is "fail early and often." I've read critiques of this approach, but agile development in software, rapid prototyping, model making in architecture, and scenario planning in futures work all support the idea that we need to explore many ideas and try things out in order to have innovation emerge. How safe people feel "playing around" is often a direct result of the way you as a team leader behave and what kinds of tools you make available. If you move in a new direction and try out different ways of working it will open up your team to do the same thing.

Visualizing Emergent Order

One of the most innovative approaches to team leadership I've encountered recently was used by Marv Adams to manage the IT function at Ford Motor Company during the mid-2000s. He had spent some time working with the Santa Fe Institute, learning how living systems work, and decided to apply evolutionary dynamics to his management team. We cocreated some effective visuals to illustrate his approach for a presentation he gave at the Pegasus Conference, an association of systems-oriented consultants and managers, and the ideas have stuck with me ever since (often the case if you draw out your thinking). He gives credit to Michael Cohen and Robert Axelrod for explaining these concepts in *Harnessing Complexity*.

Marv believed that the most effective way to stimulate innovation would be to control the three variables that drive evolutionary process—variation, replication, and selection.

1. **Variation**: This is the amount of latitude encouraged for bringing up new and/or different ideas. He believed a team leader could control this directly by how they behaved.

2. **Replication**: Marv called this one "interaction," believing that a leader could encourage or discourage the kind of meetings, communications, and connections through which ideas propagate and reproduce themselves.

3. **Selection**: In nature variations are "selected" when they successfully find a "fitness peak" where they can continue to replicate. In organizations this process is controlled by whether it's easy or difficult to get an idea sanctioned and budgeted.

Drawing Your Way Into Insights

It is actually easy to get your teams to start drawing and visualizing if you just do it. David Cawood, a strategy consultant in Vancouver, brought me up to team with him at an off-site, the

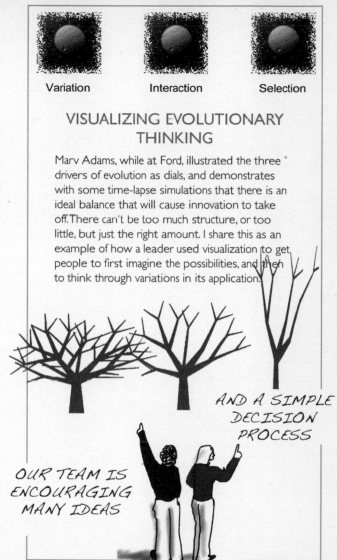

Variation   Interaction   Selection

VISUALIZING EVOLUTIONARY THINKING

Marv Adams, while at Ford, illustrated the three drivers of evolution as dials, and demonstrates with some time-lapse simulations that there is an ideal balance that will cause innovation to take off. There can't be too much structure, or too little, but just the right amount. I share this as an example of how a leader used visualization to get people to first imagine the possibilities, and then to think through variations in its application.

AND A SIMPLE DECISION PROCESS

OUR TEAM IS ENCOURAGING MANY IDEAS

goal of which was to forge a team out of the city agency heads. They were facing the challenge of hosting a large international event in the city and needed to decide on some big infrastructure projects. Because Vancouver has the mildest weather in Canada, it is a desirable professional location for people in just about every functional area of city government. Once a person gets a job as the head of public works, or health, or the police the tendency is to work at staying in the job and not take risks. So the city departments functioned more like kingdoms than teams.

They wanted to start work across some of their boundaries and loosen up for the fresh thinking that would be required by the big event they faced. They needed to work as a true team. We decided to use a right brain, visualizing strategy to get things started (in addition to my working visually throughout the retreat). We asked them to break into teams of three and draw a picture of city government as if it were a kind of vehicle, label the parts, and then describe the condition.

We didn't spend a lot of time arguing about the value of this. We just moved them into the exercise. The key, of course, was having all the supplies ready and on hand. Now imagine trying to create one drawing of something pretty far afield from your expertise, and then using it as a map to describe something you knew well—city government. It's impossible to be "professional" and "expert" at this kind of thing. You have to jump in and just create something. Well, the drawings were pretty wild—of ferry boats with one paddle not working, of buses that were too small for all the passengers, and so on. But they had a lot of fun, and more importantly, when they reported on the assignment, through humor and metaphor they were able to talk about a lot of very important things. This is what consistently happens in active sticky note processes, drawing, seeing drawing in a web conference, or making models. It's the sweet spot of innovation.

Let's turn our attention back to the team itself and start back at the creating stages. The next seven chapters walk through the process once again, with even more ideas and stories.

III: Visual Team Startup
Creating Trust, Focus, & Commitment

III: Visual Team Startup

Chapter 7: Visualizing Purpose This chapter includes best practices for getting clear about purpose and results up front, clear chartering, and making space for people to answer personal questions about fit and involvement.

Chapter 8: Seeing Yourself As a Team Visual dialogue helps people get to know each other and grow their trust, forthrightness, and openness. This chapter dives into graphic storytelling, context mapping, and group portraits as reliable strategies.

Chapter 9: Clarifying Goals Visualizing a team's goals and actions steps is a power tool for performance. This chapter steps through using the Grove's Graphic Gameplan to quick start action teams, kick off cross-functional task forces, and get people on the same page. I include examples from real action planning sessions with an architectural firm that has regularly used the gameplan template to clarify goals.

Chapter 10: Consensus or Command? Getting clear on decision-making approaches is as important bottom line as understanding purpose is top line. This chapter will lay out the basic tools for group decision making and a framework for thinking about choices about things like roles, resource deployment, and overall direction.

7: Visualizing Purpose
Orienting to Your Mission

These next two sections in *Visual Teams* step through the TPM stage by stage and explore the kinds of best practices you can use to address each one. I will treat some of the suggestions made in *Visual Meetings* in more depth, especially in relation to creating team action plans and decision making. But before we go there, let's begin at the beginning, and look at how visual teams can start out connecting with purpose, personal fit, and membership.

Teams Have A Wide Range of Purposes

Teams get started for all kinds of reasons. Some are initiated because a specific problem has popped up and needs to be addressed. A human resources development team might be asked to develop specifications for a new training program in operation excellence and recommend some consultants. A chip design team might be challenged with coming up with a device that uses less battery power. A fund-raising team on a nonprofit board needs to raise a specific amount of money. These teams all have a very clear purpose and a relatively short life.

Sometimes the problem is clear but very, very large—like the oil spill in the Gulf of Mexico in 2010, or the Japanese earthquake and resulting nuclear crisis in 2011. These kinds of problems have a clear focus, but may be quite unclear how to organize or solve the problem. There are layers of coordinating teams, logistics teams, medical, food service, water, and shelter teams—it goes on and on. The challenge of setting direction is more one of prioritizing a withering avalanche of requests and needs.

Other kinds of teams have vague purposes. I have a nonprofit client that after a retreat where they identified many communication issues, created a Culture Improvement Team to review these and suggest some communication principles that could become "norms" for staff. But the true focus of the group kept blurring as other issues having to do with the informal culture of the organization cropped up.

LET'S THINK *REALLY BIG* THIS TIME!

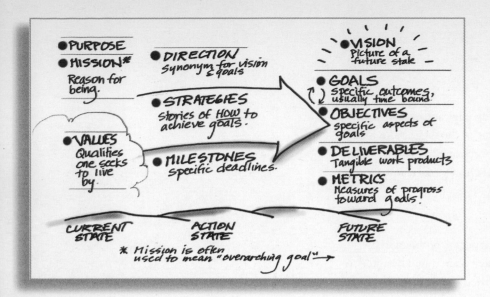

Some teams are started in organizations with very lofty, expansive purposes, like fostering world peace, or doing something about global warming. Teams in this environment face a big challenge getting clear on what they should be doing, since there are so many choices.

Because having a sense of purpose is very much a question of each individual person's awareness and consciousness, it is difficult to put into words or graphics. So the focus of best practices in this area is to provide a kind of space or "container" within which people can share and explore these questions.

THE LANGUAGE OF PURPOSES

This is a graphic chart mapping out some of the many terms that are in common usage for purpose, goals, and strategies. They vary in how forward looking they point, and how abstract they are. A graphic like this can help a team sort out how they want to use language.

Handling the Language Problem

Before you can suggest a specific activity that would clarify purpose, you might have to clarify how people are using all the language that surrounds this challenge. On this page is a graphic I've used to help people visually define how the different terms are used.

You'll see here some of the common words that become proxies for purpose in organizations—*mission, direction, vision, goals, objectives, outcomes, deliverables, strategies, core values, guiding principles.* I've placed them where they seem to gravitate. Missions generally arise from initial conditions and the reasons for being associated with a team. A vision, on the other hand, is generally considered to be a compelling picture of a future state. In the middle are the terms we use in action, like strategies.

But having a picture like this won't settle the issue. In some organizations the word *goal* describes the top level, direction-setting orientation, with *objectives* supporting the goals. In another it will be *strategic objectives* on top and *goals* supporting them. At HP for a while they used the Japanese term *hoshin* to represent the big, overarching goal of a division or unit.

I think the reason there are so many words for purpose is a direct result of its importance—just like the wide number of words Eskimos have for snow. All of these words have special and different meanings depending on where they have become established.

While the words I charted here are the ones I've encountered most frequently, I know that if your team has a spiritual orientation people talk about having *guidance*, a *calling*, or *ministry*. Grove consulting teams talk about *scope*, *intention*, or *focus*. In the military a person has *orders*, *assignments*, *details*, and *missions*—meaning the big goal.

My experience is to learn whatever language is used most widely, and tune up your team much like an orchestra would tune up before playing. Put up a chart like the one on the previous page and get some general agreement on which words you are going to use where. As much as I might like the chart I'm sharing here, I know that there are team situations where the words would be used differently, so be prepared for that and adapt!

Clarifying and Communicating Sponsor Expectations

Here I am using yet another word for goal—*expectations*. If you are a special task group or new team in an organization, there will surely be some people who were involved in starting it that have ideas about what the team should be doing. In an organization with performance management systems in place these expectations might be quite formal and tied to specific metrics, with pay and promotion linked to the results. Getting clear about sponsor expectations in Stage 1 orientation is critical if you want your team to be able to engage their help at Stage 4, when you need commitment of resources.

My experience is to learn whatever language is used most widely, and tune up your team much like an orchestra would tune up before playing . . . Getting clear about sponsor expectations in Stage 1 orientation is critical if you want your team to be able to engage their help at Stage 4, when you need commitment of resources.

COMMUNICATE THE BIG PICTURE

A task group charged with specifying guidelines for a consultative selling training program needed approval from two high-level sponsors in marketing and sales who were more focused on their own dislike of each other than on the consultative-selling task force's needs. To let the two executives understand they knew their purpose, the group created a chart that showed the overall company goals in large letters, the big initiatives that they knew the two VPs were consumed with, and in very tiny letters showed how their task force fit in. This poster was the first thing the VPs saw, and it immediately oriented them to knowing that the task force had its priorities right! It was a bit like bowing deeply before going out on the Aikido mat to spar They accepted the team's meeting outcomes and gave the go-ahead!

Practices for Clear Chartering

Here are some ways to use visualization to get clear about sponsor expectations

❏ **Graphic Interview**: Interview the sponsoring manager or manager and write out a list of their expectations on a chart so they can see you heard them correctly. Then share this with the team.

❏ **Posterize Sponsor Expectations**: Find the original e-mails or other communications where the sponsor communicates what they expect and write these up in a poster that the team can review in its first meetings.

❏ **Invite Sponsors to Kickoffs**: If your team has an initial web conference or startup meeting, have the sponsor come and provide some context and information about expectations. Write these down visibly so the sponsor sees you and others heard things correctly.

❏ **Create a Line of Sight Chart**: Leaders in organization like to believe that teams know how their work links with others. Create a chart that shows the overarching goals of the organization that your team is serving, and then nest in the other goals.

❏ **Name Your Team to Reflect Your Purpose**: When you are clear about your purpose pick a name that will remind everyone of the purpose of the team. The Boise BLAST team stood for Boise Laserjet Advanced Sales Team. The purpose was embedded in the name.

Working as a Team to Orient to Purpose

Regardless of whether or not the initial charge to a team (there's another word—*charge*) is clear, it helps to have everyone get a chance to think through the purpose of the team. These practices are useful in the beginning of a new team, or with a standing, functional team or ongoing team that may have lost sight of its purpose. These practices all seek to create a spacious container for dialogue and exchange. The intention is to let everyone create some meaning for him- or herself, and have time to think through their own sense of connection with the team's identity and his or her own fit with the team's purpose. Later on this kind of work provides grounding for the more explicit work of clarifying goals. If you move too quickly to goal formation it can close up the space for thinking about purpose.

- **Sitting in a circle**: Circles symbolize wholeness and are a great way to have a dialogue about purpose. The circle allows everyone to see each other equally. The absence of tables suggests that the people are the focus of attention, not the work itself. Having a beautiful centerpiece stimulates people's imagination and reflective selves. In the photo on this page you'll see that flip charts and large panels are ready to capture key comments. Some of the questions you might ask in this kind of setting are:

  – What brought you to this team?

  – What are you most excited about that we've been asked to do?

  – Why is this team important to you?

  – What is your story about our reason for being?

  These kind of open-ended questions pull out the inner stories that people are telling themselves.

- **Working in pairs**: Have people work in pairs and answer the same kind of questions and report out.

SIT IN A CIRCLE

One of the oldest ways of working is to meet in a circle, where everyone is equal, and you are centered on something meaningful, often represented in a centerpiece of some sort.

HUMAN WORD PROCESSOR

A fun way to work on a mission statement is to become a human word processor.

1. Have everyone throw out key words that he or she thinks ought to go into the mission statement.

2. Arrange these words on a large display (this can also be done on a whiteboard in a computer conference).

3. At this point, invite the group to propose phrases and sentences composed of the words.

4. Keep reflecting all the suggestions, moving the stickies around.

5. Keep at it until the words gel into a draft statement that everyone can sleep on.

6. As a variation you might ask a smaller group to make the original arrangement to get started.

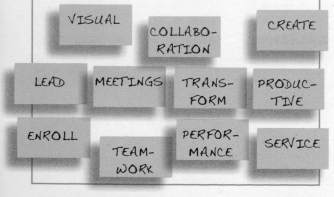

❏ **Mandala Templates**: Post a large mandala template and ask everyone to share who they are and why they are on this team. You can extend this into a trust-building activity easily by asking what skills and knowledge people bring to the team.

❏ **Go-Arounds Online**: For a team meeting on the web, ask the same kinds of questions that you would ask sitting in circle face-to-face, but record the answers with a simple tablet on whatever whiteboards are provided by the web conference software.

❏ **Human Word Processor**: Some teams want to get a clear mission statement early in their work and aren't wanting to spent time reflecting on purpose and more individual concerns. Do the exercise in the side box if you want to have some fun.

Taking time for purpose can have a powerful effect on a kickoff meeting.

Focusing on Values

Sometimes a team that is in a renewal stage is really, in a sense, starting over and needs to reconnect deeply with its purpose. This is often the case for directors who are joining the boards of an established organization. It's also the case for associations and functions in large organizations that are ongoing in the midst of personnel changes. In this case, where there is a history, you can focus the group on the value of the organization and use that as a way to bring some sense of purpose.

The Los Angeles music center was initially funded by a group of friends of Buffy Chandler, wife of the publisher of the *LA Times*. She called the group the "Club 100" and they defied all common sense and managed to succeed in getting the music center built north of the city in an area that wasn't deemed the most desirable at the time. Over the years the original group had moved on and a new group needed to reconnect with their mission. They decided they needed a workshop on how to fund-raise and engaged Coro to help lead it. I was the lead facilitator and knew that they needed to reconnect with their deeper purpose to be effective. We had an innovative design for the workshop, in that we invited some actual foundation program officers to hear proposals that the women would develop in small groups and then present. Because they were actual foundation representatives, this was more than a practice session.

I was struggling with how to begin when I remembered a story about a consumer research group that had found out that in a given year 5,000 people in the Chicago area had purchased 1/4 inch drill bits. The odd thing was no one who bought one of the bits wanted them—they wanted the hole!

I do believe this is a made-up story, but it provided a perfect, humorous frame for our work. So I began the workshop telling this story, and at the crucial moment turned and drew a circle on the large sheet of paper. Then I turned and said "no one really wanted the music center. They wanted the value it brings to the community. Let's share what we think that is."

The next half hour was an explosion of sharing about all the things that the music center meant. I simply recorded all these ideas around the open circle. The group went on to immediately apply these ideas as they created pitches for funding that small teams actually delivered to invited foundation managers, who agreed to come and provide critiques. Even though it was a workshop, the conversations were with real program executives capable of giving grants. The lessons stuck!

Telling Group Histories

A bridging practice between orienting to purpose and helping build trust is to guide the group in telling its story in a visual way. Recently, following the economic meltdown in 2008, the top management of Old Navy met to have a strategy meeting. Their internal organizational person wanted to have the session be a real team development experience in addition to being a strategy

NOBODY WANTS A DRILL BIT

Begin a values workshop by telling a story about a number of drill bits being sold in a region, but nobody wanting them!

They all wanted the hole! Nobody really wants your team, they want the value you will bring.

Draw a circle and draw out the values that everyone imagines your work will provide.

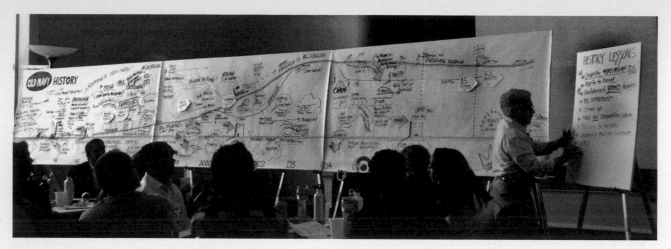

SHARE THE DEEP NARRATIVES

The purpose of a team is often embedded in its stories of origin and success. This picture shows me illustrating a history of Old Navy at a top management strategy offsite. Following the economic meltdown of 2008, the mission of Old Navy to be a value player came fully to the fore and the company experienced steady growth. This history-telling allowed everyone to celebrate their management team's purpose and mission and many accomplishments along the way.

workshop. We agreed on doing the history.

On The Grove's Graphic History template (shown here), there is light flash that says "...in the beginning." All teams have an origin story about how they came to be. For a standing functional team, a management team, a board, or staff group that has long tenure, there are probably different versions about why they got started in the first place. Letting everyone share the story they carry and simply writing it out on a history chart really opens things up. You can then continue with all the other stories about how your team came to be.

If you remember back to the BLAST team story in Chapter 1, this was one of the first things I did when meeting with the team to determine what they wanted from me regarding presentation design. If I had just stuck to the simple goal of our work, I might have missed the bigger picture. I didn't know until we told the story that there had been a history of failures that propelled that group to take risks and make a printer that connected to all computers. I didn't know that one of their internal concerns was having their experience repeat the failure of two prior teams. They had some personal reasons for wanting to be on the team, but failing wasn't one of them.

Providing Space for Orientation

Questions of personal fit and identity can't be answered explicitly in the early stages of a team process. What's important is to invite reflection about it, and give space for it. This is a personal concern, not a group matter, at this point.

Here are some suggestions for providing space for reflection on purpose, group identity, and membership.

❑ **Journal Activities**: In The Grove's workshops we have table teams begin by creating a title page for the workshop and inviting everyone to create something that reflects their reasons for being in the workshop.

❑ **Walk Abouts**: Give everyone time to walk around in nature and then come back to a meeting with reflections about why they are here and what is important to them.

❑ **Cover Story Vision**: Do the exercise described in the box to the right as way to orient everyone. This activity is also useful later on as the group is formulating a group vision. In this application its purpose would be to allow everyone to imagine success and how they contributed to it.

❑ **Writing an Obituary**: A rather powerful way to stimulate reflection on purpose and values is to have people write an obituary about they would like said about their work on the team when they die. This kind of activity would apply to boards and other critical teams that might be the subject of such remembrances. I remember doing this with a group of community foundation executives who were a special interest group in the Council on Foundations. We gave them a half hour for personal reflection, and then invited everyone to come back in a circle to share the result. Within 10 minutes several were weeping at the power of the stories they read. These were grown men and women, used to being somewhat private.

❑ **Sitting in Silence**: If a group has a stated purpose and mission that people know, you can connect them with this sense at the beginning of a teleconference or face-to-face meeting by simply inviting everyone to reflect on the reasons everyone is gathered, and to connect with the importance of that mission.

WRITE A COVER STORY VISION

One way to get team members to reflect on their upcoming work together and what it might mean to them would be to have everyone imagine being featured in a magazine or blog article. Simply writing the story in the past tense will address many of the orientation concerns on your team.

1. Invite everyone to imagine they are on the cover of a popular magazine or featured in a popular blog for the work they have accomplished on the team.

2. Have them imagine the story, using the little template shown here.

3. Come back together in 20 minutes and share what came up.

4. Make sure you create a nonjudgmental space for this kind of sharing. Its purpose is to gain insight into how people are thinking about the team.

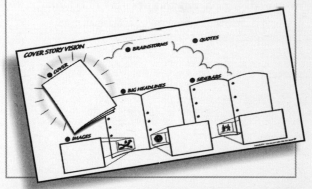

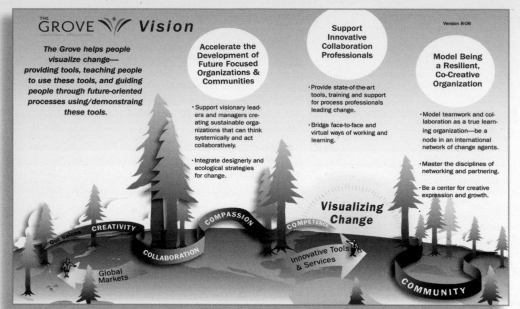

THE GROVE'S VISION

This large poster of our vision at The Grove Consultants International was created in 2008. It has remained quite steady in the midst of the ups and downs of the economy and the changes in our strategies.

In my work with Allan we have come to understand that it's not so important that everyone's different stories about purpose, identity, and membership agree, but that everyone has a story that is compelling to them personally. This is what fuels all the rest of the work together. Agreement and alignment comes at the "turn" in the TPM. Before that is a lot of exploration, trial and error, and even "storming," as Tuckman points out.

Commemorating Your Purpose and Mission Graphically

When you do get to a point of having a clear purpose and mission that can be articulated, it helps to create a visual poster that can be posted during meetings, or carried around in small size, or show up on critical presentations and documents. Some of the possibilities for visualization include:

❑ **Logos**: Create a team name and logo that reflects the purpose and mission.

❑ **Poster**: Create a special Mission Poster with text and graphics.

❑ **Desk Icon**: Create a desk item, like a 3-D pyramid or cube that has the purpose and mission on one side, the team's name on another, and maybe some of the key goals when you determine them on another.

❑ **Wallet Card**: Some organizations would have their management teams carry a plastic wallet card with the purpose and mission.

❑ **Create a special, graphic slide** that everyone can use in presentations.

You can always work backwards in regard to these kinds of visualization activities. By this I mean agreeing it would be good to have the team purpose and mission in one of those forms, and then have a process of dialogue and agreement to determine what goes on them.

Graphic designers and architects work this way all the time. They know the client wants a nice looking website, an attractive brand image, or a compelling new headquarters building. The act of beginning to create sketches and versions of what it might be provides a kind of scaffolding that supports people thinking about possibilities far beyond what they might have imagined at the beginning of the process.

If you work visually this way you can take your group into the kind of spaces a designer lives in when they are inventing and playing around. The dynamics are quite conducive to providing time for everyone to get tuned into what they are doing together and why it is important. Creating these *for* a team does not have the same impact as cocreating them.

Trusting Your Trained Intuition

When I was just starting my business I served as a selection judge for Coro along with Sam Bois, a very experienced consultant and former Jesuit who wrote *The Art of Awareness*, our guidebook to general semantics, the operating meta-language of Coro. I knew Bois was an expert on handwriting analysis and at lunch shared with him some of the visual notes I was taking of the different candidates. "What do you make of these?" I asked, in the kind of expectant way an admiring

ALIGNING ON STRATEGIES

Each year The Grove team identifies the key strategies and initiatives it will pursue as a full team. This is commemorated in The Grove's Five Bold Steps template you see on the far wall. This picture is of a quarterly team meeting in the Garden Room at The Grove's offices in the Presidio of San Francisco. As the team has repeated the practice, the depth of alignment increases.

student would approach a teacher/mentor—which he was for me at a distance through his writings. He looked at the papers, then looked at me very carefully. Then he set the papers down and said "trust your trained intuition" and went back to eating.

I've puzzled over that response for years. As I've explored the far edges of the kinds of sense I can make with pictures, symbols, words, and charts of every imaginable kind, I've discovered the worlds that lie beyond symbols. I think that these realms are accessible if we pay attention to faint signals, if we learn to trust our intuition.

But what is a "trained" intuition? I've come to believe that the human psyche is capable of pattern finding and recognition at levels that move well beyond explicit symbols. I'll return to this in Chapter 12 on high performance, when I share Hilary Austen's principles of artistry. For now let me invite you to imagine that allowing yourself to work hard with language, numbers, and pictures, and working on yourself so you actually experience the four flows I wrote about earlier with all their distinct qualities—learning to access your own spirit, emotions, mind, and body— result in something that can register as a whole, integrated impression and what my Quaker friend calls a "leading."

If you can connect at this level with what it means to have a sense of purpose, and more importantly if you can create space where your team can be open to this kind of sensibility, you will experience a current of intention and movement that may be the most important element of all in teaming.

8: Seeing Yourself As a Team
Developing Trust

The three characteristics of teams with high trust are mutual regard, forthrightness, and trust in each other's reliability and competence. These characteristics point to qualities that have a huge river of meaning for people. Who we respect and who we hold in high regard are very much functions of personal values that in turn are very influenced by culture and experience.

One day my wife, Susan, a poetry teacher in San Francisco public schools, brought in an article by former poet laureate Robert Haas. I don't have the article anymore but I can't forget its primary point, which was about how deeply the music and rhythms of language communicate beyond the explicit meaning of words. Haas had many examples of how patterns of speech call us to respond or to cringe, just through deep associations with that we find familiar.

Think about people from the southern United States, who pride themselves in appreciating life and gracious living, and have musical speech patterns that reflect this. They can find the driving cadences of a native New Yorker grating. In reverse, the New Yorker may experience the southerner as too "laid back." Extend this kind of subconscious assessment to cross-cultural communications. A person from Asia may be extraordinarily literate in his or her native language, but stumbling with English. It's hard to see through this to the respect we might have for someone from our own culture who knows all the nuances. All of this feeling and assessment of each other goes on unconsciously most of the time, but affects our relationships and trust. In this chapter I want to share some of the ways you can work visually to support teams working through all this.

Teams Sail Through Icebergs of Meaning

In our Creating and Maintaining High Performing Teams workshops at Bethel, Maine, when Allan, Russ, and I were developing the TPS, one of the exercises we would conduct involved having small work teams create a flip chart image of an iceberg, labeling three regions as shown on this page. Then we would have people share (1) Things they thought but didn't say; (2) Things

People in teams communicate only a fraction of what they actually think, feel, and observe. This is why creating trust takes time. Conduct this activity to see for yourself.

1. Draw out a picture of the iceberg shown here on a flip chart.

2. Explain that members in a team process always think things they don't say, feel things they don't express, and observe things they don't share.

3. Give people a few minutes to note some of these things for themselves.

4. Then share items, writing them around the iceberg and elaborating on those ideas that spark interest.

5. Draw the conversation to a close when the allotted time is up.

Team Iceberg

1. Thoughts not spoken
2. Feelings unexpressed
3. Observations unshared

HOPES AND FEARS

This is an exercise to get everyone to feel okay about expressing concerns, as well as dreams and visions, at the beginning of a team process.

1. Invite everyone on the team to interview each other about their hopes and fears for the team.

2. Create a large display like the one shown above.

3. Have each person introduce his or her partner to the rest of the team, sharing their hopes and fears. Record hopes as circles and fears as clouds.

The chart above was recorded during a meeting of chief information officers who were partners of a major consumer goods company.

they felt but didn't express; and (3) Things they observed but never pointed out.

It didn't take long to make the point that groups of people express only a small fraction of what is actually going on at any time. Imagine teams that are decentralized and communicating through the web! The icebergs are even larger, especially if people are multitasking, which is common. No wonder building trust is so challenging. There are many ways to trip up.

Creating Common Language

To even begin to engage deeply, people in teams need to be able to communicate, and that requires language. One of the reasons graphic facilitation has grown in popularity stems from the way it provides a second channel of visual language through which people can communicate. One time I was invited to France to facilitate a management team of a very traditional French pharmaceutical company. They had no experience in meeting as a management team. In that culture the president and two senior officers traditionally made all the decisions. But the European Union was forming and they wanted to expand outside of Europe. They knew, as a team, that they needed to expand their skills, and their language. So they had me work in English while they spoke in French. I had a translator, of course. I would listen and write down and illustrate what they were talking about. They would read the English and then respond and comment in French.

It was a very successful meeting and we developed a vision for the company that I later illustrated. I also discovered one of their reasons for having me over. They wanted to learn business English! Seeing me translate everything graphically was a perfect medium. What a great example of workplace learning this was.

The impact of graphic language goes beyond reflecting what is spoken. Graphic language engages collaborative illustration of how things connect and work in systemic ways. And the artifacts of these visual meeting sessions take the presentation of results to a new level.

In the 1990s, Procter & Gamble had a very developed internal culture of computer conferencing. In fact, they were one of the leaders in the application of this kind of software, but didn't advertise this. For instance, they had great success getting teams that were starting new plants to share information with others who already had the experience, and greatly reduced the variability in effectiveness of these kinds of projects.

As members of the Groupware Users Project they hosted a conference for the network of companies involved (see Chapter 17 for the complete story). We were discussing teamwork and the prospects of various kind of collaboration software. This was all happening when our computers still had "C" prompts—before WYSIWYG (What You See Is What You Get) interfaces and windows. The exchanges really weren't very robust. The conference wasn't peoples' main line of work and team members would touch in now and then. But one day I posted the seven stages of the TPM with a one-sentence description of each stage. The conference erupted in exchanges, with everyone using this framework to make this or that point. This happens when people have shared mental models that they can refer to. You don't have to agree with the models to use them effectively, especially if the distinctions are well-developed and useful.

Common Language Best Practices

A set of practices for creating common language would include things such as the following:

- ❏ Share the TPM early.
- ❏ Design clear, descriptive names for the stages of the team's work.

MY GIFT IS INTUITIVE VISION

❑ Identify information that everyone should know in common and make it available on a shared website or hard copy.

❑ Take time to really understand the words in any scoping documents, expectations lists, or mission statements—especially with cross-cultural teams.

Create Settings for Relationship Building

Since trust is centered in feelings, our social selves are the ones that need to be engaged. In many cultures one would be expected to know a person personally before doing any business with them. These "high context" cultures, as cross-cultural consultants call them, are places like Latin America, Japan, or Italy. One would expect to have meals with new teammates, share information about children and families, and sing and laugh together.

"Low context" cultures don't need as much personal information to relate and communicate. The German culture is proud of its precise language and trusts it. American and British cultures are in the middle somewhere, but often move right to work in meetings. But even lower context cultures depend on social time to get to know and trust each other. You feel different about someone if you've seen pictures of their children or where they grew up.

Personal Best Team Experiences

Aside from well-planned socializing time, the most effective way I've seen to develop trust fast is to let people tell stories about what, in fact, are their deep filters in regard to teamwork. These come from our past experiences working with groups and teams. One of my clients is a Leadership program in Baltimore that involves 50 community leaders in a very immersive program of learning how things work in that region. It's a cross-cultural, cross-sector program sponsored by the Greater Baltimore Committee. The participants aren't a highly interdependent team, but they do need to have high mutual respect and good communication to get the most out of the program.

In the third month the entire group goes on a two-day spring retreat to connect with their personal visions for leadership and to get to know each other much better. It's a classic trust-building experience.

The turnkey activity, which I have seen work every year for 24 years of facilitating this program without fail, is called "Personal Bests." We ask everyone to share a story of his or her own personal standard of excellence in regard to leadership. It is, by request, a personal experience coming from any aspect of life—work, family, or community. There are ten minutes for each story, with a couple of minutes of feedback about what the story reflects about each person's leadership style. After all the groups are complete everyone returns to the large group and shares themes, which are posted graphically on a large sheet of paper. They don't need to be lectured about leadership. It's embedded. I've seen small groups bond permanently. People are amazed at each other's lives.

I learned the activity at Apple Computer at our Leadership Expeditions—week-long workshops at Pajaro Dunes south of Santa Cruz, California. The same thing happened there. The small groups shared their stories and bonded. In the case of Apple, we asked everyone to use a well-developed form to fill out their story in advance, which they brought with them for the storytelling.

Ladders of Abstraction

Sometimes it helps to frame storytelling activities with an explanation of the ladder of abstraction. The chart on this page was created to set up the personal best exercises at the spring leadership retreat I just wrote about. It is a great of example of how a short story and a simple graphic

Strengthen relationships and understanding about how each person thinks about teams with the following exercise:

1. Have each person reflect on the best team experience they have ever had in their lives.

2. Write this on a sticky note and create a display of all the teams.

3. Have each person tell a short story and begin identifying the characteristics of good teams, one item per sticky note.

4. Introduce the TPM.

5. Map the characteristics onto the model, moving the sticky notes around and talking about where they seem to reside.

6. Explore all the different kinds of words that people use, and treat this session as a tune-up for learning how to listen to each other.

framework can broaden a group's ability to communicate. By encouraging real engagement and open listening, we can begin to understand another's point of view.

In *The Wisdom of Teams* (page 5), Katzenbach and Smith state as one of their "uncommon sense findings" that high performance teams are extremely rare. They go on to write that "this is largely because a high degree of personal commitment to one another differentiates people on high-performing teams from people on other teams. This kind of commitment cannot be managed," they say, "although it can be exploited and emulated to the great advantage of other teams and the broad organization."

The amount of time and energy you need to spend getting to know and trust each other on a team is a direct function of how high-performing you hope to be. One of the powerful aspects of the TPM as a visual framework is showing graphically how trust and high performance relate by operating at the same emotional level of a team's existence.

Sharing Experiences and Success Models

Larger teams can build mutual respect and forthrightness through group storytelling. The Old Navy team of VPs that I wrote about in Chapter 7 began their work by sharing pictures of each other's families. It fit with their company culture, but even so, it was impressive to see how much good feeling and positive energy was released in the room after they completed the sharing.

I then followed up by leading the group in telling their group history. I have never had a history telling session be anything other than a positive, helpful experience for people. Individual team member's stories never have as much detail as I can draw out of the team as a whole in a short period of time. Few have ever visualized it. The effect is to provoke a reorganization of everyone's internal story, making room for more differences and nuances.

Assessing Competency

The resource section in the back of this book indicates many wonderful sources of ideas of team development activities of all kinds. *Visual Meetings* itself is packed with different ideas about how you can use interactive graphic recording, sticky note activities, and idea mapping to engage a group and get them to open up to each other. I want to end this chapter with one final observation about the value of these kinds of visualization strategies.

Many teams are not struggling with interpersonal trust and mutual regard. People like each other and are open. But in today's fast-paced environment, people are not always sure the people on the team know enough or are competent enough. If you don't know the other people you simply don't know.

At Apple's Leadership Expeditions in the early days of the company we had Jim Whittaker, leader of the first American expedition to climb K2, kick off the sessions with stories of how he organized his climbing team. He stressed time and again how important it was to be bone honest about capability, because everyone's lives depended on it. He himself didn't crest K2 on that climb. Others were deemed more fit for the assault. Because altitude sickness affects climbers mentally, team members had to rely on each other to call each other on symptoms.

So how do new work teams check out each other's competencies? How do management and leadership teams do this? Deep trust probably requires moving deep into implementation and having direct experience with each other, but there are ways to work on competency assessment earlier.

One of my favorite ways with leadership teams is to do environmental scans and context maps. These outward-looking activities allow everyone a chance to add-in, and get a flavor for each

VISUAL CLUSTERING

This is a variant on the kinesthetic graphing described in Chapter 5.

1. Create sticky note labels that read VISUAL, AUDIO, and KINESTHETIC and post them in three places in a room.

2. Explain that everyone on the team probably has a preferred way to learn.

3. Even though everyone may use all three, have team members cluster by the label that represents his or her preferred mode of learning.

4. Have each person in the clusters talk about why her or she picked that mode to the others who picked it.

5. Talk as a whole group and invite people to talk about their choices and preferences.

6. Discuss the implications for your team in terms of what kind of tools and methods you need to think about using.

Another interesting kind of clustering would be to have the labels refer to the archetypal roles illustrated in Chapter 4, page 67—

VISIONARY, ANALYST, TASK-ORIENTED, and RELATIONSHIP-ORIENTED and do the same exercise.

GRAPHIC CASE STORIES

Use visual storytelling for team-building. This small group of consultants with an HR team in China received instruction to graphically illustrate one of their projects and then share it with the other team members. This allowed them to both learn something tangible about their work, and learn a lot about each other's awareness and expertise.

other's thinking. No one knows everything about the environment in which a team finds itself, so this kind of activity is usually very equitable.

Here are some of the ways you can create a discussion that creates a solid foundation of mutual understanding:

❏ **Case Stories**: Share case stories of comparable projects and map them out. Have small groups draw out stories of projects without any rehearsal and share its insights with other small groups. (See side story.)

❏ **Context Maps**: Create context maps of the relevant environment. Make sure that you have everyone contribute to the conversation and write down everything everyone says without judgment. Let the group argue with each other if need be, but focus on creating a fair, safe, conceptual playing field.

❏ **Research Reports**: Create customer research teams and have people work with other team members they don't know well and report back results from interviews.

❏ **Group Portrait**: Map out a group portrait and have people identify categories of information relevant to the work at hand. A circular, mandala format works well for this. On distributed teams have everyone send in a photo in advance and create a combined picture. Then record the information people share around their pictures using a tablet. Map out experiences relevant to teaming such as family sizes, first jobs, sports, performing arts, and community involvements.

❏ **Kinesthetic Modeling**: Earlier I described having people line up along a spectrum of interests to learn about each other and preferred styles. You can find out things such as what time of the day each person thinks is best for their work, or whether or not they like to talk out ideas or reflect individually before communicating.

The Power of Group Norms

All of the exercises I've suggested in this chapter will provide a setting where people can open up and get to know each other. The playfulness of graphics helps a great deal in this process. But none of this substitutes for the power of the informal social agreements of a team. These are called "norms" in group work, a shortening of what sociologists would characterize as "normative behavior"— meaning the behavior that is considered acceptable and standard.

A classic experiment that has been repeated many times is illustrated here in the side story. It's *Candid Camera*'s "Face the Rear" video. Repeated experiments show that everyone will go along when everyone else in a group embodies a certain kind of behavior. You can try this yourself by getting a group and going out on a crowded city street. Then have everyone in your group look up at something. Invariably nearby people will look up.

An organization has many kinds of things that everyone in the organization just simply goes along with as "understandings." Leadership is hugely influential in setting these kinds of norms, as leader behavior gets mimicked. Edie Seashore, a revered senior organization consultant, told a story at an OD Network conference about a client she had worked with successfully for several years, getting them to open up and develop a culture of sharing. On a visit several years later she was startled to see people come in the front door, walk to their offices with their heads down, and close their doors. It happened repeatedly, until she asked someone she knew well if there had been some changes.

"Oh yes," the person said. "We have a new boss who comes in every morning, doesn't talk to anyone, and marches right into his office and closes the door." The implications for team leadership

FACE THE REAR

A classic example of the power of group norms is a *Candid Camera* video called "Face the Rear," created in New York City in 1962. Here you see a man in an elevator. Three *Candid Camera* staff enter the elevator and face the rear. After a few moments of uncertainty the man is now turning to face the rear himself. The video shows repeated examples of this effect, with *Candid Camera* staff facing sideways, taking hats on and off, and reversing positions mid-floor. In every case the individuals not in on the "rules" went along with them anyway.

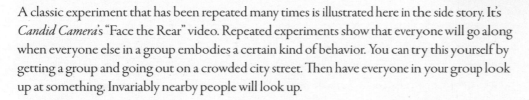

seem clear. If you want people in a team to be forthright, mutually respectful, and trusting each other's competencies, then the team leader needs to be the first to do so, and remain consistent about it. Even more importantly, the larger organization needs to cultivate a culture of teaming that supports this kind of modeling.

The Balance Beam of Trust

Tom Melohn lost his job at a large consumer goods packaging company after 25 successful years and took over leadership of a small company called North American Tool & Die in the 1970s. In his 11 years he turned the company around and became a featured story in the highly acclaimed PBS TV series *In Search of Excellence*. Our team at Apple invited him to be a regular speaker at the Leadership Expeditions to describe how he created such a high-quality result without firing employees and radically restructuring. What he did was win their trust. In many sessions I heard him tell the story of patiently and consistently telling his people the truth, loaning them trucks when they needed to move their families, and understanding and encouraging involvement. He described the "refrigerator award" that he used to graphically acknowledge people who came up with great ideas for the team. One worker had reduced errors caused by two parts getting damaged when they were being fit together by putting one in a refrigerator first to shrink it a little. So every week Tom would gather his team around that refrigerator, and pull out an envelope with someone new getting the award.

When asked what the hardest thing about his accomplishment was, he replied, "Realizing that every bit of work I spent building trust could be destroyed with one lie, one betrayal—poof." This is probably why truly high-performing teams are rare. It takes a great deal of integrity and persistence to create the kind of high trust that such teams require. But it can be done.

9. Clarifying Goals & Action Plans
Using the Graphic Gameplan

This chapter describes how to use the Grove's Graphic Gameplan to answer five basic questions that are key for launching a new team. Agreements on these will help your team get to work quickly and effectively. These questions are:

1. What are your specific **goals**?

2. What **resources** do you have to work with?

3. What **tasks** need to be done to reach your goals?

4. What **challenges** will you face?

5. What **team agreements** are needed to support success?

If these seem to be common sense, they are! Any time you do something cooperative with other people, like take a vacation for instance, you will need to know where you are going, what you have to take and spend, and how you plan to get there. It is common to compare planning to taking a journey. This is the reason this metaphor was chosen to support the Graphic Gameplan template.

Clear Goals are The Most Important

The keystone to action planning is the first question about goals. Being clear about goals involves creating a description that makes it possible for anyone who reads or hears the goal to know what it means to complete it. Agreeing on goals makes the rest of the planning process possible. A good boss can set goals for a work team in some cases without collaboration, but any team that has to work closely together needs to support goals as a group.

WE CAN ALL DO A GAMEPLAN AND COMPARE!

GRAPHIC GAMEPLAN SETUP

This illustration shows our book's little team ready to lead several breakouts—each able to sketch out a draft Grove Graphic Gameplan..

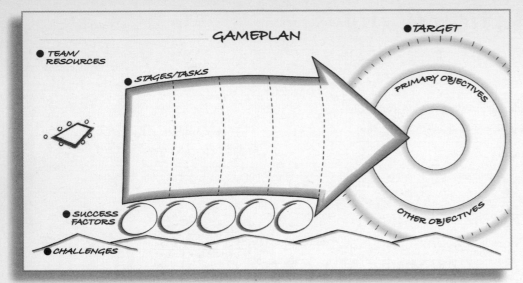

Having clear goals is different than simply having an overall purpose or direction. You may know your family wants to go on a vacation, but you still have to choose whether you will go to Europe and visit Paris, or go camping in the mountains. Until you identify the specific focus or target of your activity, it's impossible to decide what to take and how to prepare.

Graphic facilitation is at its most effective at this stage. Writing things down and using maps and diagrams to explore relationships is what human beings mean by being clear.

The Graphic Gameplan

I first saw a large, graphic template being used in a planning meeting that Geoff Ball was leading. He called it a rainbow diagram, because it had a space to indicate the goals near a pot of gold at the end of a rainbow. A large arrow provided space to write down the tasks and actions intended to reach that gold. The arrow moved over a set of hills that represented challenges. The simplicity of visualizing in this fashion made it easy for everyone to see the relationships between those elements. I knew I could use this framework myself to help a group plan. You'll probably have the same response reviewing it in its evolved form now.

Many years later I was invited to facilitate a meeting of several change teams at Levi Straus & Company. They had been working several years with a large consulting firm that spent hours and hours analyzing every aspect of the business in the context of an "re-engineering" project. The consultants formulated many suggestions for business improvement. But in all that time they had not shown the teams at Levi's how to organize for action. The change team was very unhappy with the results. Coincidentally the company's overall results had improved since the

GRAPHIC GAMEPLAN GRAPHIC GUIDE

The Grove's Graphic Gameplan template is probably the most widely used and useful of the different templates in The Grove's visual planning toolkit, and the one I recommend for doing draft #1 of an action plan.

initial contract, even though implementation had not begun. Management decided to terminate the big consulting contract and take over the job itself. The change team still needed help.

In one afternoon, using the Graphic Gameplan, our Grove team facilitated the development of three team action plans, using large sheets of paper. The change teams were ecstatic. They were so happy with the result, in fact, that they insisted that we create a detailed guide to using this tool that they would provide to all team leaders in the company. This became the first of The Grove's Leader's Guides, and one of our first published Graphic Guides. Let's look at this tool in detail.

On the facing page you will see the graphic and the spaces for answering the five questions I posed at the beginning of this chapter. This Graphic Guide is designed to support the initial meeting of a team where it takes a first look at how it will move into action.

Why Is It Called a "Gameplan"?

We call it a "game plan" because it is like the kind of plans that a sports team might develop before a game. Users also call it an action plan, because it is perfect for the kind of action teams that are often created on the heels of a special strategic offsites where management agrees on big goals and launch initiative teams. There are many examples of how effective this can be. One of the clients that I wrote about in *Visual Meetings* is an architectural firm called the DLR Group. They have dozens of offices around the country. Some 40-50 partners collectively own the firm, and like most collegial professional organizations, didn't have a long history of planning together when I first engaged with them. But following our initial planning offsite, where we identified eight strategic goals with full group support, they decided to push further and develop action plans the same way.

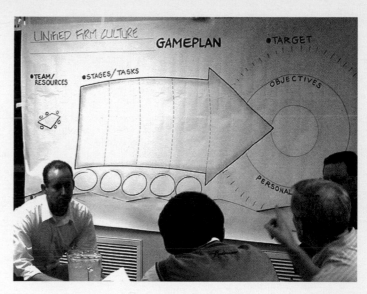

SMALL GROUP ACTION PLANNING

A team of architects from the DLR Group orientes itself to the Graphic Gameplan and the topic it chose. They are one of six groups that developed these action plans in parallel, and then shared and critiqued them in a larger group. These first drafts became the basis for a more detailed set of plans developed by teams in the different offices.

CREATING SMART GOALS

1. Hang up your Graphic Gameplan with a large sheet of paper or flat wall to its right side.

2. Review the definition of SMART goals on the next page—i.e. Specific, Measurable, Actionable, Relevant, and Time bound.

3. Ask for an example and write it on a sticky note. Check against the SMART criteria and create a model for the team.

4. Set a target date for the action plan. This date would be the time when the goals will be complete. A specific date helps make your discussion more concrete.

5. Ask people to work in pairs and identify additional potential goals for the team.

6. Group these on the workspace to the right of the target. Consolidate similar ones and number each goal.

7. Dot-vote or multi-vote for 1/3 of the total list (have each person jot down the #s of the goals he or she prefers and then raise hands).

8. Discuss and add the goals that the team agrees upon to the Graphic Gameplan target.

In a follow-up meeting, shown in the photograph on the last page, the same partners re-gathered and broke into six action-planning teams. Each was provided a Graphic Gameplan, instructions, and sticky notes. In one session they not only developed but also shared all six, with a rich amount of learning.

These initial drafts, of course, needed further development and became the basis of more formal project plans that involved many other people. But let's turn to look at the Graphic Gameplan now and see how to use it. Following are the steps you would go through to develop a good first-draft action plan.

STEP 1:
Warm up Looking at Current Team Resources

Even though the goal setting is most critical, it helps to warm up by reviewing where you are starting as a team. The left side of the Graphic Gameplan has room to list out who is on your team, who is sponsoring it, and what other resources you have to work with. What's already in place? What constraints exist? The point of starting here is to agree on what you have to work with.

If you are holding a meeting and this is the only chart you are developing, you may need to add addition flip chart pages to the left side for all the things you might want to identify. The template itself doesn't detail out all the variations. You need to think through these. Some of the things that are worth exploring in regard to the team and its current resources are:

❏ Specific names of teammates
❏ Names of sponsors and champions

- ❏ Names of associated teams & organizations
- ❏ Budget allotments
- ❏ Work already completed that you can build on
- ❏ Issues that you are carrying into the work as baggage
- ❏ Specific constraints
- ❏ Tools you have to work with

How much time you spend on this depends on how familiar or unfamiliar the team as a whole is with the current situation. In a longer planning process you might have already reviewed your team history, maybe even completed a SPOT Matrix (a four box model identifying strengths, problems, opportunities and threats). The DLR Group managers had done this, for instance. If you are doing the Graphic Gameplan in this context, begin by reviewing this other work and use the template to simply highlight some of the key points and list team members.

STEP 2:

Clarify Goals

Determining the specific goals for your team is the most important in the action planning process. If you have only a short period of time to plan, spend most of your time here. I wrote earlier about SMART goals and objectives in the section on purpose. Purpose and intention are like the containers that give goals meaning. But the goals themselves allow a team to make decisions and focus resources in effective ways. Getting group agreement on them also makes it easier to lead a team, if that is your role, or to set the goals of your direct reports if your team is a management team of a function or smaller business and you have people reporting to you who need to link to the team's work.

SMART GOALS CRITERIA

Determining the specific goals for your team is the most important in the action planning process. If you have only a short period of time to plan, spend most of your time here. A common set of criteria for clear goals is summed in the acronym—SMART. It stands for:

- ❏ **Specific**: in that goals and objectives should be concrete and clear.
- ❏ **Measurable**: you should be able to analyze results numerically
- ❏ **Actionable**: meaning there are clear actions that would lead to the goal being achieved.
- ❏ **Relevant**: (some like the word "Realistic" here) meaning it is something that needs to be done, and is possible imagine accomplishing
- ❏ **Time bound**: meaning a specific date for completion is embedded in the objective.

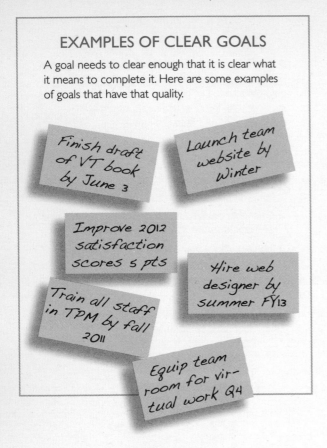

EXAMPLES OF CLEAR GOALS

A goal needs to clear enough that it is clear what it means to complete it. Here are some examples of goals that have that quality.

Finish draft of VT book by June 3

Launch team website by Winter

Improve 2012 satisfaction scores 5 pts

Hire web designer by summer FY13

Train all staff in TPM by fall 2011

Equip team room for virtual work Q4

Challenges in Setting Clear Goals

Following are suggestions of how to create your target on the Graphic Gameplan and address common challenges you may encounter.

- **Fuzzy goal statements:** It is common for people to suggest very general things like "improve our customer service" or "become more efficient" or "improve the quality of our publications." These are more statements of intention than actual goals. The way you can tell if a goal is written specifically enough is to ask, "Would we know for sure we have accomplished it?" If you have to work on a goal to get it clearer, take the sticky note and put it on a flip chart, or write it on a clean page in your web-conference notes, and then invite suggestions for how to make the goal clear enough that you would know it had been accomplished. "Become more efficient" might end up being "Reduce the time to market for new products by 25% by Q4."

- **Unrealistic goals:** When ever I've helped a team create its target goals, someone always challenges one or another goal as being "unrealistic." I think what people mean by this is they can't imagine any way to accomplish it. But what is realistic for one person may be unrealistic for another, or may seem very un-ambitious to another. Goals cannot substitute for leadership on a team. Remember the story about structural tension seeking resolution as the driver of creativity. It may be important to have some goals that are "stretch" goals, and seem unrealistic to some of the people on the team. In these cases, if you are the team leader, you need to enroll people in the possibility of going for it anyway—paint some pictures of having a breakthrough in creativity.

- **Team isn't accepting a leader's suggested goals:** In some organizations team leaders are expected to set the goals for a team and lead them skillfully to their completion. In very hierarchical organizations the team leader may be more like a commander, giving orders. In others it's simply a matter of a new team not knowing enough and needing close guidance. In both these cases you may run into a situation where the group isn't "buying in" or agreeing. Holding a gameplan session is a chance to educate the group and bring them along. If a team leader simply imposes goals and doesn't allow discussion it can drive the group to become passive and move into denial and unproductive behaviors.

- **One or two people dominate:** Goals matter and sometimes people "dig in" and get very stubborn. One of the values of working with sticky notes and dot voting is it provides a step-by-step, visual evidence of where the whole group is responding. Keep providing chances to write up all the ideas before you start narrow, and then patiently work toward agreement.

- **Too many goals:** A convenient way to avoid accountability, as a team, is to have a blizzard of goals, making it very difficult to know if progress is being made on any of them. If your team seems resistant to converging on 4-5 key goals, it may be necessary to step in as the team leader, or if you are a consultant or facilitator, encourage the team leader to step in. If you are a self managed team without a leader, then think about the problem as one of choosing which goals should lead the others, like a lead goose in a flock, or the leader of a peloton in bicycle racing. In my experience it is very productive to establish some clear priorities if you have more than 4-5 stated goals.

- **Goals are actually tasks or principles:** Groups will write down many suggestions in a goals exercise that are actually better illustrated on the gameplan as specific tasks, or held as operating principles and posted in the "Success Factors" wheels that hold up the action. There isn't a hard and fast rule for what ends up as a goal and what ends up as a task or milestone, but I follow the principle that the target should be high level enough that it truly does guide action over a period of time, say months.

- **Sticky notes get confusing:** If you are putting sticky notes on the target itself, having more than 10 or so can get visually confusing. In this case it might be better to organize the potential goals in columns to the right. If you are working with a larger team and the pairs generate a lot of notes, this column layout visually shows right away where the bulk of agreement is, by the number of variations of a similar goal. On the target itself, once you have dot voted or multi-voted, write the ranking on the sticky and rearrange them so the ones getting the most attention on toward the top. Then continue discussing until the group agrees.

Clarifying Goals & Action Plans / 123

- **Group can't decide:** If you can't get closure on the target a good response might be to suggest the team do a quick, first-pass on the rest of the action plan, then let the information "soak" a bit and come back to it in another meeting or web conference. Getting goals that aren't real goals doesn't help.

Aligning with Personal Goals

In some cases you may find it useful in a game plan session to have a dialogue about personal goals as well as team goals. You would use the space called "other objectives" for this purpose. A truly committed and aligned team will have its members feeling like they will accomplish something for themselves as well as the larger organization. The kinds of teams where this might be important are:

- Special task forces like the BLAST team that are seeking breakthroughs
- Management teams of a startup organization
- Change teams taking on big organization transformation assignments
- Teams leading special campaigns
- New product development teams
- Performing arts and sports teams
- Learning teams

These teams have in common the need for people to trust each other and work past real challenges, backing each other up and pulling together. It helps to know the personal motivations of other team members. You would support this kind of dialogue the same way you did when identifying general team goals. Invite some reflection time, then use sticky notes, then share and lead a dialogue for understanding. Because these are personal goals you don't really need to agree on them.

STEP 3:
Identify Tasks

By the time you get finished creating a clear target with its goals, you may already have some task items in the big arrow. There is enough room in the arrow to support a good brainstorm about what you need to do to reach the goals. It's important to think of this activity as creating a "first draft," since you will surely need to revisit it and work on details or rework the plan on a real roadmap linked to calendars.

There are several different ways you can approach this third step.

1. **Brainstorm tasks with sticky notes:** You can invite the team to identify tasks, having one person or everyone writing them down, and cluster them inside the big arrow.

2. **Sequence Tasks:** If there is time and interest, once you have identified tasks you might get the group to sequence them and create the first version of a more defined roadmap linked to calendars.

3. **Brainstorm tasks by stage:** If the work of the team will fall into nature stages—like Research, Identify Options, Pilot, Evaluation, Program Design—then list these stage names along the top of the arrow and identify the different tasks in columns under them.

4. **Brainstorm by week or quarter:** An alternative to stages is to mark off the arrow into weeks or quarters and identify tasks in progression. For this kind of application you might just list the items with little bullets and not use sticky notes.

5. **List out strategies:** If you use the Graphic Gameplan with the management team or high-

SORTING AND AGREEING ON TASKS

This DLR team chose to brainstorm potential tasks on sticky notes, then consolidate and write the agreed-on ones on the chart itself.

CHALLENGES FREQUENTLY IDENTIFIED IN TEAM ACTION-PLANNNING

❏ Not enough resources
❏ TIME
❏ Competing demands
❏ Complexity
❏ Weak sponsorship
❏ Conflicts with other teams
❏ Politics
❏ Uncertain environment
❏ Cultural differences

TIGHT RESOURCES

NOT ENOUGH TIME

level task force you might simply list out ideas for strategies to accomplish your goals, and move to tasks later. In these cases just write in the different items in a list inside the arrow.

You may notice a wide range of specificity in the tasks the first time you work on them. If your use of the Graphic Gameplan is a first draft, don't worry about this. Have whoever takes responsibility for the next version even out the items so they are similar levels of specificity.

Step 4:
Identify Challenges

During goal and task identification some team members will inevitably bring up reasons why things can't be done or wants to talk problems that the team will face. Instead of ignoring these comments, write them down in the challenges area down below the horizon line of little mountains. Just write them as separate bullet items. This practice acknowledges rather than discounts people who are focusing on problems, and will stimulate more thoughts about tasks that need to be in your plan to meeting these challenges.

After you have finished the tasks review the challenges you've already noted and invite the group to identify any others that seem to be missing. Challenges include anything that can stand in the way of the group achieving its goals or compromising the quality.

Step 5:
Agree on Success Factors

The wheels on the Graphic Gameplan are called "success factors." There are several different kinds of things that you can identify here, but all have the characteristic of not being tasks you can complete. Success factors are behaviors and agreements that have to be part of the team process all the way along, much like wheels on a car. Some of the kinds of things teams might want to consider are "operating agreements," "core values," or "team norms" about behavior. The strongest drivers of team behavior, as I pointed out in the last chapter on trust-building, are social norms. These are the stated or unstated expectations about what kind of behavior is acceptable. A first pass at identifying these during action planning does not create these norms, but helps open up awareness and dialogue about what they are.

If you are working cross-culturally you can assume team members will have different ideas about this part of the action planning. Discussion of the success factors may well catalyze the need to have a special session just on this subject, especially if you are a team working on culture change during a merger or reorganization.

A large leasing company from the Midwest acquired a West Coast leasing company and wanted to have a team session focused directly on values and operating agreements. The larger company had a culture that was quite process-oriented, with procedures and disciplines for many activities that were left to the individual judgment of managers in the California-based company. On the other hand the California company had a more creative and, frankly, fun, work environment. Both sides were quite wary of the other as they began working together.

The management team leader was from the Midwest company and wanted a full discussion of team values and behavior. He chose to go beyond the simple identification of norms in an action plan to a full session focusing on how values translate into action. The visual format was pretty straightforward. We created a flip chart for each of five core values that were already articulated. In the center of a three-ringed target we lettered out the value.

The process began by checking to see if the values were correct. A healthy discussion added the

EXAMPLES OF SUCCESS FACTORS

- ❏ Keep sponsors informed.
- ❏ Get buy-in from stakeholders.
- ❏ Stay on budget.
- ❏ Deal directly with conflict.
- ❏ Support each other.
- ❏ Meet deadlines.
- ❏ Time-outs to adjust.
- ❏ Equitable scheduling of teleconferences.
- ❏ Ask for help.
- ❏ Flag problems early.

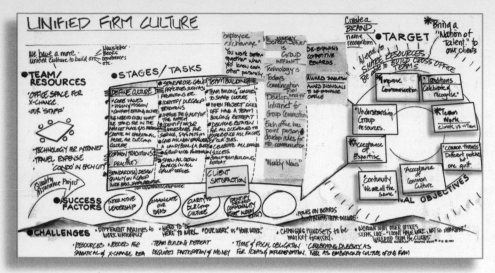

FIRST DRAFT GAMEPLAN

This is a digital copy of the final draft of the Graphic Gameplan the DLR team created at the off-site. You can see it didn't have time to transfer all the sticky notes to the chart itself. On these kinds of initial plans, encourage your team to work quickly and get a version they can share and improve, rather than overworking the first draft.

value "profitability" to the initial five. Then we reviewed each value and had members of the management team define what they meant by each one. We recorded these definitions in the second ring on each value target. The third ring was for reflections on how this value should show up in action in specific parts of the business. A good couple of hours were spent in rich conversation.

If you are in a culture where team leaders are powerful, he or she will be very influential in setting the success factors. In self-managed or more loosely managed teams, the social environment sets these norms. W. L. Gore, for instance, has a culture that is overtly collaborative and works consciously to have teams take responsibility. Colleagues will rein in a leader who is too bossy or non-inclusive.

Applying the Graphic Gameplan Virtually

A team that wants to do its action planning virtually would follow the same process as I just described, but with some technical choices about how you support the visualization.

❏ **On-Line Templates:** You can pull the digital version of the Graphic Gameplan into a drawing program like Sketchbook Pro and fill it out using a tablet and stylus.

❏ **Interactive Slides:** You can share a PowerPoint version of the Graphic Gameplan in whatever web conference platform you are using and have one of the participants fill it out as the group goes along.

❏ **Modified Slides:** A third way to work is to have a smaller group prepare a draft action plan using a digital version of the Graphic Gameplan. The on-line discussion would then involve review and input, with notes either being taken with a tablet on a whiteboard or by changing the original slides. This approach works very well if whoever is the team leader is truly receptive to input and not just going through the motions.

❑ **Shared Interactive Whiteboards**: If you are lucky enough to have a network of Smart-boards (see Section VI), your team can work on the touch-screen just like you would on a paper template and persons in remote locations will be able to participate. Smart Technology allows its board to network with iPads, PCs, Macs, and other boards, with dual-drawing capability. I think we will see a lot more of this capability developing as organizations seek to avoid travel costs.

Getting Buy-in to Your Plan

When you work with visual templates like the Graphic Gameplan, you now have a tool that makes it easy to show it to other teams, your sponsors, or whoever else needs to support the plan. Hang up the chart or give them a photocopy of it and then invite suggestions. If you incorporate their suggestions the people you involve will feel more connection to what you are doing. Your ideas might even improve in the process!

A really solid action plan probably requires two or three revisions, and time reflecting and discussion it with others to make sure it is something you can publicly commit to as a whole team. A common practice is to take a first pass at the plan during initial goal-setting meetings, then repeat the process creating new Graphic Gameplans after the team has had time to think about their commitments. If these are then transferred to a digital version (The Grove supplies PowerPoint template for all its Graphic Guides), then a third round of reflection is supported. One of the purposes of planning in an interactive way like this, is to build a stronger and stronger base of mutual understanding among all team members. If your team context is very dynamic, this may be much more important than the documented plan itself, for changes will be required. Chapter 11 has examples of how an HR team conducted several reviews of its roadmaps to get alignment,

**GRAPHIC GAMEPLAN
LEADER GUIDE**

A 20-page, step-by-step Leader Guide is available for this and other Grove Visual Planning Graphic Guides at www.grove.com.

and then used the final documents a year later for review of progress against plans. Predictably, what actually happened didn't conform precisely to the plan, but the planning introduced a level of mutual understanding that made the review sessions a real exploration of learning and preparation for the next cycle.

10. Consensus or Command?
Deciding Commitments

Allan Drexler and I had as much discussion over what to call Stage 4 in the TPM as any. We landed on the stage name COMMITMENT, wanting to emphasize that something more than just planning and being clear goes on when actual money, time, and staff are brought into the picture. This operational level of team performance is tangible and specific. It embodies the constraints that when mastered make it possible to focus on action and performance in later stages.

Think about meetings you have been in when the focus turns to "How will we work?" People immediately think of their calendar, their budgets, their staffing, and workload. The energy of the group hits ground at this point. The universality of this feeling undergirds our confidence that showing the team performance process as going "down" before it can go "up" reflects what really happens. People are pointing to this fact when they talk about team process having a "pinch point" or a "groan zone"—to use the term of Sam Kaner, author of *The Facilitator's Guide to Participatory Decision Making.* Learning how to get a team past this point, and be clear about how to make decisions going forward, follows right behind having a trusted leader and clear goals as being essential to high performance.

What Are the Choices for Decision Making?

In any group there are some who want to get going, make decisions quickly, and sometimes be the ones in charge. Others want to hear from everyone and be more thoughtful. At the turn a team needs a common language to work out these differences. If you are adventuring outdoors, the decisions may involve lives. In business it may involve efficiency, timing, and profits.

In *Visual Meetings* I shared a framework that has been well tested in our facilitation work at The Grove called the Decision Strategies Framework. It provides an excellent common language for teams. The different approaches are organized in conceptual spaces created by combining how power and loyalty shape which choices work best. If you think of the four quadrants as centers

WE HAVE TO GET MOVING AND HEAD OUT THIS WAY.

I THINK WE SHOULD HUDDLE AND POOL WHAT WE KNOW—WE COULD GET LOST.

Consensus or Command? / 131

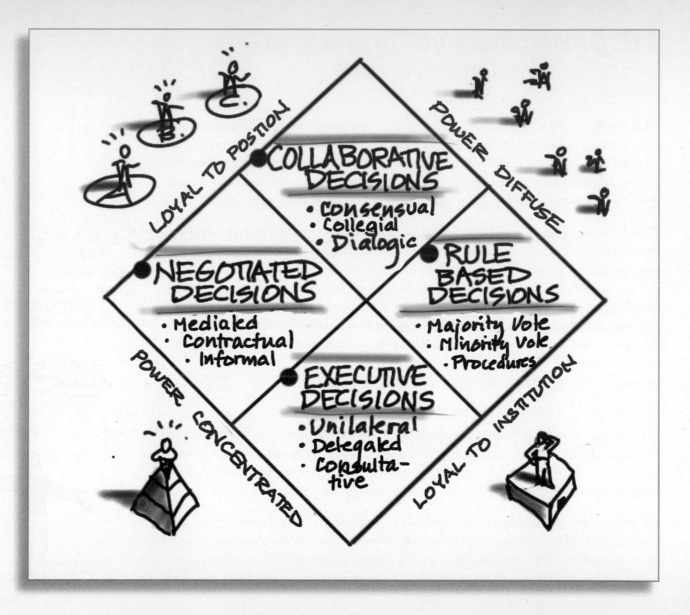

DECISION STRATEGIES FRAMEWORK

If you compare the dimensions of power and loyalty they create four zones that each provide a center of gravity for one of the decision strategies. This framework is a type of visual language, and not a precise map to the territory. You can imagine any one of the squares getting larger and the others smaller, depending on the culture and norms of the organization that sponsors your team.

LOYAL TO POSITION

POWER DIFFUSE

COLLABORATIVE DECISIONS
- Consensual
- Collegial
- Dialogic

NEGOTIATED DECISIONS
- Mediated
- Contractual
- Informal

RULE BASED DECISIONS
- Majority Vote
- Minority Vote
- Procedures

EXECUTIVE DECISIONS
- Unilateral
- Delegated
- Consultative

POWER CONCENTRATED

LOYAL TO INSTITUTION

of gravity created by the conditions that exist within the culture of the organization, then the four different choices are positioned where they work the very best. Before we get too practical looking at specific tactics, let's step back and think about why making the turn at the pinch points of process are so challenging.

Loyalty and Power, the Drivers of Decision Culture

Loyalty falls on a spectrum between loyalty to an institution or loyalty to your own positions and interests. One the one hand it is about affiliation and being completely immersed in an organization or movement, and on the other being attached to your own ideas. This is one axis of consideration in any decision process. Underpinning a sense of loyalty is the emotion of love and connection, as the side story suggests.

Power, using Adam Kahane's definition in *Power and Love* (see side story), is the built-in desire of all living things to express their essence and grow. It is what drives plants to absorb water, sunlight, and carbon dioxide and create more leaves, roots, and trunks. It is what pulls executive teams to acquire new companies and new personnel, enter new markets, and grow. In groups this desire can be diffuse, like it is a parent-teacher organization connected with a school, or a cross-boundary task force in a company, or an association of nonprofits working together on a social problem. On the other end is concentrated power with means and resources—like the concentrated power of contemporary executives of large, multinational organizations, the heads of large military organizations, elected officials, and inspirational leaders with huge followings.

I heard Kahane speak a few weeks after his book was published, and he called for more leaders to become ambidextrous about power and love. The same appeal needs to be made to teams. They need to know both the language of power and the language of love, connection, and loyalty. How does this play out in practice?

POWER AND LOVE

After years of working with groups doing scenario planning, Adam Kahane, the Royal DutchShell consultant who worked in South Africa to help end Apartheid, has written a book called *Power and Love: A Theory and Practice of Social Change*. He's worked all over the world getting teams of leaders to deal with today's toughest problems—healthy cities in the United States, equitable development in Colombia, peace in Guatemala, polarization in Israel, and child malnutrition in India. Twenty years of this work led him to an initial conclusion explored in his first book, *Solving Tough Problems*. In his words—

> I concluded that the key to creating new social realities is to open ourselves up and connect; to our own true selves, to one another, and to our context and what it demands of us. (*Power and Love*, Preface, x)

Connecting is a deep instinct. It's why we gather in teams. It's why tribes are so universal and basic. Kahane knows from experience that even in the toughest situations, if the right conditions are created people realize their connection with—their love for—each other. But he goes on.

> Five years later [after his first book] . . . I can see that this conclusion was right, but only half right, and dangerously so. In order to address our toughest challenges, we must indeed connect, but this is not enough: we must also grow. In other words, we must exercise both love (the drive to unity) and power (the drive to self realization). If we choose either love or power, we will get stuck in re-creating existing realities, or worse. (*Power and Love*, Preface, x)

LET'S AGREE ON
WHERE TO BOUNCE!

Collaborative Decision Making

When power is diffuse and loyalties are more to individual ideas and positions than to larger institutions, working in a collaborative way is required. No one has the power to order others around. There probably aren't rule books anyone agrees upon. The choices involve different way of sitting down and talking things through. On a team, when you choose a collaborative approach it can take a couple of forms.

❏ **Consensus Decisions**: Consensus is when everyone on the team agrees to a decision. The mantra for this kind of work is—"Can you work with it?," "Can you live with it?"—will you go along and pull with the team if we accept this decision? It does not mean complete agreement. If you are part of groups and teams that work this way you know that it takes time and can be quite frustrating, but if you have the patience to work through things it can result in very strong agreements. Look on the following pages for a large grid that details the specific pros and cons of this and other substrategies for decision making. My book *Visual Meetings* is full of examples of how facilitators work with sticky notes and large displays to board everyone's ideas and then find patterns of agreement. If your team works by consensus, using active visualization will be a huge help.

❏ **Collegial Decisions**: Groups of experts who work together often defer to each other's expertise and will make decisions by having the subgroups with the most knowledge make them. An unstated assumption, very common on academic teams, is to support each other and not make problems for the other colleagues. In other words, if you don't challenge our decisions we won't challenge yours. In some teams this way of working might manifest as deferring to subcommittees on a board that have more expertise than others in subjects like fund-raising, marketing, programs, and the like. Very diffuse organizations can work quite effectively this way. A way to support this kind of decision making visually is to invite subgroups that are advancing proposals to make suggestions supported by graphic template or murals. This will allow expertise to shine, and provide space for additional ideas.

❏ **Dialogic Decisions**: A growing number of groups are using dialogue instead of discussions as a way of reaching decisions. The orientation has been framed by physicist David Bohm, who describes an "implicate order" inherent in all nature that can be observed by opening and paying deep attention to its emergence. In groups this means listening behind what people say for their deeper assumptions, suspending judgment, and actively working as a group to draw out each persons' wisdom. This kind of approach is used in spiritual groups and cross-sector circles that are working to understand social change. When a work group or team decides to explore an elaborate metaphor visually, comparing itself to another kind of organization, like a musical or sports group, and maps out roles and characteristics, the quality of the exchange is dialogic. In my experience these graphic explorations work best when exploration replaces judgment. Everyone in a dialogue focuses on looking past initial ideas to the deeper patterns of insight, and trusting the group will recognize agreed-on ideas when they appear.

Executive Decisions

The opposite pole to collaborative approaches is executive decision making. This, in its simplest term, is where the leader of the team makes the decisions. Many groups work this way, but it requires concentrated power and loyalty to the organization that provides the power. Its most complete realization would be the command and control approach used in military organizations. However, there are different approaches to wielding this kind of power. They are:

❏ **Unilateral Decision Making**: This is fairly easy to understand. The team leader decides what to do and tells the others. As you will note on the Decisions Strategies Grid, this is a very efficient style and often a preferred one in emergencies where speed is of the essence. Paramedical teams would work this way, following a leader. It's a tempting role for high-performing individuals who are expert in their fields and have been promoted to team leadership. Relying on just this approach would be like a musician playing one note.

When a team decides to explore an elaborate metaphor visually, say comparing itself to another kind of organization like a musical or sports group, and mapping out roles and characteristics, the quality of the exchange is dialogic.

Following is a simple visual exercise for tuning up your group and empowering more distributed, delegative decision making:

1. Give each team member paper and markers.

2. Ask each person to list out their responsibilities, making sure to indicate all areas where they have decision authority.

3. Have each team member read the other persons' charts, and initial one of three things:
   – Things that are missing
   – Disagreements
   – Items that aren't clear

4. Take one of the lists and go over the initials as a team. Clarify any confusion, add missing elements, and make decisions about areas of disagreement. (In my experience only about 10 percent of the items will fall in this latter category.)

5. Delegate as many of the disagreed-on items to the parties involved.

6. Discuss as a group items that involve everyone, and work to come an agreement.

7. Have the team leader settle differences if you work in an executive style. Work by consensus if not.

❏ **Delegative Decision Making**: On a complex project a team leader cannot make all the decisions, even if they are expert. Boards, project teams, executive teams, and even design teams will delegate out different kinds of decisions so that many are involved. Each delegate has executive power, and if aligned, experiences all the collective decisions pulling together. Nonprofit boards will delegate personnel decisions to executive committees. Production teams empower quality professionals to decide when standards have been met. You can see, if you think about it, that this kind of decision strategy relies on having a good amount of organizational loyalty that counterbalances special interests. Visual teams apply this strategy when diagramming out the different areas of delegative authority. This is where explicit exercises to define roles and responsibilities help clarify the boundaries and authorities. (See side panel for a visual approach.)

❏ **Consultative Decision Making**: Many effective executives and team leaders use a consultative style of decisions. This means the leader is seeking advice from other team members, outside experts, and stakeholders, but retains the ability to make the decision in the end. In a compressed meeting where action is necessary by its conclusion, a team leader might announce that he or she wants to work by consensus as long as possible, but will make a decision if the group can't come to agreement. This blending of styles can be very effective. A requirement goes along with this style. If a leader seeks advice but never listens to it or makes any adjustments as a result, then the contributions will stop coming, or he or she will implicitly train the team to just mirror back what they know the leader alread agrees with. A visual teams practice is to invite subteams and individuals to create draft proposals using graphic templates and slides as a starting point for discussions with the leader. Murals work wonderfully with leaders who prefer just having a conversation to a formal slide presentation. Murals are up and can be visually scanned all through the conversation. They lend themselves to both linear and nonlinear review, depending on what emerges.

The shadow side of executive decision making by powerful leaders is becoming insulated from outside opinions by rings of supporters who agree and go along. The more powerful the leader the harder it is to really know what is going on outside the umbrella of his or her influence. Mixing decision strategies in special workshops where titles are dropped can offset this problem.

Negotiation Style Decision-Making

When power is concentrated and loyalties are leaning toward positions and special interests, then negotiation is usually required. Negotiations assume vested interests and attachments to positions. As a result the strategies are all about drawing out all the details from all sides, and looking carefully for middle ground. There are three main types of negotiation strategies:

❏ **Mediated**: When team members are so polarized and positioned that they won't even talk with each other, then you may have to approach the situation as a third party and meet with first one side, then another, then back with the first side and back to the other, ferrying solutions back and forth. Lawyers work this way frequently, as do deal makers. Top executive teams are often quite competitive and need this kind of approach for someone both sides trust. The mediation approach focuses on slowly building mutual understanding about interests on both sides, trying to get behind positions. Graphic recording provides some real advantages when the results of one set of conversations are carried into the other side.

❏ **Contractual**: A common way to work with people who have strong interests is to work with a common source document that circulates until everyone agrees with its contents. This kind of contractual work is common in formal legal agreements, but works just as well with shared visual displays that will be used in public ways. When an executive team creates a vision mural, or a team creates a public action plan, the graphic serves the same purpose as a legal contract, and goes through versions as different parties add their changes and request representation of their interests. For a team that wants to engender strong support from its larger organization, creating a graphic charter that reflects sponsor interests is a good way to develop a de facto contract with those stakeholders. Taking a graphic action plan and sharing it with sponsors to get input is another kind of de facto contracting.

Many effective executives and team leaders use a consultative style of decisions. This means the leader is seeking advice from other team members, outside experts, and stakeholders, but retains the ability to make the decision in the final regard ... If a leader seeks advice but never listens to it or makes any adjustments as a result, then the contributions will stop coming.

INFORMAL ROLE NEGOTIATIONS

If you are a team leader and have two sponsors in different parts of the organization, follow this process to get clear on scope and roles.

1. Ask each of your sponsors to have a meeting with you to talk about your team scope and role.

2. Invite each person to write down answers to two questions:

   "What do you need from the team?"

   "What will you do to support the team?"

3. Compare answers and find out where the needs and supports align.

4. Discuss those areas that need clarification and decision.

5. Write down the agreements about expectations as to scope and roles.

❏ **Informal Negotiations**: In matrix organizations where workers report to more than one boss, teaching everyone informal ways to negotiate roles helps a great deal with conflict. This was one of the practices I learned early on from Allan. He would have the matrixed party ask for a meeting of the two bosses, and then have each of the people list out what they wanted out of the situation, and what they would give to make it work. Sharing these lists consistently results in any number of conflicts resolving right away, leaving a few others that needed discussion and agreement. Getting this kind of information understanding in advance of conflicts is a huge help.

Rule-Based Decision Making

When power is diffuse but organizational loyalties are strong, teams can resort to rules and procedures to make some kinds of decisions. In democracies, identification with the rule of law allows legislatures to take binding votes on major issues. Boards of directors will often use this approach to key decisions. There are three major types:

❏ **Majority Vote**: In this approach, if more than 50 percent of a group agrees on something then that is the decision. Teams would rarely use this kind of decision unless they are an executive team or a board, because it creates winners and losers. If, however, team loyalty is very strong and there is a premium on making decisions quickly without having the leader decide, voting is efficient. Visual teams can use different kinds of tools to show the results of votes. In larger groups decision support tools will immediately visualize the results of polls and votes of the group as a whole. There are now tools that utilize smartphones, special keypads, and software on portable computers to do this. Many of these systems will show the final tallies with bar graphics and others visuals to get an immediate sense of where the agreements are moving. Graphic facilitators use sticky notes to do the same thing.

❏ **Minority Votes**: In boards and legislative bodies some issues are sufficiently important that it takes a two-thirds or more vote to get a decision. In this approach the minority votes have the power since it takes a larger agreement to get a decision. A variant on this is where a subgroup is given the power to vote for the larger group and make the decision. Executive committees sometimes work this way.

❏ **Procedural Decision Making**: Decisions can be made "by the book" when processes are very clear or when legal requirements are specified. This, of course, requires the "book," and requires that people have a degree of commitment and loyalty to following it. Cultures vary widely in how much respect they have for the procedures and laws. If you are working in a global corporation and interfacing with a culture that works by relationship and not by the book, you need to be careful of assuming that people will conform. A visual team that makes its action plans and processes explicit and graphic can use these charts to help guide decisions. At The Grove we have our annual goals and initiatives visualized on a large chart and keep it up during important meetings as a reference. Turning strategies into reference documents creates a "book" that can help with subsequent decisions.

The next two pages lay out a matrix of all these choices in summary form, including definitions, pros and cons, and uses.

Decision-Making Tactics

Let's assume that your team has been able to clearly choose the kind of decision strategies that it will use in relation to different decisions. Having a clear range of strategies gives a team a vocabulary of choices.

- Allocating budget might require one kind, perhaps of the executive sort.
- Determining quality standards might be done "by the book," if you are in an industry where certain standards are required.
- Determining roles and responsibility might be by consensus or negotiated. Having a range of strategies gives a team a vocabulary of choices.
- Setting goals and strategy for your team might be collaborative.

Decisions can be made "by the book" when processes are very clear or when legal requirements are specified. This, of course, requires the "book," and requires that people have a degree of commitment and loyalty to following it.

DECISION STRATEGIES MATRIX

The chart on this page and the next details some of the guidelines for the four different kinds of decision strategies and their substrategies. It really helps a team to share a common language for the full range of choices, even though you may, on your team, only use a few of them. It will also help your team as it interfaces with the rest of the organization, which may make decisions in a different way than you do.

COLLABORATIVE DECISIONS	Definition
❏ **Consensual**	Decisions are reached when everyone can "work with" or "buy into" the decision. Minority opinions are explored and win/win solutions sought.
❏ **Collegial**	People with shared points of view synthesize their ideas into a common document or proposal, present them, and look for common ground.
❏ **Dialogic**	By suspending judgement and exploring underlying assumptions, mutual understanding develops and insights emerge from the implicit wisdom of the group.
NEGOTIATED DECISIONS	
❏ **Mediated**	Adversaries work through an intermediary who travels back and forth between parties, crafting a compromise that will be mutually agreeable.
❏ **Contractual**	Friendly parties create a document or clear position that is modified back and forth until each party is willing to sign off on the agreement. (Mural designs work this way.)
❏ **Informal**	Individual or subgroups declare what they want from the other parties and what they are willing to give in order to agree on decisions.
EXECUTIVE DECISIONS	
❏ **Unilateral**	Individual leader makes decisions and communicates orders.
❏ **Delegative**	Decisions are made by the person who knows the most about the subject. Leaders or team delegates decisions to qualified personnel.
❏ **Consultative**	Team leader retains the right to make decisions, but seeks input and advice from other team members and other stakeholders.
RULE-BASED DECISIONS	
❏ **Majority Vote**	Voting guided by *Robert's Rules of Order* or other rule set. Decisions are made in favor of the 50 percent or more who favor a given idea.
❏ **Minority Vote**	Votes require a two-thirds majority, giving minority votes more power. This approach includes special subcommittees that make decisions for others on a representative basis.
❏ **Rule-Based**	Decision are made "by the book" by team members or outside authorities.

COLLABORATION	Pros	Cons	Use when...
Consensual	+ Participation and ownership + Understanding decision	– Time consuming – Not always best decision	• Power is distributed • It is important to have buy-in
Collegial	+ Pooling of expertise + Arguments clarify decisions	– Can be exclusive – Tough issues may be skirted	• Diverse expertise is present • Expert exploration is needed
Dialogic	+ Focus on listening for common ground + Reveals implicit agreements	– Requires openness and trust – Can be circuitous, takes time	• Assumptions need testing • You want deep understanding
NEGOTIATION			
Mediated	+ Accommodates strong positions + Brings in outside perspectives	– Parties are separated – Reinforces positions	• Players are locked in position • Compromise is essential
Contractual	+ Single document focus + Enforceable by reference to document	– Tough if parties aren't equal – Can hang up on details	• Disagreements are likely later on • Stakes are high
Informal	+ Disclosure reveals potential agreements + Respects strong interests	– Relies on willingness to disclose – More difficult with power differences	• Dual reporting requires alignment • Team members are stuck in subgroups
EXECUTIVE			
Unilateral	+ Efficient + Timely	– Misses inputs/low buy-in – Requires respect for leader	• Emergencies require quick action • Timing is of the essence
Delegative	+ Likely to get an informed decision + Utilizes experience	– Others may not understand decision – Low participation and ownership	• Decisions are technical • Correctness is critical
Consultative	+ Uses group info and judgment + Involves others without delaying decisions	– Responsibility isn't shared – Disagreements aren't resolved in group	• Responsibility is focused on the leader • Project management requires consistency
RULE-BASED			
Majority Vote	+ Allows debate/forces resolution + Good for large groups	– Winners and losers – Decision may not be the best	• Interests are very diverse • Power is widely distributed
Minority Vote	+ Uncovers special concerns + Taps special expertise	– Potentially unhappy majority – Resistance to taking risks	• Decisions require substantial agreement • Decision tasks need to be subdivided
Rule-Based	+ Equitable if enforced fairly + Doesn't require understanding	– Can be cumbersome, impersonal – Doesn't handle exceptions well	• Decisions are routine and proscribed • Impartiality is critical

Within each strategic choice, however, there are specific tactics that work, especially if you choose the collaborative approaches. In *Visual Meetings* I shared a Decision Funnel, which is a graphic way of remembering how to guide a group through a range of closure techniques to get to a final decision when working by consensus. When I first learned this approach it was compared to the trial closes that salespeople use. A "trial close" is question you might ask a prospective client to which they will probably say "yes." The side story explains this metaphor.

On the facing page you will find a series of specific activities that are consistently useful in team decision making if you are working collaboratively. Depending on how much divergence of opinion there is, or how attached people are to different positions, you would do more or less of these. Sometimes a good decision just requires a series of proposals, dot voting, and voicing the agreement. Sometimes it takes several hours of discussion and reassessing. You should at least know how to do all the activities described on the next page.

Allocating Resources and Roles

Two additional criteria shape stage 4 of team performance. One is clear allocation of resources and the second is clear designation of roles. Something that designers know is that constraints are actually catalytic to good design. It is the boundary conditions that channel and focus attention and creativity. On a team, coming to agreement on specific budgets and roles, far from being a limited condition, actually frees the group to focus on creative action within those constraints. When these are not clear and you begin implementing, considerable energy and time can get pulled into confusion about roles and resources.

Agreeing on budgets and roles both involve making decisions, and can be approached with any of the methods previously described. Visual teams, of course, would approach both of these problems as a design challenge.

INVITE PROPOSALS

1. Ask for specific proposals regarding whatever you need to decide.

2. Title each one on a big sticky.

3. Array all the proposals on a chart as they are identified and described.

DISCUSS PROPOSALS

1. Scan the array of proposals and invite the team to ask questions.

2. Bring out differences and nuances.

3. Perhaps write pros and cons near each one.

AGREE ON CRITERIA

1. Review whatever overarching goals are relevant.

2. Invite the team to identify potential decision criteria.

3. List criteria on a flip chart or sticky notes.

4. Circle the criteria that everyone agrees upon.

DECISION FUNNEL

This page illustrates a sequence of activities you can follow to get convergence and decisions on a team.

DOT VOTE

1. Provide sticky dots (dark colors photograph better).

2. Ask everyone to vote for 1/3 the total list of choices, whatever they are.

3. Have everyone put the dots in a consistent place, so the graphic pattern shows up easily.

4. Count the dots and indicate the number of votes between two diagonal slash lines (to make them differentiate in any photos).

5. Discuss what this tells you about what the group decision should be.

SORT ON A HI-LO GRID

If you still don't have a decision, create a four-box chart labeled "HIGH" on top and "LOW" on the bottom, for "high payoff" and "low payoff."

1. Sort out the top dozen sticky notes using this spectrum.

2. For variety, put "EASY" on the left and "HARD" on the right to create four quadrants.

CHECK COMMITMENT

1. Draw out a scale from 0–10 with "10" = 100 percent agreement this is the right decision. "0" = wrong decision.

2. Have everyone pick a number, then call out and mark "x"s on the scale.

3. Have people explain what's needed to make their commitment stronger.

VOICE AGREEMENT

1. Look at all the different steps you have taken in regard to the decision.

2. Ask for someone to voice what he or she believes to be the agreed-upon team decision.

3. Circle the choice that is suggested.

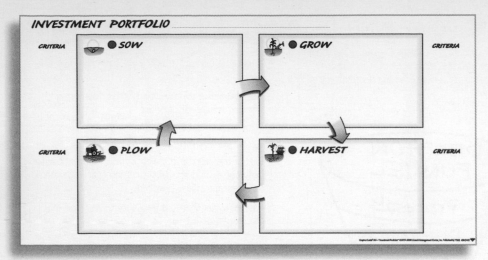

INVESTMENT PORTFOLIO

This template is copyrighted by Rob Eskridge of the Growth Management Centers and reproduced here with permission. It is part of the Grove's Strategic Visioning Graphic Guides, which also have Leader Guides available that explain how they work.

The Grove included a graphic template developed by Rob Eskridge in its Strategic Visioning Process that is a terrific tool for making decisions about resources. It's called the *Portfolio Graphic Guide*, and borrows from a farming metaphor in asking a team to look at four categories for spending money:

1. **Sow**—projects and tasks that need to be started up.

2. **Grow**—projects and tasks that already have some history, and need more resources to get stronger and bigger.

3. **Harvest**—projects and tasks that already work, still get results, and need to be sustained, but not necessarily with more resources.

4. **Plow**—projects and tasks that need to end, in order to free up resources for the other three quadrants.

Look at Current and Future Plans for Resources

At an annual business planning meeting, a customer support function had small teams of five each complete a chart like the one on this page. First they identified the criteria for each of the four categories, based on what the larger organization set as its overarching strategy. Then the teams identified in one color where resources were currently being spent. Another color indicated where each team would like to have changed resources allocation. The small teams designated dollar amounts or FTEs (full time equivalent staff) for the items. Because this was not a formal part of their budgeting, but an exercise in connection with strategy, the team did not push to final agreement, but used the portfolio as an initial activity. A second pass would refine the choices and drive the budget process.

Using sticky dots that stand for simulated money is another way of visually reviewing resource allocation. First, board all the potential activities a team might need to fund, and then have little sticky notes or sticky dots represent a budget of money that each person would "spend" on the projects. This graphically pops out where people place the most emphasis. You may need to work through a decision funnel to get to final agreement, since the dots simply provide a springboard for discussion.

The value of working with sticky notes and dots during a resource allocation process is being able to build a funnel of convergence. First the criteria get developed—one step of closure. Then the items are identified—second step. Then the team dot votes for a third step. Then discussion and consensus, or discussion and the team leader makes the final call.

Role Decisions

If you need to clarify and decide on roles on your team, there are several ways to do this.

1. **Volunteers**: In some team situations the most important thing is to have someone in a role who wants to be there. Asking for volunteers greatly increases the possibility of this happening. In our community garden, for instance, most of the roles get filled this way. Often in a planning session that ends with a number of action teams, management will ask for volunteers to head up this or that group.

2. **Team leader decides**: In instances where a team has a strong leader and/or specific expertise seems required, final role decisions are made by the leader. In describing his ascent

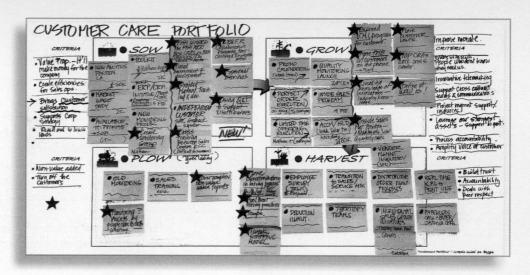

CUSTOMER CARE PORTFOLIO

This chart illustrates how one of three small teams in a customer care function analyzed their current and desired use of resources. You can see the criteria identified for the sow, grow, harvest, plow categories written around the edges. I starred the proposed changes in this black and white reproduction, because you can't see the color differences on the sticky note. This chart supported a good several-hour conversation about resource allocation.

RASI ROLE CLARIFICATION

1. Create a large grid on the wall (or in an Excel spreadsheet if you are online).

2. List names of the team on the right and the key tasks or jobs along the top.

3. Review the RASI distinctions described in the text for who is Responsible, has Authority, Supports, and needs to be Informed.

4. Go over each task and make your decisions.

LOOKS LIKE I'M LEADING ON TWO AND SUPPORTING ON TWO!

up K2, Jim Whittaker was very directive about who he thought should summit, based on his assessment of strength and capability played against the conditions they faced. He did not ascend himself. Sometimes team members need to be stretched to take on something they won't volunteer for, but will perform if asked. Often at the end of strategy sessions when action teams form, top management would like to tap specific individuals as the lead, knowing their capabilities and preferences.

3. **RASI approach**: A graphic and analytical way to determine roles is to put up a large grid and list all the team names on the left and all the different key tasks along the top. It's a tough workout but really clears up confusion. The team discusses and agrees who has the following:

❑ **R**esponsibility: This role is team leader, the person at the point of the arrow of action.

❑ **A**uthority: These are persons who must approve decisions and resource expenditures

❑ **S**upport: These roles support the action.

❑ **I**nformed: This role is to be informed as things go along.

4. **Explore Metaphors**: A more right-brained way to determine roles is to invite everyone on the team to think of other teams that might be similar in challenge and structure to theirs. Once a metaphor is shared, then the roles can be mapped onto the metaphor. A partnership team consisting of a high-tech instrument company and a peripheral supplier decided that their joint team was like an America's Cup sailing team. Several of the members were sailors and knew the metaphor. They could then talk about who was the captain, the chase boat, the sponsors, and the other roles. Getting the group to draw pictures of these ideas helps support the discussion. Another HR team in a high-technology company was having a great deal of confusion and tension between the trainers and the consultants. Each group was annoying the others with differences in how they liked to work—with one wanting more structure and the other wanting more improvisation. They explored past experiences and found that a majority of the team had participated in theater at one time or another.

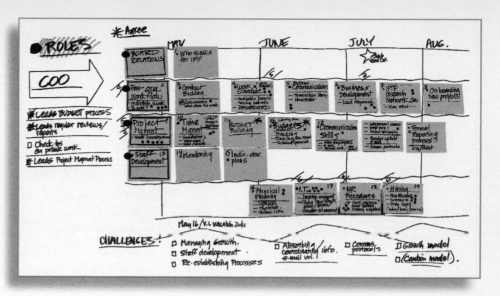

Once the team settled on that metaphor, and examined what it takes to be a good theater company, everyone realized that some of the program would be standard and scheduled and some would be improvised and ad hoc. They also came to appreciate the need for operation roles as well as performance-oriented roles.

5. **Swim Lanes Discussion**: An activity that bridges to implementation involves putting up a large chart and determining the "swim lanes" of activity that the team needs to manage. You then identify persons to lead each lane, and the specific tasks they will have as responsibilities. An example of such a chart is included here.

Managing Your Organizational Infrastructure

In Section II when I addressed the tasks a team leader faces, I stressed the importance of getting organizational support for your team. This is graphically represented in the TPM by the large platform. When teams are collocated the other parts of the organization are available for negotiation and support. When teams are distributed this is a much more challenging job.

On virtual teams, your communications infrastructure is the platform that the team needs to "bounce" off of to get performance. This is why I'm devoting the last section of this book to new technology. Too many team managers claim they still have to fly and meet everyone individually to keep things moving smoothly. It's a burnout task. I actually think that the new technologies like telepresence, interactive whiteboards, and tablets are making it possible to have much richer exchanges without being physically face-to-face. In any event, clear and timely decisions need to be made about communications infrastructure, even if it is simply what teleconference numbers

COO ROLE

This is an example of a roles chart created for the Chief Operating Officer on a management team. It illustrates the four main areas of work and the subresponsibilities. The team worked up this kind of display for each member as a way to get clear about roles.

to use, what web conference platforms are available, and where and how you will store and share large documents and graphics.

Go Slow to Go Fast

In any kind of team process you will be making trade-offs between handling early stages thoroughly and moving ahead more quickly. It is tempting to think that rushing to implementation will get better results than investing in team-building and goal clarification. If your team is facing more rather than less complex challenges, you may be served better by going more slowly and thoroughly in the beginning. Strong orientation, trust, goal clarity, and commitments position you to move very quickly when it comes to implementing. Teams that rush through the first stages may find their time disappearing as they encounter resistance to their work and have to spend additional time selling others on what they are trying to accomplish.

As we move our attention to the "sustaining" part of teamwork, be prepared for revisiting the more fundamental elements when you find out they aren't as developed as they need to be for what you are trying to accomplish.

IV. Sustaining Results
Innovating for High Performance

IV: Sustaining Results

Chapter 11: Graphics & Project Management This chapter reviews the way Otis Spunkmeyer brought visual strategies to the job of implementing strategies within their functions across a multisite company. It features the HR team, which learned to work this way virtually, as well as exemplary applications of large murals for leadership communication.

Chapter 12: Visualizing & Innovating The RE-AMP Infrastructure support team modeled being a high-performing visual team. I tell this story pulling out examples of all the specific tools and methods that made this possible, and end with a set of principles about what distinguishes a truly artistic effort from ones that simply get results.

Chapter 13: Assessments, Dialogues, & Sharing Rallies Handling learning, change, and renewal is the key to ongoing team excellence. This chapter shares how you can use TPS assessment and team dialogues, sharing rallies, theatrical embodiment, and carefully crafted visual models to support rich learning and best-practice development.

11. Graphics & Project Management
Implementation You Can Literally See

Otis Spunkmeyer is a very successful midsized corporation specializing in fresh baked goods like cookies, bread, and muffins. They applied visual strategies over several years to implement their strategic vision and build a visual planning culture within the organization. They utilized a full set of visual meeting strategies to get alignment and action following commitments of the management team to overall direction. Remember that the keys to this stage of team performance are clear processes, alignment, and disciplined execution. The Otis experience is a lesson in how to do all three. As you read through the story, notice that the early stages of team performance repeat, but in the context of having a clear strategy and set of organization-wide commitments.

At the start of the process management was very clear about its strategy, which it was communicating in a lengthy slide deck that had many graphs, charts, and pages of bullet points. But John Schiavo, the CEO, felt that the company was not engaged beyond the management team. When he first came aboard he had been very active communicating throughout the organization, but several years of work that ended up in the company being purchased by an Irish-owned fresh baked goods company had left the employees a bit uncertain as to the future.

Otis Loved the Idea of Large-Scale Visualization

John wanted to bring everyone into the conversation around their new strategies and agreed that a graphic vision would help. Over several months and several iterations the management

OTIS' STRATEGIC VISION

The top management at Otis Spunkmeyer created this Storymap mural in 2008 to provide a strategic framework for all business planning throughout the company. It portrays the key points in their history that leadership needed to emphasize, a review of the overall vision (on the right side) and a visualization of their ten key strategies in the middle. Each person on the management team could tell this story, and knew the detail that lay under the strategic "cookies." These strategies mapped onto the little "cookie man" in intuitive ways (erased to respect confidentiality). The strategies mapped on the bottom provided the "legs" that allowed the upper arms, which required more "reach," to be implemented.

JOHN SCHIAVO ORIENTS THE INFORMATION TECHNOLOGY TEAM

This picture shows Otis CEO John Schiavo telling the story of the company's Strategic Vision to the IT function within the company. The IT function was on the edge of a very large enterprise resource planning project that would integrate all the company's critical information, and needed to align with the overarching strategy. This session helped a great deal.

team created a large mural that any of them could talk about in upcoming business meetings. The process of agreeing on the mural, and then actively rehearsing how to tell the story, went a long way to getting the management team aligned for action. But it needed to translate into the functions.

Aligning the Business Functions

The first year after creating the Otis Strategic Vision, John asked each of his functional managers to lead their teams through a business planning process that would result in each function articulating its own vision and goals that would support the overall plan. These meetings were all framed by the overall strategic vision and were graphically facilitated using The Grove's Graphic Guides.

The functional meetings were classic visual meetings. Each team told its history, developed a context map and chart of strengths, problems, opportunities, and threats, and developed a bold steps picture of the key goals and strategies for the next year. These were all face-to-face meetings taking place at the different units around the country.

Because functional teams were holding business planning sessions and not strategy sessions, the focus was on implementing the larger company strategy. They culminated in an alignment meeting where each function brought their following year goals and strategies charts to a big meeting room, and together reviewed all suggestions in concert. During this session any decision that needed to be taken to remove roadblocks and support implementation found its way onto a sticky note. In the final hour of the meeting the executive team responded to and settled the main issues. Four task groups got organized. A dozen or so decisions were delegated. A couple of decisions were taken on by the executive team for resolution right there.

Human Resources Takes Off

A key goal that initial planning year was the support of the internal Otis workforce, mapped into the strategic vision as "Passionate People." John hired Robyn Meltzer, a dynamic HR manager with previous experience at Levi Strauss, Lucas Digital, and Genentech. Within a year she had assembled a brand new human resources team with members at each of the key Otis facilities and at headquarters. Robyn loved the visual way of working and made it a centerpiece of her own implementation of the Otis strategy

She held an initial face-to-face off-site in 2008 to have everyone meet each other, review the company strategy with John Schiavo and other top managers, identify goals, team build, and take a first pass at a calendar-based road map for their work. (See chart on next page.) She even included some graphic facilitation training so that her team could begin working as a visual team. On the next page is a copy of the first road map they created. When you look at it imagine it in full color with sticky notes and a large, 4' by 8' format.

Robyn's team decided to work virtually after the initial off-site due to cost controls following the economic meltdown in 2008, and the fact that Otis' factories are spread from the East to the West Coast. She wanted to continue the collaborative spirit of the initial off-site and ensure that everyone had input on the goals. It was critical to developing a sense of trust and teamwork in addition to goal clarity, and that took persistence over time. She planned several webinars using graphic recording on a tablet over a web conference, using the same visual formats..

"This process held everyone accountable for providing input," she said in an interview for this book. "I wanted people to visually see that they were being taken into account even though they were not in the same location. This kept them engaged even though they were working virtually.

WEBINARS LINKED THE HR TEAM

Following an initial face-to-face meeting, the Otis Human Resources team used webinars to fine-tune their implementation plans, and check in annually to develop their goals for the year. Here is one of the opening team portraits used to support an interactive check-in, where each person updated the others on key activities, seeing his or her comments recorded and visible through the "share desktop" function on the web conference software.

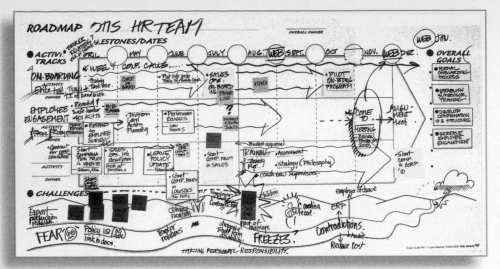

OTIS HR ROAD MAP
CREATED LIVE

This implementation plan was created as a first draft at the conclusion of a two-day team-building off-site that Robyn Meltzer organized for her new Otis HR team. It was translated into a PowerPoint version that became a reference document going forward (see next page).

They also created a pyramid of interdependency/dependency to create a three-year plan. This helped everyone visualize where each player was dependent on other company staff."

Checking the Road Map

The second year of her team, Robyn held a planning web conference rather than a face-to-face meeting. It involved reviewing the overall company strategy, making suggestions for goals, dot voting, visualizing the goals on a graphic template, and then revisiting them for final input. In this process Robyn provided more directive leadership but stayed open all the while to input from all directions.

The road map was translated into a slide version that provided a target document for reviewing what had been accomplished and what needed to carry over. Robyn was very careful to support everyone and have it be a learning event, not a meeting for passing judgments. Everyone was pulling hard and she projected real confidence in everyone's abilities and intentions. On the next page is an image of what the working display looked like after the review. You can compare the original with the tuned-up version to get a sense of how things refined.

Results for the HR Team in Going Visual

A year later Robyn reflected on the results achieved by this regular virtual work with graphic displays and recording. "It created an opportunity to create unity around the HR organization's goals and a road map linked to what Otis was doing at a larger scale," she said. She reported that the visual products had a built-in process that kept the team on track and kept it aligned even though everyone was in different geographical locations. Utilizing visual facilitation via the webinars allowed for the goal development process to be less "dreaded" because individuals did not have to travel; no extensive planning was required (i.e., identifying a venue, hotels, etc.); and there was a minimal amount of disruption to their work. The visual facilitation process was "much more dynamic, rather than boring like traditional strategic meetings."

"Web meetings bring an interactive and engaged approach for alignment and focus for virtual teams. It brings vision and energy that was extremely effective," Robyn says.

"What is great about the webinars is that you see that the input is live. As the participants are talking, they are seeing their input being put into the document. It's kind of like a virtual classroom—and what you say is already noted—you see it being put up."

I will focus in a little closer on some of the techniques for online graphic facilitation in Chapter 18. You will see that the Otis story is being repeated in many companies that are learning how to offset travel and face-to-face meeting expenses with truly interactive online work.

Summary of Visual Tools for Implementation

The Otis results came from a combination of strategies, summarized here. The different levels of documentation and visual work provide a great checklist for using visual meetings and visualization strategies to support implementation of strategy. Here are the tools they used:

1. **Orientation murals**: High-level charts that visualized strategies and visions helped keep teams and units focused. The process of creating the mural and the process of rehearsing and presenting from it gave the executive team a way to align on Otis' strategic vision.

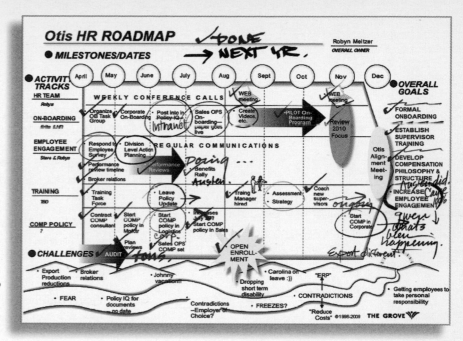

OTIS HR ROAD MAP REFINED IN A SLIDE

Here is the HR road map shown on the previous page translated into one of Grove's digital Roadmap Graphic Guides. The check marks and notes were added during a team web conference facilitated with tablet-based recording.

Getting our management team on one page brought real excitement to our strategic implementation. I was impressed how arguing over the visuals ignited important conversations and supported alignment.

Ahmad Hamade
CFO, Otis Spunkmeyer

2. **Visual planning sessions and graphic documentation**: Both the top management and functional teams—HR, IT, marketing, sales, manufacturing, and customer service—held two-day, face-to-face business planning sessions supported by graphic recording, and framed by the big strategic vision. These sessions produced very graphic 11x17 meeting reports that allowed anyone attending to tell the story of the meeting to persons who did not attend.

3. **Graphic guides for alignment**: By asking all functional teams to report using a standard visual format, the management team was able to visually support an alignment process that allowed leadership to literally see the company as a whole and all the goals and initiatives being proposed for the upcoming year.

4. **Visual online meetings for follow-through and accountability**: Robyn Meltzer's application of web meetings to review progress, road map commitments, and overall alignment built a tradition of team accountability into her far-flung team. The fact that the visual templates from the face-to-face gatherings matched those used online allowed the group to see the linkage between communication events.

5. **Online graphics training for human resources**: The HR team handled the business planning in the years after the initial rollout of the vision. They all participated in online training about how to handle both the face-to-face and the online planning.

6. **Consistent messaging**: An implementation challenge in any distributed organization is sending a steady and reliable message. The fact that Otis pursued its visual strategies over several years, made sure all offices had the strategic visions posted, and circled back to evaluate progress in alignment meetings went a long way to move Otis to a new level of involvement and alignment.

7. **Celebrations**: Otis brought the visual approach into annual sales meetings with celebratory skils and visualization in break-out groups.

Visuals for Implementing Large-Scale Projects

The Otis story so far has focused on business planning and alignment. The same tools and approaches apply to projects, especially large projects that require clear processes, alignment, and disciplined execution. Otis faced such a challenge several years after launching its business planning process when its parent company, Aryzta, agreed to use Otis as the lead company in their group to implement a system-wide enterprise resource planning (ERP) process that integrated all data with SAP software.

Like all processes of this sort, a large consulting firm with expertise in SAP led the process of identifying key internal processes, mobilizing the subject matter experts into a dedicated task team to create specifications, help customize the software where needed, and coordinate the massive organization change project that successful utilization would require.

Ahmad Hamade, Otis' Chief Financial Officer, agreed that the ERP team would benefit from having to align its own work by creating a large implementation mural that would tie to the strategic vision. The project leaders met in a special meeting to agree on the overall project vision and roadmap. This meeting followed many weeks of planning and the team was quite clear on what it had to do in detail, but had not taken the time to develop this into an aligned communication that the rest of the company could understand. The consultants and internal Otis leaders appreciated that the behavior change challenges would need to be addressed directly, and people needed to know the real reasons and benefits of going through all the changes required.

PROJECT FUSION LAUNCH PLAN

This Storymap mural supported the communications surrounding the implementation of a large enterprise resource planning system at Otis Spunkmeyer. The project team aligned on all these top-level messages in several iterations of the design. It purposely links with the Otis Strategic Vision shared earlier. You will have to imagine it in full color!

BLEND VIDEO AND BIG PAPER

If you are working with panoramic visuals and need to connect with persons calling in remotely, use this application of a standard video conference unit.

1. Arrange a standard video conference unit with a controllable camera so it can scan the big chart you are creating.

2. Check lighting and focus. Rehearse having a controller move the camera.

3. Invite the remote members to log in to the video conference and/or audio conference.

4. Be aware of where you are standing and explicitly review critical parts of the chart as you go along.

The image shown on the previous page was the result. The team named the ERP effort Project Fusion. The process of agreeing on all the information on this mural served to help align the team. Its publication anchored everyone's commitment to this overall schedule. The focal image allowed the entire leadership of Otis to tell the story of the benefits. This tool was not a single factor by any means, but was very helpful in a successful implementation of this project. Its linkage to the strategic vision communicated a degree of organization and thoughtfulness that was appreciated in the larger organization.

Blended Implementation Meetings

Because implementation requires frequent team meetings, more often than not it involves linking in remote team members. The Otis ERP team needed to involve three key members who were not able to come to San Leandro. They improvised using an internal video conferencing system and were able to visually link everyone without sacrificing the large-scale graphics used in the main meeting to map out the Project Fusion initial design and key messages. The little drawing here illustrates how they set up the room.

There is a footnote this story. In 2010 Otis' parent company, Aryzta, acquired another US fresh-baked goods company and moved its bread operations into Otis, doubling the number of factories and moving Otis even closer to its growth goals. Project Fusion is up and running, with the big lift of organizational integration ahead. Implementation is a way of life in a company like Otis.

12. Visualizing & Innovating
Understanding High Performance

Imagine the TPM and its "bouncing ball" design. A team becomes a real team when it commits to a common direction at Stage 4 and an interdependent way of working at Stage 5. You can directly experience this "turn" as activity accelerates and everyone pulls together to implement plans. But a team doesn't really deserve to be called a high-performance team until it begins to encounter challenges and rises to meet them with innovation and adaptation. The RE-AMP infrastructure team was such a team and is the lens through which we can see how this works in action.

We Are Cleaning Up the Midwest Energy Sector

In late 2004 I received a call from Rick Reed, a program officer at the Garfield Foundation. He was looking for a facilitator to help a new collaboration of 60 environmental NGOs (nongovernmental organizations) and six foundations developing strategies for cleaning up global warming pollutants in the upper Midwest energy sector. They called themselves RE-AMP, for Renewable Energy Alignment Mapping Project. It had been operating for a year with the initial goal of seeing how it could get more results from philanthropic investments in renewable energy, he explained. But the goal had already expanded to one of reducing global warming pollutants 80 percent by 2050 in the region bounded by Illinois, Wisconsin, Minnesota, Iowa, North Dakota, and South Dakota. My mental jaw dropped. This was an extraordinary goal. How in the world had they come to this kind of commitment?

As Rick told the story, a working group had spent a year studying how the energy system worked in order to find out how renewable energy could grow. Not much was happening so far. He and his fellow program officer Jennie Curtis convinced their Garfield Board to fund a collaboration between philanthropists and environmental nonprofits to develop a systemic approach to the

THE RE-AMP INFRASTRUCTURE TEAM

The Infrastructure Team (I-Team) for the RE-AMP network after its first annual meeting was, from left Sissel Waage, Sunni Brown, Ruth Rominger, Laurie Durnell, Rick Reed, and David Sibbet. Rick, a program officer from the Garfield Foundation, led the team. We'd been working together nearly a year when Laurie and Sunni joined us for this initial meeting. Our story is a lens for understanding what high performance means in action.

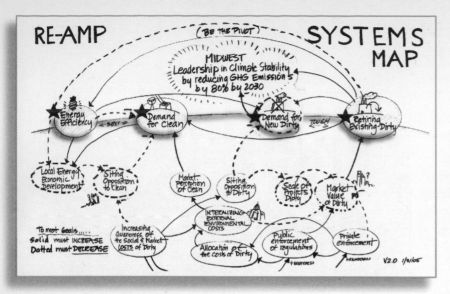

RE-AMP SYSTEMS MAP

This is an image of the map that oriented new people to the four initial RE-AMP working groups. It's an example of a formal way of graphically depicting dynamic systems called "causal loop diagramming" and is a visualization method developed by scientists studying ecosystems— which work in dynamic, nonmechanical ways. The original had colors. In this version the dotted factors (circles) need to decrease, with a resulting decrease in the negative, dampening effect of the dotted lines. The solid circles need to increase, with an increasing effect of their solid lines. Coal was labeled "dirty," because of coal's huge contribution of global warming pollution. Some 70 plants in that region contribute 25 percent of the United States' global warming pollutants.

issue. The initial year involved several workshops and a contract with a research consultant named Scott Spann. He helped produce a 175-factor systems map drawn from 35-plus interviews and vetting with several expert sessions. Reduced to a more refined, 16-factor map (shown here), the group concluded that the problem of creating a clean, renewable energy sector would have to be approached systemically to have any impact at all. The map made it possible to think this way at a team level.

If you study it you will appreciate that these kinds of diagrams are not intuitively clear. But after careful thought the RE-AMP Steering Committee agreed that four factors needed to be addressed in parallel.

1. **Old Coal**: The 70 existing plants in the region needed to be retired or cleaned up.

2. **New Coal**: The 25 proposals for new coal plants, the "Demand for new Dirty" as they called it, needed to be stopped.

3. **Renewable Energy**: The demand for and availability of renewable energy needed to increase.

4. **Energy Efficiency**: Energy saving efforts needed to expand.

They had, according to Rick, organized four working groups to address each one of these four areas with a deadline of producing strategic plans over the next six months. They were looking for consultants to facilitate that process.

"But how did 80 percent by 2050 come to be the goal?" I asked. Rick said that another graphic exercise had been catalytic for the steering committee stepping up to their extraordinary goal. It was called a "Behavior Over Time" graph. It is reproduced here. In seeing the gap, everyone realized that without an 80 percent effort, their time would be wasted.

I joined the RE-AMP effort in December of 2004 at a Steering Committee Meeting at the McKnight Foundation in Minneapolis where Scott briefed the committee on his work and I began to work with the group to create an action plan for the strategy formation process. It was the beginning of a team experience that became a standard for high performance for me.

Innovation and Visualization Required

The RE-AMP story is a complex one, and telling it fully is not the purpose of this chapter. I want to focus here on the staff team that ended up supporting the process, and describe how we faced and met the challenges and became a truly high-performing team. The challenges were considerable. The RE-AMP effort was an unprecedented kind of collaboration between NGOs and foundations in the environmental funding world. We had changing members, limited funding, rapidly evolving politics, emergent strategies, and no offices. Our commitment was to "think systemically and act collaboratively." Since visual thinking is required for systems thinking, it became a signature element in our approach. We "lived" collaboration on our team.

Garfield was farsighted in funding the kind of support staff Rick assembled. The steering committee and NGOs connected with the project felt that creating another organization was not their goal. They wanted RE-AMP to be a true consortium, with all the member organizations sharing in the support tasks. But in the beginning the network was not a committed one, and the 27 people on the initial steering committee needed dedicated help. They needed staff—not a team that would build itself another organization, but a truly empowerment oriented team. We

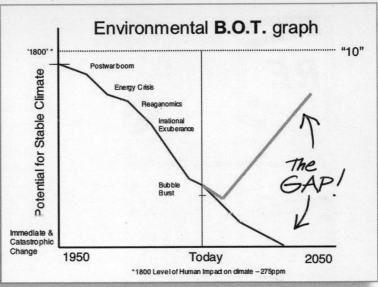

BEHAVIOR OVER TIME GRAPH

This graphic is yet another way of conceptualizing a dynamic system. It illustrates time on the x-axis and the potential for a stable climate on the y-axis. The dotted line across the top is where the atmosphere was in 1800 at 275ppm, a benchmark for atmospheric stability. The descending line indicates the increasing inability of the atmosphere to stabilize itself, with some of the historic events that mark the time indicated. The RE-AMP group used this graphic to think through how much of a difference its current philanthropic and NGO effort would make. It barely changed the slope. Seeing the huge GAP catalyzed a shared realization. If they didn't try to clean up 80 percent, nothing they were working on would make any difference.

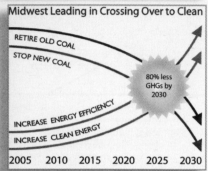

RE-AMP'S IDENTITY LOGO

The discussions about this image brought the entire RE-AMP Steering Committee and network to a simple way to explain what they were doing. The concept was initially diagrammed as a graphic summary of the strategy (shown below) and evolved into the logo (shown above) over the first year. The target represents the big goal. The black arrows represent less dependency on coal. The two (green in full color) arrows rising up are renewable energy and energy efficiency. The RE-AMP name stuck in spite of the move away from just focusing on renewable energy.

called ourselves the "infrastructure team" (I-Team). It was composed of:

- Rick Reed as the project manager from Garfield
- Ruth Rominger from the Monterey Institute for Technology and Education as designer of a digital commons for information sharing
- Sissel Waage from Natural Step as an evaluator developing "indicators" of success
- David Sibbet from The Grove Consultants International as lead facilitator
- Michael Goldberg and Dick Brooks of Action Media, two experts in "framing" and communications who would help with messaging

Michael and Dick worked relatively independently on the communications projects, but Rick, Ruth, Sissel, and I became a truly high-performing team. While we each had specific roles, our regular strategy meetings were true collaborations across each of our areas of expertise.

Visualization Emerges As a Core Tool

For the four "fronts" (as we called them) to succeed in creating strategies in six months, we needed to work rapidly and visually. The I-Team agreed on some initial tools:

- A **graphic action plan** from the Steering Committee to guide our work.
- A **project identity and logo**.
- **Special templates** to support workgroup strategy formation.
- A **graphic history map** to tell the origin story.
- A **simple Systems Map** to explain reasons for the strategy.

We decided to develop each of these charts with the steering committee, using the graphic design process as a way to get alignment.

A Graphic Gameplan, as described in Chapter 9, emerged from the very first meeting.

We then developed a logo that reflected the systems idea of new and old coal decreasing and renewable energy and energy efficiency increasing.

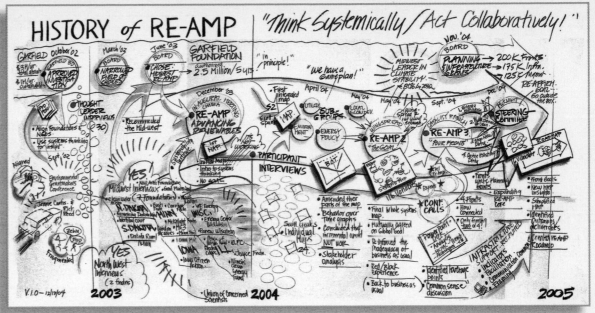

And we needed a graphic history right away to orient all the new people being recruited onto the working groups. I remember Rick Reed and I mapping out the one shown here in a hotel one evening. It became our consistent orientation map, along with the system diagram shared earlier. All these murals were created in full color with magic markers and chalk. You will have to imagine them from these two-color versions.

Supporting the Workgroups

The first six months of 2005 involved a crush of face-to-face and virtual meetings with the four working groups. Because they themselves were distributed across different locations, they determined that they could only afford to meet twice face-to-face and the rest of the time would work virtually. Our infrastructure team felt that this argued even more forcefully for a standard visual vocabulary across the groups. After each meeting, PDF reports containing all the charts and

HISTORY OF RE-AMP

This chart records the initial years of the RE-AMP project. It illustrates the many environmental organizations in the upper Midwest that led Garfield Foundation to focus this project in that region. The circles represent key meetings. The little pictures of charts and documents record the pivotal visuals used to bring coherence to the project.

graphs were sent to all participants, and added to the digital commons that Ruth was helping create. Having a central repository for all documents proved invaluable in this cross-organizational effort where everyone had slightly different standards for sharing these sorts of things.

Infrastructure Team Becomes a Real Team

Our infrastructure team developed as a very smoothly running group over these first months. We had a very clear agreement on our purpose and desire to be a part of the project; we met face-to-face a half dozen times in the beginning phases of the project and came to trust each other completely and understand our different competencies. It helped that we all were "producer" types with lots of experience under pressure. None of us were seeking glory or credit. Our goals were clear. Our commitment to working on the problem of global warming was a professional one in each case that ran far beyond this project.

It helped immeasurably to have Rick as our lead. As a Garfield Program officer he had the authority to deal with budgets in consultation with Garfield. In that regard our decision making was clear. We worked by consensus and on important budget matters Rick and Jennie made the decisions, or took requests to the Garfield Board. Rick was also a key fund-raiser and recruiter of additional foundation support, so we had access to resources, even though they were limited.

In order to keep all the moving pieces clear for us and for the Steering Committee, we created a road map every year that was then updated at the end of the year as a summary report (see next page for an example). These plans allowed us to implement with a great amount of discipline.

Becoming High Performance

If you examine the road map, you might notice a bigger rectangle in the middle labeled "CROSS TEAM Action Planning Charrette." It was here that our I-Team stepped up to high perfor-

We had a very clear agreement on our purpose and desire to be a part of the project; we met face-to-face a half dozen times in the beginning phases of the project and came to trust each other completely and understand our different competencies. It helped that we all were "producer" types with lots of experience under pressure.

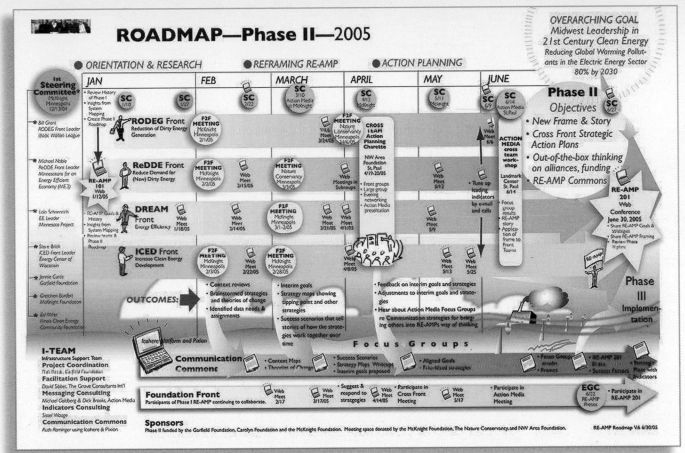

ROADMAP—Phase II—2005

● ORIENTATION & RESEARCH ● REFRAMING RE-AMP ● ACTION PLANNING

This chart guided the working groups and the I-Team in managing the RE-AMP process, and was used to report on it at the end of each year. It was created originally in Adobe Illustrator and shared as a PDF. The circles all represent meetings. The little computers are web conferences. The channels (which were in color on the original) are the working groups. It illustrates how output documents would flow down into the Communications Commons, our online repository. The Foundations formed their own working group, illustrated on the bottom. The key teams and their leaders are depicted on the left. The goals are on the right. This kind of map provided an integrated overview for orientation and tracking.

mance. The challenge we faced was a growing sense that all the issues on the different working groups were interrelated. But the working groups were functioning separately. The renewables group, for instance, was very concerned about technologies like carbon sequestration, an untested approach to reinserting carbon from coal-fired plants back into the ground. Others were concerned about nuclear energy. Environmental issues attract passionate people.

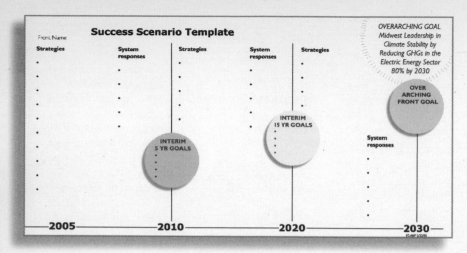

Success Scenario Template

Front Name

Strategies | System responses | Strategies | System responses | Strategies

OVERARCHING GOAL
Midwest Leadership in Climate Stability by Reducing GHGs in the Electric Energy Sector 80% by 2030

OVER ARCHING FRONT GOAL

INTERIM 5 YR GOALS

INTERIM 15 YR GOALS

INTERIM 5 YR GOALS

System responses

2005 — 2010 — 2020 — 2030

SUCCESS SCENARIO TEMPLATE

The I-Team knew we were facing a daunting strategy issue with our big 80 percent goal. One assumption we made is that if people cannot see how day-to-day actions are moving toward stated goals, they become bogged down in politics, as everyone seeks approval of individuals in lieu of knowing whether or not their work is actually effective. In this regard we wanted the working groups to set 5 year, 15 year, and overarching goals as an expression of the big RE-AMP Goal. To support this we created the template on this page. This format allowed the four workgroups to clearly understand each group's intentions, and provide input.

Our project initially called for two one-day meetings with the combined teams to align their project, but our I-Team began to see that in these initial stages people needed more face time to deal with the size of issues they were considering. At one of the critical Steering Committee meetings we had the idea of consolidating the two meetings into one two-day meeting, and making it a very well-designed, cross-team process. Our I-Team came to consensus, and then talked to individual leaders on the Steering Committee. We argued that the work groups needed the more intense face-to-face experience to support working virtually. We also knew that system-level thinking requires more time. After initial resistance we succeeded in getting agreement and changed our plans.

This decision put our I-Team on the spot. How were we actually going to run the process to facilitate true cross working group awareness? We moved to a visual solution. We knew each team would have the big Success Scenario charts shown here. We also knew that we had a large room at a local nonprofit in Minneapolis. "What if we set up a work group breakout in each corner of the big room with a set of walls for charts," we thought. Then we would have the work groups initially meet, then rotate and attend the other work groups and provide input, then rotate back to consider all the input from the others and align their strategies. All inputs would be recorded graphically to make this possible.

This idea required two additional people for our team to graphically facilitate the small groups. Adding team members to a tight team is tricky. It can sometimes drop things back to beginning stages in team performance. We needed our support team to remain focused and flexible, and decided to bring on Laurie Durnell and Sunni Brown as two additional graphics people from

The Grove. They would take two groups. Rick needed to work closely with the Steering Committee. Sissel was evaluating. I handled a third group and Ruth handled a fourth.

It was essential to have all The Grove people sharing a common visual vocabulary and understanding the graphic template way of working, or the cross-team process would be difficult. Even though Laurie and Sunni hadn't been in on earlier meetings, the I-Team trusted me and therefore trusted them. We also had the history, systems map, and road map as orientation documents, so our prep meetings were very efficient.

An Annual Meeting Tradition Is Born

The meeting went very well. In fact, the cross-group inputs and considerations facilitated by the large charts and breakout groups created real excitement as the network began to see the system as a whole and break out of their individual focuses. The ultimate testimony was the network deciding to hold an event like this every year.

The RE-AMP network grew rapidly. By 2010 it had over 140 NGO members and 15 foundations. Many states formed global warming task forces at the state level and began to activate energy efficiency standards and explore a regional carbon trading scheme. The Steering Committee adopted rotating terms and elections drawn from at-large and working group members. A Media Center emerged from the communication work of Action Media. The Communications Commons went through two complete redesigns and has become a backbone of the movement in that part of the country. Michigan and Ohio joined the network, and a special Transportation Working Group and Global Warming Strategy Working Group emerged out of subsequent annual meetings. The RE-AMP organization became a pass-through funder for millions of philanthropic dollars working on global warming issues and one of the best organized collaborations in the country.

WORKING GROUP MEETINGS

Laurie Durnell from The Grove facilitates the RE-AMP group that was working on reducing the demand for coal energy. After sharing its success strategies and getting feedback from other groups, each group met again to lay out next steps. All of the charts from each breakout went into the final visual document of the meeting.

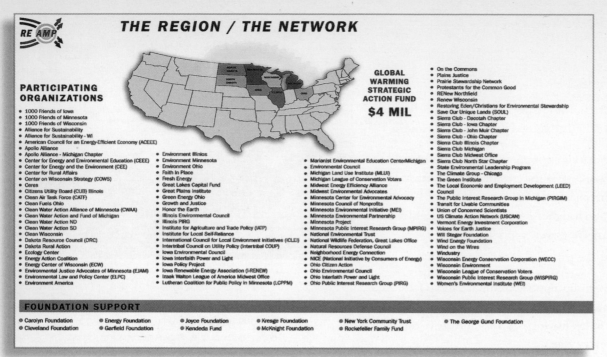

PARTICIPATING ORGANIZATIONS

- 1000 Friends of Iowa
- 1000 Friends of Minnesota
- 1000 Friends of Wisconsin
- Alliance for Sustainability
- Alliance for Sustainability - WI
- American Council for an Energy-Efficient Economy (ACEEE)
- Apollo Alliance
- Apollo Alliance - Michigan Chapter
- Center for Energy and Environmental Education (CEEE)
- Center for Energy and the Environment (CEE)
- Center for Rural Affairs
- Center on Wisconsin Strategy (COWS)
- Ceres
- Citizens Utility Board (CUB) Illinois
- Clean Air Task Force (CATF)
- Clean Fuels Ohio
- Clean Water Action Alliance of Minnesota (CWAA)
- Clean Water Action and Fund of Michigan
- Clean Water Action ND
- Clean Water Action SD
- Clean Wisconsin
- Dakota Resource Council (DRC)
- Dakota Rural Action
- Ecology Center
- Energy Action Coalition
- Energy Center of Wisconsin (ECW)
- Environmental Justice Advocates of Minnesota (EJAM)
- Environmental Law and Policy Center (ELPC)
- Environment America

- Environment Illinois
- Environment Minnesota
- Environment Ohio
- Faith In Place
- Fresh Energy
- Great Lakes Capital Fund
- Great Plains Institute
- Green Energy Ohio
- Growth and Justice
- Honor the Earth
- Illinois Environmental Council
- Illinois PIRG
- Institute for Agriculture and Trade Policy (IATP)
- Institute for Local Self-Reliance
- International Council for Local Environment Initiatives (ICLEI)
- Intertribal Council on Utility Policy (Intertribal COUP)
- Iowa Environmental Council
- Iowa Interfaith Power and Light
- Iowa Policy Project
- Iowa Renewable Energy Association (I-RENEW)
- Izaak Walton League of America Midwest Office
- Lutheran Coalition for Public Policy in Minnesota (LCPPM)

- Marianist Environmental Education Center Michigan
- Environmental Council
- Michigan Land Use Institute (MLUI)
- Michigan League of Conservation Voters
- Midwest Energy Efficiency Alliance
- Midwest Environmental Advocates
- Minnesota Center for Environmental Advocacy
- Minnesota Council of Nonprofits
- Minnesota Environmental Initiative (MEI)
- Minnesota Environmental Partnership
- Minnesota Project
- Minnesota Public Interest Research Group (MPIRG)
- National Environmental Trust
- National Wildlife Federation, Great Lakes Office
- Natural Resources Defense Council
- Neighborhood Energy Connection
- NICE (National Initiative by Consumers of Energy)
- Ohio Citizen Action
- Ohio Environmental Council
- Ohio Interfaith Power and Light
- Ohio Public Interest Research Group (PIRG)

- On the Commons
- Plains Justice
- Prairie Stewardship Network
- Protestants for the Common Good
- RENew Northfield
- Renew Wisconsin
- Restoring Eden/Christians for Environmental Stewardship
- Save Our Unique Lands (SOUL)
- Sierra Club - Dacotah Chapter
- Sierra Club - Iowa Chapter
- Sierra Club - John Muir Chapter
- Sierra Club - Ohio Chapter
- Sierra Club Illinois Chapter
- Sierra Club Michigan
- Sierra Club Midwest Office
- Sierra Club North Star Chapter
- State Environmental Leadership Program
- The Climate Group - Chicago
- The Green Institute
- The Local Economic and Employment Development (LEED) Council
- The Public Interest Research Group in Michigan (PIRGIM)
- Transit for Livable Communities
- Union of Concerned Scientists
- US Climate Action Network (USCAN)
- Vermont Energy Investment Corporation
- Voices for Earth Justice
- Will Steger Foundation
- Wind Energy Foundation
- Wind on the Wires
- Windustry
- Wisconsin Energy Conservation Corporation (WECC)
- Wisconsin Environment
- Wisconsin League of Conservation Voters
- Wisconsin Public Interest Research Group (WISPIRG)
- Women's Environmental Institute (WEI)

GLOBAL WARMING STRATEGIC ACTION FUND $4 MIL

FOUNDATION SUPPORT

- Carolyn Foundation
- Cleveland Foundation
- Energy Foundation
- Garfield Foundation
- Joyce Foundation
- Kendeda Fund
- Kresge Foundation
- McKnight Foundation
- New York Community Trust
- Rockefeller Family Fund
- The George Gund Foundation

RE-AMP STORYMAP

This Storymap and the graphic on the following page (they were split here for publication) together provided a large mural backdrop for RE-AMP's annual meetings. The part shown here illustrates the membership. The one on the right illustrates the working groups, media center, documentation strategy, and goals.

On this page (and the next page) is a large Storymap that Tiffany Forner on The Grove team created in the third year of the project to illustrate the organizational system and membership of the network. This mural has provided a backdrop for all subsequent gatherings.

In *Visual Meetings* I told the story of a recent RE-AMP annual meeting where we reviewed all the action in eight states in a 2.5-hour visual review with another set of standard graphic templates. Since the economic meltdown in 2008 jobs have become a predominant political concern in the region so there has been some retrenching, but the strength of the relationships in RE-AMP network are allowing it to persist and provide a model for other regional efforts.

By year three the I-Team had transferred most of its jobs to other people. At this point, RE-AMP hired an executive director, and then part-time staff for each working committee. All staff are hosted by member organizations, so there is still no central office. There were, of course, many factors that have contributed to RE-AMP's success besides working visually, but graphic methods were a key success factor in giving the far-flung movement a sense of alignment and identity as it organized. The I-Team became for me a model for what a visual team can accomplish when it is literate across different kinds of media with a common visual language for systems thinking.

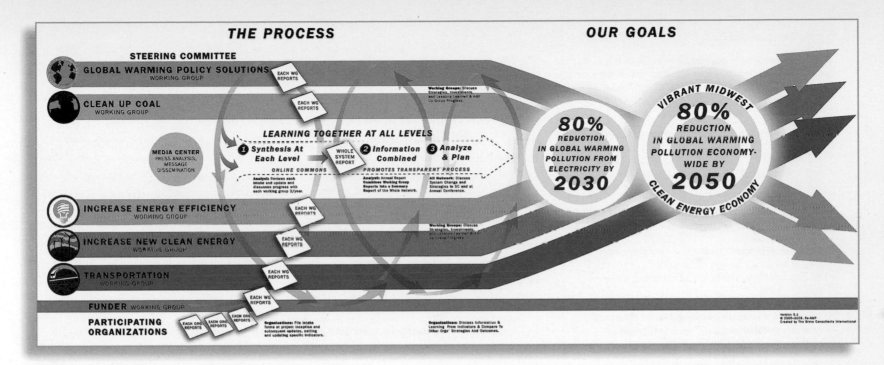

THE PROCESS ... **OUR GOALS**

STEERING COMMITTEE
GLOBAL WARMING POLICY SOLUTIONS
WORKING GROUP

CLEAN UP COAL
WORKING GROUP

MEDIA CENTER
PRESS ANALYSIS,
MESSAGE
DISSEMINATION

LEARNING TOGETHER AT ALL LEVELS
1 Synthesis At Each Level
WHOLE SYSTEM REPORT
2 Information Combined
3 Analyze & Plan
ONLINE COMMONS
PROMOTES TRANSPARENT PROCESS

80% REDUCTION IN GLOBAL WARMING POLLUTION FROM ELECTRICITY BY 2030

VIBRANT MIDWEST 80% REDUCTION IN GLOBAL WARMING POLLUTION ECONOMY-WIDE BY 2050 CLEAN ENERGY ECONOMY

INCREASE ENERGY EFFICIENCY
WORKING GROUP

INCREASE NEW CLEAN ENERGY
WORKING GROUP

TRANSPORTATION
WORKING GROUP

FUNDER WORKING GROUP

PARTICIPATING ORGANIZATIONS

High Performance As Artistry

High-performing teams have a lot of synergy, where the results of the whole are truly greater than any of the parts could achieve. And they are characterized by spontaneity and improvisation, and by getting results that surpass original expectations. All these were true of the RE-AMP I-Team and the other high-performing teams I write about. An interesting challenge for visual teams who want to rise to high performance stems from the very benefits of working visually—clarity of concepts, ideas, and plans. High performance requires having this kind of clarity and *not* being attached to it.

In writing this book I came across the work of a consultant named Hilary Austen, who has written *Artistry Unleashed: A Guide to Pursuing Great Performance in Work and Life.* I read it coincident

RE-AMP PROCESS MAP

This part of the large mural (whose left side is on the prior page) illustrates the way the working groups, the media center, and the digital commons all interact as they work to achieve the RE-AMP goals illustrated in the large circles.

to writing this chapter and experienced a breakthrough. All these years of working with the TPM I have endeavored to refine the distinctions, especially between a good implementation team and one that is high performing. I know that implementation means achieving goals. I also know that high performance is more than that. It's about having something new emerge, some-thing unexpected, and having the flexibility to absorb the changes and keep the momentum. In sports and music it's being in the flow state.

Austen researched this topic with the hypothesis that artistry occurs in any field, and that it has something to do with the same qualities—rising above competency to greet surprise. She inter-viewed and analyzed many creative people, and sums it up with seven principles that characterize artistic process. I got excited. She was echoing reflexive process!

I've summarized Austen's principles here in the side story as another set of lenses for looking at high performance. She found it's about working on both ends and means at the same time. She found that artists master the medium they work in. Our I-Team members were all long-time, serious students of groups process, I realized. She says artists balance mastery and originality, stay-ing open to surprise. They remain unfazed by failure and unfixed on success. And they express personal ideals, understanding, and awareness in action. All these were true of the I-Team.

What stopped me were two of her principles: "Reason with Qualities" and "Develop Cognitive Emotions." Cooks taste, dancers move, musicians hear music—these people reason with more than words and symbols. I realized that excellent team processes sustain an energetic field that must be felt. Leaders and facilitators need as much emotional intelligence as visual clarity. These principles reminded me that some things are known by very accomplished people and aren't symbolized in text or graphics. As I reflect back, this acceptance may have been the secret sauce in the I-Team. We all embraced the mystery in our process, each other, and RE-AMP itself.

13. Assessments, Dialogues, & Sharing Rallies
The Importance of Learning & Renewal

A central reason the TPM shifts from a "building" to a "performance" metaphor is to underline the reality that team process is ongoing, and high performance experiences in particular are vulnerable to change and not steady-state. This puts a premium on learning for any team that wants to sustain its performance. In addition, any organization that wants to foster a team culture will want to support learning that moves between different teams.

Where flexibility and ability to change is necessary, then competency is a function of breadth of repertoire. This is especially true for performing artists, athletes, and facilitators. It's why musicians have rehearsals and athletes have locker room talks. Reflection and renewal is essential for true high-performing teams. This chapter will share key tools that will help you support renewal.

Strategies for Renewal

The success factors identified in the TPM for renewal are recognition and celebration, change mastery, and staying power. Visual teams apply a number of strategies for these.

1. **Team performance assessments and dialogue**: One of the principle ways to support team development is to generate reliable information about the need to change. This comes most usefully from the team itself, through structured assessment tools. People have to believe there is a need to change before spending time on it. In this chapter I will describe the different assessment choices that are available within the Team Performance System, and some of the graphic tools that help support the feedback and learning sessions.

2. **Sharing rallies**: Getting teams to share learning and suggest improvements in an organization can be supported very creatively. We'll look at two examples, one from National Semiconductor and one from Agilent Technologies high performance leadership program.

GRAPHIC TEAM ASSESSMENT

1. Hang up a large sheet of paper and divide it into seven columns and two rows as illustrated here.

2. Invite the team to begin exploring the IP report and identify where they have successfully addressed some of the keys. List these as strengths.

3. Invite the team to look for gaps and issues, as reflected by those parts of the report where scores are split and there aren't agreements.

4. Toward the end of the review identify one or two areas where improving on things would boost performance or support change.

The TPS assessments are created to deliver a report that is catalytic to discussion, not necessarily one that somehow describes the team apart from conversation about what people thought when they made the ratings.

3. **Ritual enactments and transition workshops**: Theater provides many tools for exceptionally graphic enactments. I will share some examples from an unusually creative organizational consultant at HP who conducted courtroom dramas and funerals as a way to deal with renewal. Bold, graphic statements by leadership can be very effective in acknowledging hard work. Have you considered riding an elephant or landing a plane as tools in a visual team repertoire?

4. **Change charrettes**: *Charrette* is a French term for "wagon" and is used in design to refer to the kind of compressed planning that designers used on their way to the king, making changes "en charrette." Well-designed face-to-face experiences that fully engage everyone in the need to change are key tools in any performance toolkit. I'll share about how Chris McGoff forged a new level of effort out of a working team aimed at increasing the effectiveness of US logistics responses to crises like the earthquake in Haiti and Hurricane Katrina in the Gulf of Mexico.

The high performance and renewal stages of team process are interactive, in that the work done for renewal helps sustain performance. You don't have to wait to the end of a team process to put these ideas into practice.

Visualizing Progress and Needs: Team Performance Assessments

In the early years of developing the Team Performance System, Allan Drexler and I, with the help of Russ Forrester, one of Allan's colleagues, developed a 72-question assessment called the Team Performance Inventory. It poses three questions for each of the three keys in each of the seven stages of the TPM, plus seven questions relating to the team leader. This assessment has evolved over the years with extensive client testing by Allan and Russ through their company, Quality Team Performance. Feedback from the many applications informed updates of the TPM itself as the distinctions were refined in response to clients' observations about the keys. In the 2000s

Allan and Russ developed a paper-based, self-scoring assessment of 42 questions called the Team Performance Indicator and a guide to using it that are also available through The Grove.

The Grove has now developed, in addition, a Team Performance Online Survey of 21 questions, plus three for the leader, in response to client demand for a simpler assessment.

In all these cases, the value of the surveys lies in facilitating a dialogue for learning on the team, using their own data as a springboard. We found through many years of work that there aren't rigid formulas for what makes a team successful. While the seven challenges outlined in the TPM have held up all around the world, the best practices teams use to respond to these challenges are very diverse, and in many cases closely linked to the culture and norms of the specific organization. For this reason the TPS assessments are created to deliver a report that is catalytic to discussion, not necessarily one that somehow describes the team apart from conversation about what people thought when they made the ratings.

The strategies for providing this feedback draw on good visualization methods.

Mapping Strengths and Opportunities

The most straightforward way to lead a team learning session is to take one of the assessments after contracting that it will not be used for individual performance assessment or disciplinary actions. A team performance facilitator, usually an HR staff or external consultant knowledgeable about the TPS, will then make the report available and schedule a learning session—most productively three to four hours long. The illustration on the prior page shows a way to use a large grid to reflect team insights. This same approach may be used in a virtual meeting and a target document with graphic recording of suggestions and reflections.

GRAPHIC FEEDBACK REPORTS

The various TP assessments use graphics to show the composite responses of the team and tables to show the clustering and disagreements. These provide a basis for group dialogue about performance.

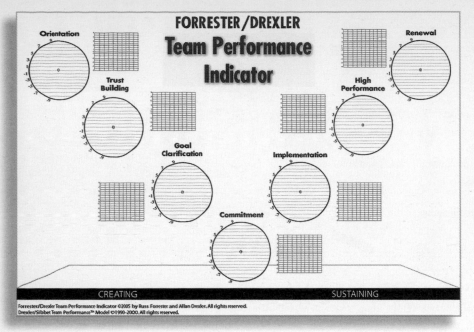

FORRESTER/DREXLER

Team Performance Indicator

Orientation

Renewal

Trust Building

High Performance

Goal Clarification

Implementation

Commitment

CREATING   SUSTAINING

TEAM PERFORMANCE INDICATOR CHART

The results of a self-scoring paper-based TPI designed by Russ Forrester and Allan Drexler can be mapped onto this template, averaged, and the circles filled in to indicate graphically how resolved or unresolved the different areas are. This template and other TP tools are available at www. grove.com.

The reports themselves are very graphic, and contain charts that anonymously show how each person rated each stage. You can see visually looking across the seven stages how aligned or dispersed the team is in its assessment. Each stage them illustrates all the specific ratings for each question in tables that highlight when the team is split in its feelings about performance and where everyone agrees. Because the assessment has succinct descriptions of all the stages and keys, it serves as an educational support for the team about team performance in addition to providing team data.

A special mapping template for the TP Indicator allows teams to display the results in a graphic depiction of where the team has resolved issues and where they still need work. The TP Indicator comes with instructions on how to use the wall template.

Most professional human resources professionals use many kinds of assessments to provide feedback to teams on performance. The Meyers-Briggs instrument has adaptations for this purpose. Style assessments of different kinds, like True Colors, also facilitate understanding of differences. Many of these, plus the TPS assessments, are referenced in the resources part of the book. The distinguishing feature of a visual team would be learning how to use large charts and graphics to support assessments of this sort, so the team can actually see the patterns of agreement as they develop.

Sharing Rallies

In 1994 during the turnaround of National Semiconductor (NSC), the organization change team arranged for a top management field trip to Milliken Carpet, a successful multinational organization in Georgia that has institutionalized what it calls "Sharing Rallies" to acknowledge employee contributions to the business. The NSC executives came back deeply moved by what they had experienced. They saw the founders of Milliken attending a large event almost like an Academy Awards celebration, with dozens of teams and persons called out and acknowledged for what they were contributing. The atmosphere was contagious, and the NSC executives were impressed with how successfully Milliken was sustaining a culture of contribution. The National execs wanted to initiate a similar process.

A special team was empowered to begin organizing a first-ever sharing rally for NSC manufacturing and packaging sites in Asia. They rented a hotel in Sentosa, a small island just south of Singapore, and invited each facility to tap several teams that had contributed special work to NSC over the past year. When they arrived in Singapore, each team had some time and materials to create a county fair-style booth of the learning and results they had achieved. These were staged in a large ballroom at the hotel, and one afternoon opened to general presentation and visitation by management. For many of the people it was the first conference they had ever attended. The energy was electric.

Creating an Agilent Action Learning Fair

I remembered the National Semiconductor experience ten years later working with Agilent Technologies on a the culminating event for their high potential teams involved in a six-month action learning program. Could we replicate the excitement of the NSC sharing rally in an

AGILENT ACTION LEARNING FAIR

This picture shows a small set of the 20 booths created by the action learning teams at Agilent during the 2005 action learning fair. Each team received graphic materials and access to printers and other media at the beginning of a week-long Global Leadership Forum. Between Monday and the fair on Thursday, each team created these booths about their team results.

ACTION LEARNING BOOTH

This picture shows part of one of the 20 action learning team booths created for the Action Learning Fair at Agilent Technologies in the mid-2000s. The Grove worked with each team and their project, teaching them the TPM and how to work virtually, so it was fun to see this team reflecting that learning in their booth. Most of this graphic work was created during the context of the Global Leadership Forum.

action learning fair? The design team for the Global Leadership Forum liked the idea.

We provided each of 20 teams poster board material, markers, color printers, LCD displays, and other graphic materials to create a booth that would communicate what they learned on the team and what they contributed to Agilent. The event was on day four of a five-day Global Leadership Forum, so each team had several open times during which they could prepare their booths. Their instructions were to prepare murals and displays that would allow a member or members of their team to share their results with others. An example is shown here.

To ensure that everyone would engage in this activity, each team participant was asked to score everyone else's booth on four different criteria. These were:

1. **Business results**: Tangible ideas for improving either products or processes.

2. **Creativity**: This related to both the booth presentation and the way the project was conducted.

3. **Teamwork**: This rated evidence of the team working together well.

4. **Learning**: If the project didn't get specific results, could the team show what they learned?

To add even more energy, each team was asked to prepare a two-minute "infomercial" advertising their booth that would be presented in a big plenary session in the morning. Following that session the fair would open and everyone would have a couple hours, including lunch, to visit the booths and absorb team learning. Top management and the key managers who had sponsored action learning teams were also invited to the event, and would also score the booths, adding to the visibility of the high-potential participants.

The result was exciting. Many of the teams had done most of their work virtually, so the creation of the booths was the first time they had a chance to work through their learning as a group. Having a wide range of choices of media to use also catalyzed the teams, and provided ways for everyone to participate. Some got very creative in their expressions.

The groups all invested in the two-minute presentations. In the first year of this program about half were skits. In the second and third years teams knew about this feature and created amazing slide and video presentations.

The country fair motif worked perfectly. Everyone had a great time. And the event capped with an awards ceremony that evening. The first year the team that proposed a new low-cost oscilloscope for China received the "business results" award. When the product turned out to be a big success the reputation of the action learning program jumped up, and subsequent presentations received even more attention.

Using Ritual to Facilitate Transition

One of the most creative organization consultants I've known is Geoff Ainscow, who worked for several decades at HP. His use of ritual enactments for key renewal events has shaped my own standards of excellence for this kind of thing. For instance, in the 1990s HP needed to close a manufacturing plant in the southwest. They asked Geoff to work on the transition. At the time HP was still famous for its employee-oriented culture and the "HP Way." This approach has been challenged by the tough economies of the 2000s, but Geoff's approach to this plant closing remains a sensitive and wonderful response. He and the workers there decided that instead of pretending nothing big was happening, that they would stage a New Orleans-style funeral and celebrate their long years of working together. On the day of the big event a group of workers, all dressed in black garbage sacks and carrying a coffin, wound their way through the office in the

---

ROLE OF GRAPHICS FOR AGILENT ACTION LEARNING TEAMS

Leslie Camino-Markowitz is leader of Agilent Technology's high potential leadership programs. These are her answers to an interview about working visually with their action learning teams.

Q. What was the biggest contribution of visual tools in the development of the Next-Gen leadership development program?

A. Visual tools facilitate learning, team dynamics, creativity, and innovation. They support our cross-functional and cross-geographical team collaboration to produce results driven projects.

Along with increasing individuals' capability, action learning projects have impacted revenue generating products (profit improvements, new product introductions, upgrades to financial models, etc.).

Graphics serve as tools to access right brain thinking—creative, intuitive, and big picture—in logical, engineering cultures and support understanding of multifaceted, complex systems. Graphics, properly used, can move folks from rational to emotional engagement, and support successful projects with clarity on deliverables.

The Project Fair led the way to similar fairs within the company, like the Innovation Fair, which is core to our Innovation initiative. Though people were skeptical at first, it proved to be a phenomenal learning experience because of the high quality of work, the level of engagement produced, the positive impact on team dynamics, and the awards becoming a high honor. The fairs have continued to evolve to include virtual fairs.

plant behind musicians playing a classical funeral lament. As they passed through, everyone put some favorite object from their desks and workstations into the casket.

Outside, the families of all the workers greeted the mourners. They marched to a grave and buried the casket, then proceeded to tear off the black garbage sacks to reveal tee shirts with phoenixes rising up and partook in a huge picnic celebration. The families were very touched that a company would support this kind of event. The transition went smoothly. Of course, HP also worked to get as many employees as possible other jobs within the company.

Plans on Trial

The second wonderful story I heard about Geoff's work was about the time he put an HP division's strategic plan on trial. Knowing that getting buy-in from the next level of management is always a key to success in planning work, he felt that something more engaging than a communication session was needed. The O. J. Simpson trial was happening at the time, and he convinced the executive team to put their plan on trial.

In the lead up to the big event Geoff interviewed employees about their understanding about the plan and questions they had about it. Then he hired an acting company to be the prosecuting attorneys in the case. The execs were arraigned on charges of (1) inadequate funding, (2) lack of boldness in the plan, (3) nonalignment, and (4) ignoring customers' needs.

For two days the executives were put on trial, with their direct reports being the jury. The prosecuting attorneys pummeled them with all the questions and concerns that had been gathered during the interviews. The trial set and the lawyers costumes worn by the executives put them into a different role and mindset that brought forth unseen talents and a passion for what they really believed about the business plan. Their new conviction won over the jury. At the end of

The shift from being a cost center to revenue producer was a massive culture change, and required a renewal event that would have deep, experiential impact on the management team and their direct reports to be successful.

the very exciting session, the execs were acquitted on all counts, and the division had a plan that everyone understood inside and out.

Reporting on the Good News

I had the privilege of actually working with Geoff on a third project for the Integrated Circuit Business Division (ICBD) at HP. The company was shifting from a policy of supporting large-scale chip design with a standard budget to a profit and loss model where the division would be retained by other divisions for fees. This shift from being a cost center to revenue producer required a significant culture change, and a renewal event that would have deep, experiential impact on the management team and their direct reports to be successful.

From long experience, Geoff knew that leadership and their followers had to feel the change, not

METAPHORS FOR CHANGE

When the Integrated Circuit Business Division of HP needed to change to a P&L culture from one supported by corporate budgets, the management team immersed itself, 200 key managers, and 2,500 virtual attendees in a two-day strategic visioning event anchoring the change in a rich experience of a different way of working. I drew this representation of the 2B2K "news" organization the design team created in a journal post that began, "this is one of the best meetings I've ever seen."

THE EVOLUTION OF ICBD

At the Station 2B2K, culture change off-site for HP's Integrated Circuit Business Division, an extra evening event proved to be a real turning point in the process.

Drawing from success in prior experiential meetings, the design team hired a theatrical company to come and interview employees about the history and culture of ICBD and create a script that traced the evolution of the division from the Stone Age through modern times.

In a twist, top management actually did the acting, coming out in costumes and reading the scripts from clipboards. This evening was hysterical. I've never seen adults laughing so hard, as they experienced their execs willing to make fools of themselves in public. The statement was undeniable. Change was on, and the leaders were at the forefront of the learning that would be required!!!

just think about it. Geoff insisted that the execs be central members of a design team, to assure buy-in. At the level he wanted to work they would need to be fully supportive, and the design sessions were the places where a lot of shifts in thinking and learning would occur.

The team decided to embed a two-day event in a metaphor of a news organization. The top managers would be the anchor newscasters, announcing the new policies and strategies in live newscasts. I would be the weather reporter, graphically mapping the responses and reactions on large "weather maps" and providing overviews from time to time. Their top 200 engineers and staff would be the reporters and were asked to write stories of the future about how the goals and strategies would be realized.

To add as much realism as possible, a set of "on air" and "off air" lights and signs and an anchor news desk transformed the hotel ballroom. The station name, 2B2K, symbolized their revenue goals—$2 billion by 2000. In the back a special news wire team manned several computers that were "broadcasting" a live computer conference for anyone else in the company that wished to attend. As participants entered, each received a small digital camera that they could use to take pictures and post stories whenever they felt like it.

The event was a huge success. The same dynamic happened at the newsroom meeting as in the jury trial. All 2,500 employees were invited online and they could "attend" if they fulfilled a set of conditions. (1) Read the bus plan, (2) Verbally participate, (3) Take notes, and (4) Commit to hold a report-out meeting with their co-workers who didn't attend. The news room set, and the graphics, put them into the role of news reporters, which helped change their mindset. Over 175 stories and pictures got posted. The "reporters" created 20 tables full of stories of the future, which were graphically illustrated in a huge sunburst vision in the front of the room.

Charrettes to Galvanize Action

The types of activities one might do for renewal are often similar to what happens to kick off new processes. Holding a special face-to-face meeting that invites everyone to face up to new realities and step up to change is a time-honored way to galvanize teams to sign up for a new process.

Chris McGoff is the founder of The Clearing, a consulting company in Washington, DC, dedicated to taking on the really tough problems of our time. He modeled being a visual team working with a task group of logistics experts convened by a three-star Army general. "They feel that the time is ripe, following the challenges of the earthquake in Haiti and Hurricane Katrina," Chris said, "to coordinate how the US Government can coordinate its logistics responses." He was facilitating a charrette for this purpose and decided that graphic support and process consulting would help.

Chris and I share a common mentor in Michael Doyle, the cofounder of Interaction Associates. Michael has passed on, but his ideas live on. In fact, at the end of Michael's life, he and Chris were working on a book that would share the key consulting concepts that were at the heart of their consulting success. Chris finished the book. It's called *The PRIMES: How Any Group Can Solve Any Problem.* At its heart is a concept called the "CORE PRIME." Chris' application to the interagency logistics team helped them get to a new level of operation. The agenda literally followed the diagram shown here:

1. First the team mapped the current situation in graphic detail—telling stories of Haiti and Katrina.

2. They then looked at the current environment and all the forces and factors surrounding such responses.

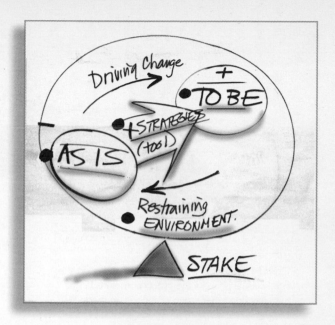

THE CORE PRIME

This is a graphic illustration of the CORE PRIME described by Chris McGoff in his book *The PRIMES: How Any Group Can Solve Any Problem*. It is the model that drives most change consulting. While many others depict the core process the same way—comparing analysis of the current state with projection of a future state and then exploring strategies—what the CORE PRIME adds is a focus on the hard work of making sure that leadership has a true stake in change. The balance must tip toward the future if real change is to occur. Mentally flip the little triangle over to get the TPM arc. "Stake" is all about making a real and not a pseudo "turn" toward implementation.

3. The team then looked squarely at how much was at stake if they made no change. Without an agreement that the "as is" state is unacceptable, no work would gain traction.

4. They then developed a future vision.

5. This provided a context for outlining action strategies and empowering a task group or direct reports to begin developing a picture of a "whole of government" crisis response.

INTERAGENCY LOGISTICS TASK FORCE

Chris McGoff of The Clearing is reflecting on the highly visual process the group completed in its two-day implementation of a decision made by their chiefs to explore an interagency approach to logistics. This effort is far from finished, and confidential at this point, so I've blurred the faces of the participants. It is such a beautiful example of how effective visual team processes can be that I wanted to include it here.

This picture and references to The PRIMES on the prior page are used with permission of The Clearing., Inc.

Chris took this offsite to a new level at the crux point when he was testing the stake people had in change. He broke the team into three groups and had each of them prepare an argument for why an integrated government effort should take place. Following the initial presentation he then invited the other two groups to tear the first presentation apart!!! The second group could then incorporate whatever additional ideas emerged from this process. The same thing happened with the second group. By the third group the arguments were gut-deep. Out on the plaza in the late afternoon, with calls coming in from the oil spill in the Gulf, the key leadership signed onto change. The rest of the off-site was very productive, as was the follow-up workshop with logistics experts empowered by their chiefs to get this process going.

These kinds of intense charrettes almost always employ large-scale graphics and visual meeting methods to achieve their results. When combined with clear and memorable mental models about why the process is designed the way it is, people can move to extraordinary levels of cooperation and creativity. This charrette was, of course, not the end of this team's work but a new beginning, such as it is with renewal and team performance.

V: Growing a Visual Team Culture

Chapter 14: Introducing Visual Teams If you like the idea of visual teams, how can you get support for working this way? What is the formula for change? What kinds of demonstration projects seem to work best? What is the role of top management in supporting a culture of visual thinking and visual communications?

Chapter 15: Developing Visual Team Skills The Team Performance Model is an application of a powerful theory of process that helps integrate the fragmented ways in which people think about groups, collaboration, and teamwork. This chapter explains how you can learn to use graphic process thinking to make sense out of diverse approaches to team development.

Chapter 16: Shared Visual Language Cultivating a learning network of visual practitioners is the key to having visual teams become a viral way of working. What does it take? Where has it happened before? What roles are most important for learning and development? This chapter has stories of successful applications.

14: Introducing Visual Teams
Communicating Benefits

Let us assume that you are excited about visual meetings and working visually as a team and appreciate the benefits of working more like designers. But your organization is running lean, prefers to present with slides, uses e-mail, text, and teleconferences to coordinate, and avoids meetings if possible. Feel familiar? It's amazing how many organizations are working this way. And they won't change until people experience something different and more effective. Even then people resist change, especially if it means you have to learn something new.

A Formula for Change—DxVxA>R

Change consultants use a little formula to remember what is required for organizations to change. This would include teams, of course. The formula DxVxA>R stands for *Discontent times Vision times Action must be greater than Resistance*. This is a variant on the Core Prime illustrated in the last chapter. It means that you and others need to be discontented with the way things are now—with the "as is" state of affairs. But that discontent needs to be multiplied by attraction to a vision of a "to be" state. And this all needs to be multiplied by having some clear action steps for going forward. And these combined need to be greater than resistance. People put down a stake for change when these conditions are met. Let's build the case for changing to visual teams.

"D"—Build Discontent with the Current Condition

The first step in bringing visual teams into your organization is to fully appreciate why *not* working this way is such a handicap. My best arguments are listed in the box on this page. Underlying these arguments against nonvisual communication is the value of being explicit and collaborative about things versus being competitive and manipulative. I do not mean to imply that there aren't times for deep dialogue with no charts in sight, or informal talks and open discussion that aren't recorded. The discontent needs to be with never having a chance to interact, play, prototype, and be creative as a group.

THE CASE AGAINST WORKING NONVISUALLY

Poor Engagement
- ❏ Tougher to get everyone's contribution.
- ❏ No public acknowledgement of being heard when someone speaks.
- ❏ Team members default to people who seem to have a clear picture in their minds.
- ❏ Sitting around is a lot less healthy than moving around in meetings.

No Group Level Systems Thinking
- ❏ Can't think at a systemic level as a group.
- ❏ Can't see the panorama and connections.
- ❏ No chance to create a collective picture of what is happening out of all the little bits.
- ❏ Work often focuses on tactics and transactions.

No Creative Stimulation of Visuals
- ❏ Teams miss the stimulation and creativity of working with imagery—no direct support for right-brain, intuitive thinking.
- ❏ New designs need visible manifestation to evolve.

Weak Group Memory
- ❏ Can't easily show others what you are doing.
- ❏ No effective group memory to bridge the gap between meetings.
- ❏ People seldom read or study retyped minutes
- ❏ Your team misses out on all the attention you get with great visuals.

THE CASE FOR WORKING VISUALLY

High Participation / Efficiency

❏ Everyone who participates gets acknowledged graphically.

❏ The content of meeting records is publicly validated and corrected.

❏ Team drawing and working with sticky notes is a *lot* more active than sitting and talking.

❏ Graphic templates support rapid collecting and reviewing data.

Big Picture Thinking

❏ Visual working displays support team-level systems thinking.

❏ Images stimulate right-brain, creative thinking.

❏ Visualization opens up awareness of our mental models.

❏ Cocreating graphic murals supports understanding and alignment.

❏ Large displays support seeing new relationships.

Memorability / Sharability

❏ Meeting notes and action plans are easy to share and invite input.

❏ Digital capture of working displays support group memory.

❏ Everyone remembers more of what happened.

❏ Visual practice allows teams to track what is going on over time.

Big Architecture Firm
Strategic Visioning Process

© 2009   GROVE

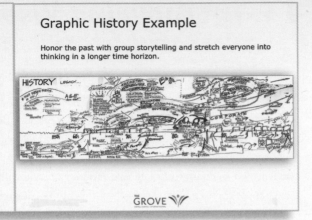

Graphic History Example

Honor the past with group storytelling and stretch everyone into thinking in a longer time horizon.

GROVE

"V"—Develop a Personal Vision of Where You Can Succeed

All the way through Chapter 3, where I describe the TPM, I listed out how visual teams would handle each stage. If you want to introduce this way of working to your organization, you need to determine where your team is stuck in a way that would break loose if you tried something new and visual. You need to have a personal sense of where you could really get a payoff from working visually. The specific opportunities you face will be unique to your situation, of course, but there are some common benefits that visual teams experience. These are also listed in the box on this page.

Far and away the most effective way to get your manager or team to envision what is possible is to show them the work output from another visual team. The reproduction of a visual meeting report on this page is a sample. Imagine this report at its full size with 11" x 17" pages. To the person reading a report, the size of the charts visually is almost the same as when a meeting participant is looking at the wall. Participants feel like they are back in the meeting.

These kinds of reports work best when you use them to personally tell the story of the meeting, and help navigate the visuals. For people who were not at the meeting they can seem confusing.

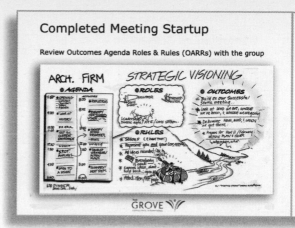

Completed Meeting Startup

Review Outcomes Agenda Roles & Rules (OARRs) with the group

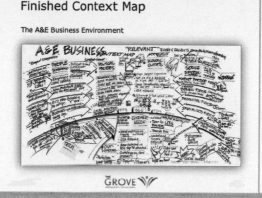

Finished Context Map

The A&E Business Environment

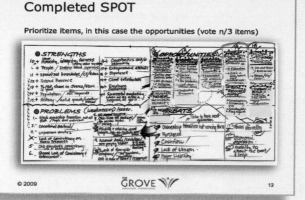

Completed SPOT

Prioritize items, in this case the opportunities (vote n/3 items)

© 2009

12

"A"—Propose Some Concrete Action Steps

Being personally convinced of the value of visual teams and painting a vision of possibilities isn't enough. You will need to propose some specific action steps that whomever you are talking to can concretely imagine implementing. Here are some tried and true first moves:

- **Take graphic notes in your meetings and share them**: Most people who get comfortable working with visual language use it for their own note taking. If you get some practice here and a little proficiency, share your notes with your team members, and suggest that you could do this at a bigger scale.

- **Jump up and record yourself**: Grab some markers and record your agenda, action steps, and/or agreements on a flip chart without asking. Your teammates will appreciate it, and probably be open to more. You don't have to be expert at drawing to have this be useful.

- **Brainstorm with large rather than small sticky notes**: If supplies are a problem, use loops of tape on the back of half sheets of 8.5" x 11" inch paper. There are, however, quite a few sources of large sticky notes (including The Grove).

- **Use a tablet for web conference recording**: The simple shift from slides and presentation to discussion and graphic recording on a web conference will change the

GRAPHIC MEETING REPORTS

Reports like the one shown in part here makes the case for working as a visual team as well as anything else you could do. This is a small sample of what could be a 20–30 page visual report. It's perfect for telling stories to people not at the meeting. The chart on the left is a Grove Meeting Startup Graphic Guide. The middle one is a Context Map. The one following is a SPOT Grid. The report continues on the next page to give you a sense of how panoramic these can be.

Cover Story Vision Example

Visioning—1 hour

"Imagine your firm is the cover story of an important magazine"

Final Strategic Vision

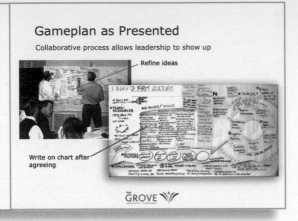

Gameplan as Presented

Collaborative process allows leadership to show up

Refine ideas

Write on chart after agreeing

MEETING REPORT, Continued

In this part of the visual meeting report for an architecture firm, the off-site process turned to visioning and action planning. The Graphic Guide on the left is the Cover Story Vision. The one in the middle is the Five Bold Steps. The one on the right is the Graphic Gameplan. The architecture firm doing this planning had the final strategic vision reproduced and posted as you see it in more than a dozen offices around the country. Because it represented a true consensus of the partner owners, it had very high credibility. (All these Graphic Guides are available in blank form at www.grove.com.)

engagement from a one-way presentation with a little bit of feedback to a real discussion with proposals and responses. Get a simple tablet and a graphics program and see what you can do (see Section VI for ideas).

- **Use simple graphic templates for breakout groups**: A tried-and-true way of getting started graphically is to have small groups codevelop their ideas on a graphic template, then compare the results with other groups to identify the ideas that cut across. There are many examples in this book of such templates. The Context Map Graphic Guide shown in the meeting report on the previous page works terrifically with small breakout groups.

- **Debrief a project with a graphic history**: Another tried-and-true process is to debrief an important project by graphically mapping out what happened and mining for insights and learning. There are a couple of ways to do this as a whole group. One is to have everyone bring visual artifacts from the project—slides, maps, pictures, diagrams, and charts of any sort—and collage them on a time line. Then tell the story of the project, mapping out what happened on a second big timeline, or writing notes around the collaged items. The value of this kind of activity isn't the quality of the drawing, but the doing of it.

- **Create a team vision or charter**: Suggesting that your team create a visual poster of your vision or charter will provide immediate validation of the value of working visually.

The arguments about how to visualize the purpose of the team will be fun. The process will be remembered. And you will have an artifact you can use for alignment purposes after that.

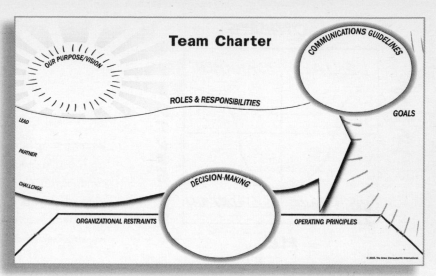

- **Create a team road map**: The single most productive thing you can suggest if your team isn't working visually at all would be to map out your plans on a calendar time line. Chapter 11 has clear examples in the case of the Otis HR team. This again is not a drawing challenge, but one of getting big paper and big sticky notes, a very easy challenge to overcome.

- **Use a Graphic Gameplan for your next team planning session**: Many leaders appreciate that using slides at management team meetings prevents having good, meaty conversations and dialogue about what is possible and what should be done. Presenters come in "loaded" and grind through the slides, with everyone else pretending to be involved. This may be a bit of an exaggeration but not much. If you feel that your action planning meetings are bogging down, using graphic templates and recorded discussion instead of slides and experience the change. I make the case in full detail in *Visual Meetings* that the interactive, participatory experience of working with graphic recording, sticky notes, and idea mapping will transform levels of engagement. A simple way to shift is to work with a Graphic Gameplan at your next planning meeting and see what happens.

- **Organize a Visual Meetings or Graphic Facilitation workshop**: If you can get a small group of people to have a common experience in a hands-on training program, they become a network that supports each other. Chapter 16 elaborates on how to create this kind of learning network. Not surprisingly, seeing is believing for this kind of work. If your team gets to work on real problems as the content for the workshop, they get a double benefit from this activity.

CHARTER TEMPLATE

This is a sample Team Charter Graphic Guide that The Grove has used with different teams to get clarity about the indicated fields. Taking this kind of worksheet and then developing a special mural that reflects a mini-vision for the team anchors the agreements even more firmly in everyone's imagination.

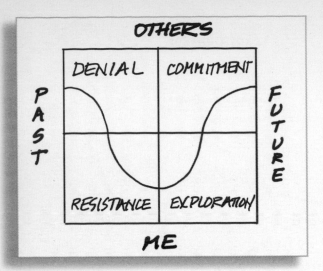

CHANGEWORKS
TRANSITION CURVE

Dr. Cynthia Scott, a senior change consultant, describes the process that people predictably experience during change. Initially, most people think it will involve others and that things won't change that much for them. When it becomes clear that the change might have an impact, the next step is to resist. If the change persists, people move to exploration of the new and eventually group commitment to the change. She used this model to help leaders see that resistance is actually progress. It is also a great example of the persistence of the "down to go up" visual as a way to explain process. For a full treatment check out the book she wrote with Dennis Jaffe called *Getting Your Organization to Change: A Guide for Putting Your Strategy Into Action.*

"R"—Respond to Resistance by Working with It Respectfully

It's interesting how resistant people can be to adopt even clearly useful ideas. All of us rely on our habits in order to work quickly and effectively. Changing something basic, like how you conduct your team meetings, will require everyone to go through a learning process. This takes time and intention. It isn't always pleasant. It helps to appreciate what kinds of resistance will rise up, patiently accept them, and come back again with a new tack. Eventually the team will have a real success experience that allows the process to take root.

Some of the ways people resist are listed in the tables on this and the next page. As the side box explains, resistance is not only normal, but a sign that change is actually happening. Denial and passivity during change are the real impediments. When people actively resist it means something has caught hold and warrants active resistance. If you learn to accept resistance as a hopeful sign, and a window into what people's real interests are, you will be able to find the win-win path.

Enrolling Leadership

If you can get the key leadership in your organization to experience success working visually, that will telegraph to the entire organization that this way of working is effective. The Grove's most widespread successes in organizations have often had this characteristic. Here are a few examples.

- **National Semiconductor**: When Gill Amelio used a graphic Storymap to share the top management vision at National's Leading Change workshop, strategic visioning became a preferred way of working and more than a dozen divisions copied the process. The change team members became very proficient working with visual planning templates and have continued working this way as they've moved to other jobs and companies.

RESISTANCE AND RESPONSES TO WORKING VISUALLY

RESISTANCE	POTENTIAL RESPONSE
❏ People think it takes too much time	❏ It takes more time when teams forget what they did or said. Demonstrate efficiency by having your first application save time—like doing an action plan, using sticky notes to brainstorm.
❏ No one understands how to take digital pictures and share them	❏ Get a camera and learn how to set the exposures. Any point-and-shoot camera takes clear enough pictures to share. Picasa or iPhoto can easily sharpen and brighten them up.
❏ Fear of looking bad at the charts	❏ Focus on listening and appreciating others' ideas rather than looking good.
❏ No experience using graphics on web conferences	❏ Get a tablet and try it out. All it takes is clicking on "share desktop" in Skype or another web conference program.
❏ Don't know how easy it is to Skype	❏ Test it out with your family and friends, then just do it!
❏ Some people who focus on listening find visualization distracting	❏ People don't have to look at the charts. Survey your team and find out how many prefer to just listen to looking and listening.
❏ Some want to take their own notes	❏ Encourage them to do so. Again, no one has to look at the public charts. But having both personal notes and wall charts will help the personal note-takers catch missing items. Explain that the public notes will also help orient people not at the meeting.

❏ Leaders don't really want collaboration	❏ There is no easy response to this one, except to demonstrate that his or her goals would be better met with engagement. It means understanding what the leader is really trying to achieve.
❏ Broadcast communication seems safer	❏ Encourage predesigned murals if a person wants visual control. Then add inputs with sticky notes.
❏ People prefer predictability to creativity	❏ Link your suggestions to specific goals your organization or team needs to achieve that require creativity. Using sticky notes for brainstorming is a fairly universally well-received intervention.
❏ Some think pictures are for dummies	❏ Frame what you are doing as mapping and pattern finding rather than illustration. Be more linear and analytic in the kinds of charts you use initially.
❏ No need to think about things systemically	❏ Suggest visualization where you are sure it will be useful, say for problem definition or action planning.
❏ Bad past experiences with recorders who didn't listen well	❏ Make sure you are oriented to serving the group and not your own interests. If your intention to do that is strong, the group will work with you to have the charts reflect what the group as a whole is saying and doing.
❏ Wall surfaces aren't great for paper	❏ Get some large foam core boards and rest them on two easels and hang your paper on them. Use flip charts side by side. Project from a tablet and your computer.

BE CONSCIOUS ABOUT MEDIA

Increasingly, one of the roles of top management is guiding the extent to which the organization learns to use different kinds of media for communications. There are so many choices that this issue cannot be left to chance or systems begin to fragment.

It's quite common for CEOs to be very clear about how they prefer their direct reports to communicate in management meetings. If you can get your top leader to support visual teams, encourage training, and use the methods themselves with the top management team, you will find the doors wide open to create a real visual teams culture in your organization.

- **Apple Computer**: When the Leadership Experience workshop for high potential managers used visual meetings methods extensively in the 1980s during John Scully's presidency, it caught on for marketing, software development, Apple University, and Apple's labs.

- **Nike**: As top execs in Treasury, IT, and HR held visual strategic planning processes for their management teams, other teams experienced the results and are beginning to work visually. The internal transition managers have adopted the TPM as a key framework.

- **Hewlett Packard Labs**: In the 1990s when Joel Birnbaum led the labs, he became convinced that visual language was essential to seeing cross-lab synergies and business opportunities. His openness to this process at off-sites with the center and lab directors led to a cascade of visual applications on R&D teams and other parts of HP.

- **Procter & Gamble**: Several CEOs have worked with the Institute for the Future and benefited from their visual mapping of future trends and scenarios. Other business groups have followed suit, and several internal practitioners have become experts.

- **San Francisco Foundation**: In the 1970s Martin Paley, an unusually creative Executive Director, became convinced of the usefulness of graphic facilitation and made it a central part of the different initiatives the foundation made to convene nonprofits and encourage cross-organizational collaborations.

- **US Army**: When Colin Powell was Chief of Staff of the army he had his staff brief him using graphic charts. This built on extensive training in Group Graphics at the Fort Ord organizational effectiveness unit in the 1970s.

As I will explore in Chapter 16, developing a grassroots network of practitioners helps support this kind of leadership from the top.

15. Developing Visual Team Skills
Learning Tips & Tools

Moving your organization and teams to a new way of working will succeed if you can stimulate a network of people to begin working visually and teach each other. This is how all innovations spread. People who know show people who want to learn. Formal training and design workshops can help plant the initial seeds and support ones that are growing, but real adoption happens informally, day by day. A team-based culture needs combinations of support.

Communities of Practice

People in organizations learn in different ways. The Institute for Research on Learning (IRL), a historic adjunct of Xerox's Palo Alto Research Lab, conducted research inside organizations during the 1980s and 1990s and formulated a graphic model of the choices that I've illustrated on this page. One main finding was that people reported learning the most from informal groups—around coffee, in the halls, finding and talking to people who could help directly with whatever you were working on. Etienne Wenger, one of the IRL researchers, has since gone on to write books and consult about what are now called "Communities of Practice," or COPs. In The Grove's experience, the most evolved visual teams have been those that developed these kinds of informal learning networks.

The change team at National Semiconductor in the early 1990s was one such team. The initiating request was from CEO Gil Amelio, who sponsored the creation of a large mural of the company's turnaround strategy. Its success led to many graphically facilitated implementation events, the development of visual planning templates, and a team of internal change consultants who all learned to work this way. Much of our learning was through our projects.

Formal Training Plays a Part

After people see what visual meetings can accomplish, and begin to see the value of having common graphic language and practices on teams, then workshops can accelerate the learning

THAT VISUAL TEAMS WORKSHOP JUST MIGHT SUPPORT OUR NETWORK OF VISUALIZERS!

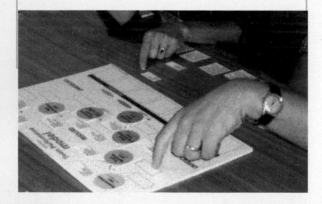

of those who can imagine these tools being helpful. The Grove approaches this development challenge with workshops that immerse participants in practicing and playing with visualization, much as they would in the workplace, and arming everyone with very thorough reference tools that support workplace learning after the workshops. I'll describe some of these activities here to inspire you to try them yourself.

Install New Mental Models by Constructing Them

I'm convinced, after years of teaching people to think and work visually, that the best way to develop a new mental model is to play with it through drawing and sticky notes. It's a process that is really the same as learning any kind of software tool. Dive in and find out what all the commands and menus do when you click on them. Markers, paper, tablets, and computers are very permissive. Making mistakes and doing versions is the way you begin to find out how things work.

In the field of architecture, making models is a time-honored way to think through problems and gain new insight. Designers create layers of drawings on tracing paper. This way of working is being challenged by computer-aided design, and a debate is raging in the design professions about whether or not this facilitates or hinders innovation. Some say that getting too detailed too early makes it hard to stay focused on the big picture and reduces sensitivity to context and environment. Others say that young designers at home with CAD can sketch and do different versions on it. Either way, it is making and testing a wide range of ideas that leads to good design.

Play with the Team Puzzles

The "construct to learn" approach is possible by letting groups play with puzzles. The Grove has created a Team Performance Puzzle where all the resolved and unresolved indicators for the different keys in the TPM are on small rectangles that small groups need to associate with the stages of the model. This kind of small group learning results in the people on the team learning the system by playing with it, talking informally, and then addressing questions to a larger group. Learning maps work the same way. They include a lot of information that needs to be linked to understand, requiring team discussion and agreement.

Use the TPM to Map Best Practices

Another kind of team-based learning is to have the team itself figure out team dynamics using either a small or large version of the TPM. I described earlier a simple exercise of asking small groups where they think the team is focused and then discussing their choices. A more elaborate exercise is to map best practices onto the TPM. In the picture on this page a training group brainstormed ways to introduce the model to the larger organization.

Share Case Studies and Debrief with the Model

A yet more experiential way to have your team come to understand its own dynamics and practices is to work with a specific project or team process. Schedule a project review or team workshop where everyone graphically illustrates the process you have gone through on a time line. Make it easy on yourself and use sticky notes. Tape on artifacts. Tell the story. When you have a full chart, step back and hand out a small version of the TPM. Then see if you can identify how the team in the project handled the different stages, and when each became the focus of the team's attention. Remember that the TPM is organized in a hierarchy of simple to complex, and the stages can find themselves at the focus of group attention in different patterns.

You will probably be able to identify places where the team worked on trust and perhaps got a little "stormy," in Tuckman's terms. You may find other times when agreements gelled and the

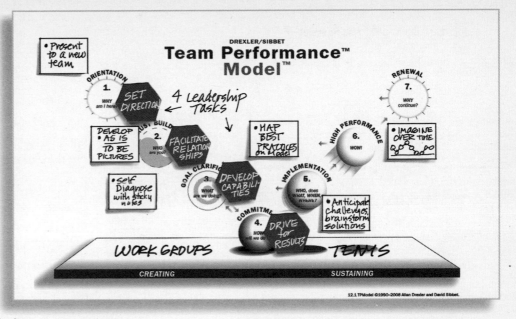

PLAYING WITH A TPM POSTER

A group learning the TPM mapped the four leadership jobs discussed in Chapter 4 on the model, as well as brainstormed sticky notes about how the model can be introduced to other people. This display emerged from a team workshop devoted to learning more about team performance and how it can be improved.

WORK-GROUP PROCESS?

energy took a turn to implementation. You might locate little turns here and there inside of the implementation story. There may be places where you bumped up into high performance, like dolphins leaping up out of the water. But these times will probably be short and fluctuate back to other concerns.

I've illustrated some fictional team process maps here to indicate the variety in processes you might uncover with these active case studies. Doing this kind of work visually is how I developed a sense of how different the mental model (the keyboard-type instrument) is from the real life playing out of the "music" of group process.

HAVE YOU EVER SEEN A TEAM PROCESS LIKE THIS ONE?

This is a story with more problems than inspiration and insight. Things can bump along for a long time with persistent problems if you and others don't feel a need to address the issues. Communicating about it may feel like work, but little progress is actually being made without a stronger sense of purpose and a shared commitment to change.

Encourage Meetings Without Slides

Throughout this book I've emphasized the value of working interactively with visual displays, creating examples and proposals on the fly, and working as a group to develop presentations—as the BLAST team did at HP. Working this way may require you to break a slide fixation, if you happen to have that on your team or in your organization. It may require actually banning slides completely from some meetings to get a different result and experience active visualization. I know of several management teams that have encouraged murals and real dialogue at key strategy sessions, believing that understanding each other is more important than moving through a lot of data. The rewards are the following:

- ❏ Teams instead of individuals develop murals. This extends the engagement and dialogue.
- ❏ Murals allow for both linear and nonlinear presentation.
- ❏ Murals stay up and can be revisited easily.
- ❏ A group of murals can be scanned for similarities and disagreements, boosting pattern finding.

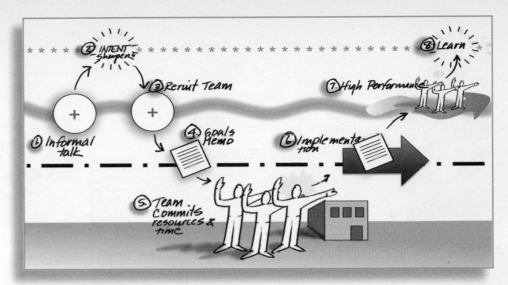

☐ Murals invite response and input more readily than slides.

☐ Murals require the presenters to distill their message and really think it through.

Make It Easy to Work Visually

The most important way to support visual teams is to create an environment where working visually is easy and encouraged. The R&D labs and innovation centers universally have lots of whiteboards and places to display things. So do rapid decision-support centers. As we will see in the next section, there are many kinds of tools that are making it possible for teams to work visually. Supplying key teams with these tools and encouraging their use will remove some of the barriers.

It bears repeating to say that the norms of an organization are probably the most controlling forces on behavior. What is allowed and not allowed is very much a function of what leadership encourages and discourages. Young people are full of experiences working with multimedia, video, digital photography, social networking, and visual thinking. They may be more inhibited when it comes to writing on charts and drawing, however, and need to be encouraged. Having paper, large templates, and decent watercolor markers goes a long way.

Black Pen, Yellow Pen, and Red Pen People

Dan Roam, author of *Back of the Napkin*, loves to share his informal research about people's orientation to visualization. In his sessions he always conducts a poll about this.

- **Black pen people** can't resist drawing if there is paper, a whiteboard, and markers.

OR IS YOUR TEAM LIKE THIS?

Your process might have a more classical pattern and look like this second map. You may notice on these two drawings the symbols are consistent. The operational, physical layer is represented by 3-D graphics. The communications layer is represented by images of the media. The interpersonal or energetic layer, illustrated by the wavy line, is illustrated as circles representing meetings or conversations. Insights about purpose and direction are shown as auras. You can use this kind of symbol system plus words to map out a project on a four-flows template.

SHARING A PROPOSED PROCESS

A team of HR consultants in China use the Graphic Gameplan to present a proposed process and brief other members of the team about what it would entail. Instead of sitting and listening to a slide talk, everyone was able to stand around and interact, ask questions, and soak up the big picture of what was involved.

- **Yellow pen people** can't resist highlighting and interacting with drawings and diagrams after they are introduced.

- **Red pen people** think that drawing and visualization misses the nuances, ignores true expertise, and encourages simplistic thinking.

According to his reports, a consistent 25 percent report being "black pen." Another 50 percent report being "yellow pen." About 25 percent admit to being "red pen."

There will always be people who do not want to work in groups or teams, and don't enjoy collaboration, cocreation, or working like designers. But the great majority of people do, and many problems that organizations face require the kind of creativity and productivity visual teams can provide.

Lead Team Development Experiences with Thorough Reflection

If you are in a situation where people really do not get the value of visual displays and visual thinking, you might need to cultivate awareness with more indirect activities. A very powerful example of how important our visual sense is to thinking is revealed in a classic team development activity call "blind squares." On the next page is a picture of Laurie Durnell of The Grove leading this exercise with a team. The directions are in the margin box. The breakdown of strictly verbal communications becomes very apparent, as well as a bounty of other insights about personal styles, response to confusion, and the impulse to lead. This exercise makes it abundantly clear that it would be much simpler if everyone could see what they are doing.

These and many other experience-based activities are available for teams. See the resource section of this book for ideas. My intent in this book is to bring forward the visualization opportunities for teams within a context of understanding overall team dynamics, but not to provide the full range of practices you would benefit from knowing.

Quite apart from team development experiences that directly address the power of seeing what you are doing, active visualization is an important tool for debriefing and team development activities. One mistake people make with ropes courses and other experiential team activities is cutting short the time spent mapping understanding back to real work settings. Immediately after one of these kinds of experiences, invite the teams involved to do some reflection. Put up a flip chart or large sheet of paper, sketch out the TPM framework, and use it as a guide to reviewing the experience, reflecting on how the team handled orientation, trust, clarification, and commitment. In games like this it often becomes very clear what it feels like when a team commits to an implementation plan and turns to aligned action.

Explicit Training in Visual Meetings

One of the ironies of our times is that more and more people find excitement in tablets and multimedia visualization, and fewer people than ever feel confident about their drawing and chart-writing capabilities. The good news is that anyone can learn how to do the simple graphics and lettering required to run good online or face-to-face visual meetings. It's much more of a practice issue than one of capability. The simple drawings that work are rooted in gestures that are universal. People just have to learn to hold a pen! The Grove offers many self-study guides for this sort of thing, so you could just supply your team with tools like the *Fundamental of Visual Language* (available at www.grove.com), which actually outlines hundreds of simple icons with specific stroke order. My books *Graphic Facilitation: Tapping the Power of Groups Through Visual Listening* (available at www.grove.com) and *Visual Meetings: How Graphics, Sticky Notes & Idea Mapping Can*

BLIND SQUARES

1. Take a long climbing rope and create a giant loop by tying the two ends together. Blindfold each person on the team.

2. Have each person grab the rope with two hands with instructions: *"Do not let go of the rope or reposition hands; you can slide the rope back and forth, but not jump over someone else's hands."*

3. Ask the team to make a perfect square while remaining blindfolded. *(You can either let the team talk as they go along or not. In any event, each person's coping strategies will come to the fore.)*

4. When the team thinks it has the square ask them to put it on the ground.

5. Take off the blindfolds and discuss the process Use the TPM to debrief the different stages.

GROUP GRAPHICS IN CHINA

In the mid-2000s the IWNC Group in China asked The Grove to come and train their consultants in graphic facilitation. The need for human resources support in growing Chinese companies was outstripping available resources. Web searches found The Grove. This is a picture of the group learning the Group Graphics Keyboard at a conference center near the Great Wall of China. Asian cultures are already very visual due to the use of character-based languages. This kind of modern application makes a lot of sense. The IWNC group was 50 percent native Chinese and 50 percent foreign-born nationals who have made their home in China.

Transform Group Productivity (available on www.Amazon.com) are loaded with specific guidance on how to work with visually active display making.

The most effective implementation of visual meetings and visual teams inside larger organizations has usually involved conducting customized workshops where participants work on real work challenges while learning the craft. The picture on this page is of an HR development company in Asia that invested in this kind of training.

After the following chapter, where I make a case for a visual operating system for thinking about organizational process, I will be describing all the new technology tools that are available for distributed teams, many of which make working visually very possible. If you like theory, this next chapter will be very interesting. If you don't skip right to Section VI.

16. Shared Visual Language
Toward an Operating System for Visual Teams

As you bring the Team Performance System into your organization, you'll want to know more about the underlying design. It is intentionally created to support teams the way software supports creativity. In the computer world there is a common visual way of thinking about the layers of technology that need to work together. It is called the "wedding cake" or "stack." It starts at the level of the code that allows machines to connect. At the next level up are hardware protocols, the machine language that makes a computer work. Above that is the operating system (OS)—a program that runs the central processing unit, random access memory, power control, and the like. On top of this are the applications such as word processors, spreadsheets, page design programs, presentation programs, and now "apps" for the tablets. The top level is the interface level, where a human being interacts with the programs. User intent activates the whole system. The success of software tools lies in how well their designers can anticipate the range of intentions users will bring to the tools, and how elegantly they organize access. Problems and inconsistencies in the operating system make it very hard to have anything flexible happen at the application level. The same is true for tools for collaboration like the TPS.

Organizations Have Operating Systems

When humans understand a common way to work and adopt collective, interoperable processes like the TPS that everyone uses, it functions like an operating system for the organization. In a time when managing information and communications is a dominant form of work, and visual information is a critical element in the mix, it makes sense to embrace mental tools that are stable, and provide a platform for a wide range of integrated applications. And it's important they use visual language in a sophisticated way. It sounds like a constraint, but a robust OS is actually the doorway to flexibility and creativity.

I remember in the mid-1980s when HP decided to standardize its company on the HP 3000, a minicomputer it was selling. This meant that everyone had to use that same machine to support

THE "STACK"

- User Intent & Understanding
- Interface Design
- Application Program
- Operating System
- Hardware
- Network
- Connection Protocols

THE TECHNOLOGY STACK

Technology works in layers, with the flexible high levels relying on stable lower levels. This picture is a layman's visual translation of this architecture.

the different divisions. This constraining choice supported a fountain of creativity, and led HP to be one of the first companies to support enterprise-wide e-mail. Everyone's energy was focused on applications. My hope for the TPS is that it can bring the same kind of creativity to team-based organizations. One reason for my optimism is the fact that underlying the TPS is a Theory of Process based on the latest findings of science about how process works in nature. If this chapter feels like a little too much theory, just skip ahead to the last section about tools. For those of you who want to know how to think visually about the deep structure of process, read on!

What Does It Mean to Be Organized?

When people say, "We are organized," I think they mean that everyone shares a common picture in their head about how the different parts of the organization fit together. You would say you are "well-organized" if this pattern works over time and everyone's different activities support each other to get a result. If you agree with this view, then it is a strategic issue to be clear about what mental models people use to think about organizations and teams and how these models work.

If members of a team have very different models of teamwork, decisions will be taken that don't necessarily integrate. If the tools a team uses are not flexible enough to handle all the different kinds of things it wants to think about, it will experience the frustration individuals experience with software that is too simplistic. Software users want applications that work together across different platforms. So should teams. Think how much organizational effort is spent trying to reconcile competing ideas of how to collaborate.

I think visuals provide a fresh way into thinking about this question of how our thinking about teams can fit together, because the whole idea of "fit" is rooted in visual representation. Scan the graphic on the next page with all the little symbols. Ask yourself, "How is it organized?" To know that one thing goes with another, you need to first identify one of the elements—say, one of the

When people say, "We are organized," I think they mean that everyone shares a common picture in their head about how the different parts of the organization fit together. People say they are "well-organized" if this pattern works over time and everyone's different activities support each other to get a result.

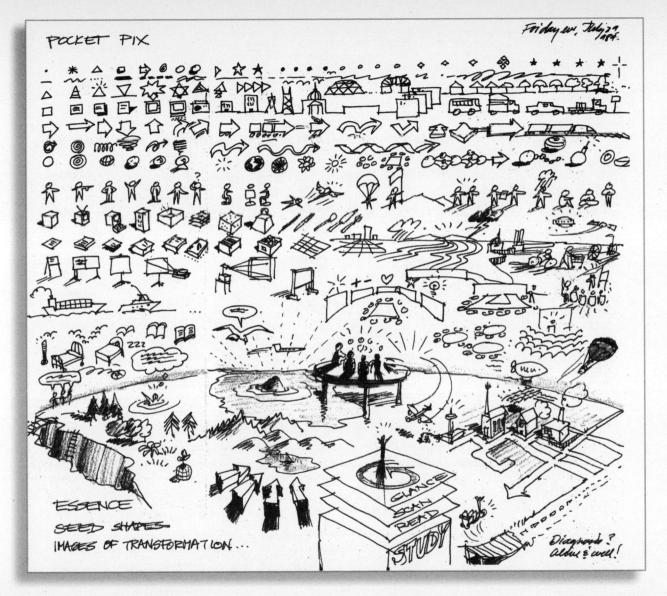

POCKET PIX

Friday eve. July 29 '04

ESSENCE

SEED SHAPES.

IMAGES OF TRANSFORMATION...

GLANCE
SCAN
READ
STUDY

Diagrams? above & well!

WHAT DOES IT MEAN TO BE ORGANIZED?

I found this page in one of my journals and think it visually demonstrates what humans mean by organization. At the top are little "atoms" of visual information, separate and not linked together. They are in a neat line, however, as one kind of organization. As they flow down the page, some of them begin to group and cluster— another form of organization. Toward the bottom they fall into little visual scenarios and settings—a canyon land, a lake, a meeting room, and a small town. At the very bottom is a conceptual diagram, a type of hierarchical mental model that you could use to see yet another form of organization. What parts of this drawing pop out at a glance? What do you see when you scan rapidly? Can you "read" the visuals like text? If you study it for dates and links what do you see? I think at root being organized means understanding the pattern that is connecting elements in whatever you are considering.

GUIDE TO MENTAL MODELS

1. STATIC	2. MECHANICAL	3. SELF-REGULATING	4. SELF-REPRODUCING	5. SELF-EXPANDING	6. SELF-MOVING	7. SELF-REFLEXIVE
FRAME WORKS	**CLOCK WORKS**	**CYBERNETIC SYSTEMS**	**CELLS**	**PLANTS**	**ANIMALS**	**HUMANS**
Parts connect	Parts connect and **move**	Parts connect, move, and **adapt**	Parts connect, move, adapt, and **reproduce**	Parts connect, move, adapt, reproduce, and **grow**	Parts connect, move, adapt, reproduce, grow, and **self-move**	Parts connect, move, adapt, reproduce, grow, self-move, and are **self-aware**
Includes buildings, scaffolding, bridges, banks, and static structures of all kinds.	Includes clocks, engines, cars, boats, airplanes, and mechanical machines of all kinds.	Includes thermostats, regulators, computer systems, and intelligent software.	Includes living cells, viruses, single-celled plants.	Includes flowers, vegetables, bushes, trees, and plant ecosystems.	Includes birds, mammals, insects, and fish.	Includes families gangs, teams, organizations, communities, and civilizations.

LOW ————————————————————— COMPLEXITY ————————————————————— HIGH

Group Graphics® Keyboard
A Process Oriented Grammar for Visual Language

little star people—and then look at another element, say, a picture of a computer—and see if you can see a connection. All the patterns of connection are examples of different kinds of organization. My argument is that the more stable and robust your underlying frameworks are, the more flexible your application-level activity becomes. But just like a computer OS, the simplicity comes with some complexity.

A Guide to Mental Models

In my 2006 book, *Graphic Facilitation: Transforming Group Process With the Power of Visual Listening* (a book for professional facilitators available through The Grove), I share a framework for thinking-about-thinking from Kenneth Boulding, author of *The Image*. He describes a hierarchy of mental models that, in my experience, has held up under extensive application and provides a key to the question of how to begin thinking about the organization of visual thinking on teams. The graphic on the facing page explains his concept visually (using a matrix format).

You can see that it builds from models that illustrate how parts connect, to ones adding movement, to ones allowing adaptation, then reproduction, then expansion, mobility, and consciousness. This pattern has a similarity to the patterns of evolutionary process that I learned from Young, which begins with simple forces and elements that combine, learn to reproduce, move, and become conscious.

From Simple to Complex

I've noticed over the years that the very simple static and mechanical metaphors are favorites because they are so universal and simple. At the other end we use human metaphors because

GROUP GRAPHICS KEYBOARD

In *Graphic Facilitation* and later in *Visual Meetings*, I describe a formal system for visual thinking called the *Group Graphics Keyboard*—my first formal application of the Theory of Process to work that I understood. It employs one of the architectural features of a visual operating system in that the simpler graphic formats nest into more complicated ones, as in the Boulding frameworks. The **Poster** makes a point by focusing attention. Focal images can be subelements in a **List** that flows in a linear form of organization. These can be subelements in a **Cluster**, like a group of sticky notes without connections. All these can be included in a **Grid** that formally compares categories of information. It continues like this through the **Diagram**, where elements are connected in branching patterns, and **Drawings**, where metaphor and graphic analogies animate the graphics. The final format, a **Mandala**, which has all information organized around a common center, can actually embody all the prior formats.

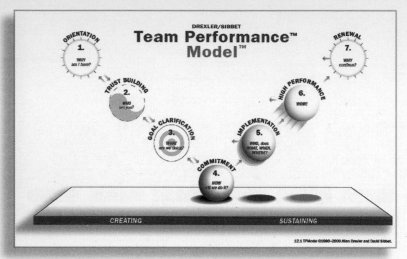

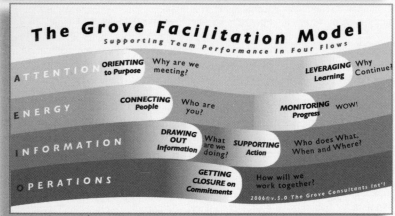

THE GROVE'S TPM AND FACILITATION MODELS

These two process models are both application-level models using the Theory of Process as an OS.

they are familiar—comparing business teams to sports teams, for instance. But the middle metaphors of cybernetic systems, cells, plants, and animals aren't as well understood. Average persons in the past probably understood plants and animals better than we do now, because people spent more time with them. But in today's organizations the working knowledge of biology, agriculture, ecosystems, and animal systems are quite limited. On the other hand ,contemporary science technically knows far more about all these middle ways of thinking now than prior generations. Crafting accessible graphical users interfaces to this kind of knowledge is one of my passions.

Toward an Operating System for Visual Teams

As I noted at the beginning of this chapter, the TPM is built upon a very stable and robust operating system called the Theory of Process, articulated by Arthur M. Young (see appendix for a review of the formal theory). The Group Graphics Keyboard was my first application of this theory to what I knew well—group process. It resulted in a conceptual breakthrough as I began to look at visualization as a set of processes with the patterns being artifacts. This is what the book *Visual Meetings* explains in detail. The Drexler/Sibbet Team Performance Model was my second application, worked out all during the 1980s. The Grove Facilitation Model shown here was a third, to illustrate what a facilitator does in relation to the stages of team performance. You will notice they all share a similar design. Let's look in broad strokes at how this kind of visual system works, starting with the applications layer and working down into the operating system.

The GG Keyboard is flat rather than reflecting a right angle at the turn to accommodate several banks of "keys," but the same movement from freedom to constraint and back to freedom is embodied in the distinctions. You may notice that the seven steps in the Team Performance Model are included in the second row of "keys."

On an organ keyboard, there are several rows of keys that make different sounds. Their arrangement is logical, and sequenced by increasing frequency of the sound. The keys on The Grove's process models are sequenced by increasing degrees of complexity. But the fact that they are in a progression from left to right does not mean you have to "play" them in that order. It just means that they are arranged that way so you can remember their properties. The TPM processes identified above each of the formats on the keyboard have a resonance with the formats below, but not a mechanical linkage. Just as in music, it's possible to have dissonant and differently juxtaposed elements—for instance, using a grid display format for trust building. Because these models all share a similar underlying OS, with practice one can move one's awareness up and down and backwards and forwards in what I think of informally as "helicopter quality thinking."

On this page are several of the other applications I've made using this same visual structure. The Grove Facilitation Model indicates what a facilitator would be doing resonant with the different stages of Team Performance. This could be considered a guide for facilitative team leadership as well. The Communities of Practice Development Model was created for the US Navy. Bear in mind that COPs, as they are called, are inherently informal and organized around flows of best practice, hence the background band. A final model is the Sibbet/LeSaget Sustainable Organizations Model. This one describes the choices leadership has when it is structuring the overall organization. It will be the subject of future books. These models, like any good computer program, have been years in refinement. I don't

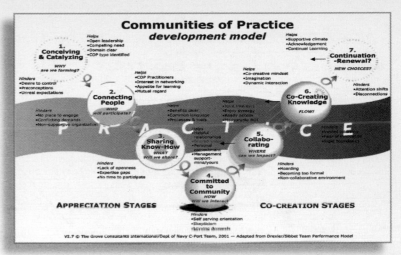

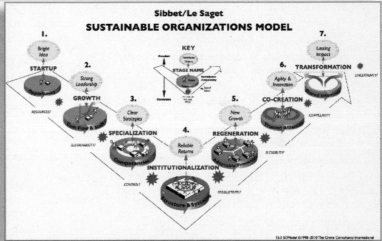

THE COMMUNITIES OF PRACTICE AND SUSTAINABLE ORGANIZATIONS MODELS

These models also reflect archetypal process patterns.

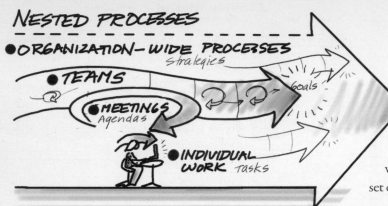

NESTED PROCESSES

● **ORGANIZATION-WIDE PROCESSES** *strategies*

● **TEAMS**

● **MEETINGS** *Agendas*

goals

● **INDIVIDUAL WORK** *tasks*

expect they will pop to life with meaning just seeing them here. You have to play around with them and apply them to see why they are so useful. The rest of this chapter is focused on helping you understand the underlying assumptions and design principles enough that you can feel comfortable beginning to work with them yourself, and experience the excitement of having a well-integrated set of leadership and team-management tools.

"Chunking" and Nested Processes

A key principle in visual organization is "chunking." This involves breaking information up into logical clusters, appreciating that short-term memory doesn't do well when there are more than four to seven top-level chunks. At a very abstract level, for instance, it is helpful to see organization processes as operating at four levels, in a stack not unlike the one illustrated at the beginning of this chapter. A text list would describe these as:

1. **Individual work**: All the processes you use to do e-mail, write reports, provide a direct service, and so forth.

2. **Meetings**: This is where you check out how your individual work relates to others.

3. **Teams**: These link meetings and individual work into projects over time with specific goals.

4. **Organization-Wide Processes**: Strategic change, cross boundary initiatives, and large-scale culture change processes integrate many different teams.

Think about this text-based way of expressing this idea and then look at the graphic of the same idea on this page.

The visual illustrates a second principle reflected in living systems—"nesting." This is the idea that

SCALING AND FRACTALS

"Nesting," or what is technically called "scaling" or "fractals," is a characteristic scientists are discovering in all living systems. It means the levels of complexity and the types of processes found at the macro levels of a system are mirrored in the subsystems, sometimes all the way down, layer upon layer. Benoit Mandelbrot simulated these kinds of systems with mathematics and created amazing visual patterns that have these "fractal" properties. It arises from the fact that the complexity in the system arises from simple processes repeated endless numbers of times at all different levels.

phenomena in nature have similar levels of complexity at every different level, from macro to micro. This is possible because core processes that run throughout a system are manifesting the visible structures you see. If you have ever been a part of an organizational redesign project in connection with implementing an enterprise resource management system, you will know that there are hundreds and hundreds of processes in any organization. Consultants who are expert in this kind of work winnow these down to the core processes and make sure the system works for them. I'm suggesting the same approach be applied to what you choose to support system-wide ways of visual thinking. I'm suggesting personal work, meetings, teams, and organization-wide initiatives are such core processes.

Wouldn't it be useful, I have imagined, having sets of tools that work up and down this whole stack? What if the blizzard of models and languages that seem to cluster around each level of work had a deeper, integrating pattern of connection that everyone understood? You probably already saw that the Group Graphic Keyboard and Facilitation Model guides the individual work of a facilitator and helps shape choices in meetings. The TPM, COP Models operate as application programs at the team level. The Sustainable Organization Model functions at the organizational leadership level.

Assuming Wholeness—Mechanism with Parts or Unified Organism?

So far I've still been describing application layer features of a visual OS. What are the assumptions that are common across the whole stack?

An initial, fundamental assumption is that all elements in a team process are interconnected in some way, and different teams and other parts of an organization are interconnected, and organizations are interconnected with each other, their customers, suppliers, and other stakeholders. Wholeness, of course, is an assumption and not provable in an objective sense. And even if you

MECHANICAL MODELS

How many "pillars" does your organization have? Are you "on or off the bus?" Are you open to "feedback"? Do you "build" your teams? We are immersed in metaphors from the industrial age. We love them for their familiarity and simplicity. They have tremendous pull in chaotic times when our minds are screaming for simplicity. I sometimes compare these simple little models all consultants love to mental sleds. They are easy to jump on and go down a snowy hill. But if you really want to maneuver and have fun you will soon want skis. They take more time to learn, but provide a lifetime of enjoyment. The Grove's process models are more like mental skis.

ECOLOGICAL MODELS

These are some of the words that are the growing tips of new understandings about organization. They draw their meaning from living systems. Interestingly, the more complex living systems metaphors can embody the more mechanical ones, but not the reverse.

accept this stance, there are different ways to think about wholeness and interconnection. It is one thing to think your organization is interconnected like a big machine. It's a completely different perspective to see it as interconnected fields of energy and information, in constant flux.

Our concepts about organization have been shaped by an industrial age. Everyone has rich experience with mechanisms, and most of us are trained to elevate "objective" thinking over inner knowing. Mechanisms are satisfying. They can be analyzed by taking them apart. The elements have rather precise ways of connecting. They can often be substituted. Objects can be measured, evaluated, and described precisely. It's a way of thinking that at its simplest sees organization as a big building block challenge, with the grid-like organization chart and its boxes the iconic symbol. Many people still think about problems of management in these terms.

The convenience of a mechanical way of thinking is its clarity. If these kinds of models are appreciated as lenses and windows, and not as blueprints and architectures, they are useful. But the downside of these ways of thinking is that organizations don't work like that. Trying to see "wholeness" in an organization through an objective lens feels like looking through a kaleidoscope. All the little bits look different and don't "fit" together. The messy parts get ignored or even expelled.

I love constructing and making things. But my sense of "wholeness" in regard to living systems (which is what organizations are) is deeply informed by early work in agribusiness and being a lifetime gardener. I personally believe civilization is moving steadily toward a biological, ecologically based way of thinking, driven by our own survival needs. The disruption to our agricultural system from global warming will necessitate understandings and innovations other generations could only imagine. The growth and urbanization of populations carries with it acceleration in the adaptation of viruses and diseases to human countermeasures. Declining birth rates, aging

❑ Organisms operate with arrays of independent elements aggregating and cooperating, with deeply interconnected systems.

❑ Organisms organize around flows of energy and resources more than structures.

❑ Structures are diverse and branching.

❑ Organisms grow, reproduce, and die.

❑ Organisms are affected by and affect their environments, and are in continuous, intimate exchange with them.

❑ Organisms communicate in subtle and multilayered ways.

❑ Living organisms are in constant motion and are continuously changing.

❑ Organization patterns in organisms often emerge from complex interactions rather than being centrally "designed."

❑ Organisms have sets of built-in but not completely consistent "models" in their DNA that are distributed throughout the organism.

populations, and the side effects of ever increasing levels of toxicity from our own industrial processes are all pushing for more understanding and response. The fact that many still look at health, agriculture, and environment through the filters of industrial age, mechanistic mental models does not mean that the more inclusive and complex ways of thinking from biology aren't more effective. They are. But they take a little more effort to learn. The good news is that the old models nest into the new (but not vice versa).

Organizational Development Requires Thinking About Open Systems

I think that upgrading our mental models about teaming and collaboration is a first order of business in these times. The field of organizational development, my professional and intellectual base, stemmed from this assumption of wholeness in systems. It grew from a network of organization thinkers who saw organizations as organisms, much more like living things than mechanisms. The root of the very word is "organ," which is a biological term. Being organized like organisms has a very different set of qualities. Some of the characteristics of living organisms are listed in the side box. You can also detect the growing edge of the new ways of thinking in the kinds of terms businesses and organizations are using as common language today:

- Value webs
- Business ecosystems
- Economic health
- Social networking
- Partnership
- Collaboration
- Cocreation
- Sustained growth
- Evolution of technology
- Biotechnology
- Bifurcation
- Climate

WE'RE ALL CONNECTED!

The mental models from cell upward that Boulding describes are all examples of ways of thinking rooted in understanding of living systems. Cells reproduce and it's no accident we call terrorist cells "cells." Plants grow and produce fruit. Again, it's no accident we call manufacturing plants "plants." When Kevin Kelly wrote about self-sustaining systems in his book *Out of Control: The New Biology of Machines, Social Systems, and the Economic World*, he chose the image of a beehive for the cover. His message is that this new world is one of connections that are in constant motion. It's a world where digital natives "swarm" and companies "crowd-source." Animals don't work as individuals. They are found in flocks, herds, gaggles, pods, swarms, coveys, mounds, and packs.

SNAPSHOTS OR MOVIES?

Everything you see has form, and it also moves. You appreciate structures and designs by taking literal and mental snapshots. You appreciate processes and change with stories, scripts, and by making movies. I've drawn a little cartoon of the difference here. Each perspective has a set of visual fundamentals that should be a part of everyone's understanding. They integrate inside our brains.

This all adds up to an argument for having a visual operation system that, at its root, emphasizes process over structure, for in living systems the flow of energy is more fundamental than form.

Thinking from a Process Point of View

The snapshot perspective illustrated on this page reveals pattern and shape. The Group Graphics Keyboard's seven archetypes are these basic patterns. But I'm arguing that an operating system for a visual organization should put a premium on visualizing from a process perspective, since movement and change are fundamental in living systems. So even though the Group Graphics Keyboard looks static in print, the different formats are actually the artifacts of seven little processes, or what I label as "procedures," in the Keyboard. If you use these formats as a graphic recorder you will experience the increasing complexity of the *processes* as you move left to right.

The Team Performance Model is intentionally more biased toward seeing the process—of appreciating the movie of life. At first glance it looks like seven separate balls and could be con-

TOP LINE — Purposes, Aspirations

Free

VISION

Dynamic
Tension

Constrained

BOTTOM LINE — Budgets, Resources

fused with a static snapshot model emphasizing fixed structure. But Allan and I used the metaphor of the "bouncing ball" to coax the viewer into imagining the movement. In practice, you will find that not only is the overall process constantly moving in different patterns, much like music, but also the seven stages are all little processes within their own right. With practice, you can come to see the TPM as a 48-key keyboard, with each of the seven stages mirrored in each one. You can also imagine the little circles in the model as "lenses" through which you look at the real moving world, in all its richness. Each lens guides you into see a different quality, all of which are working in concert in a developed team.

The Twofold Operator

After accepting an assumption of unity (a living system perspective in my case), Young's formal process theory defines archetypal ways humans begin dividing things up in order to understand them consciously, beginning simply and articulating a set of nested mental models at the most abstract level. These patterns are those Young saw reflected in the findings of contemporary science, and reinforced by traditional understanding. His bias as a mathematician and inventor was to keep these as elegant as possible, and like a good optical lens, polish the distinctions carefully.

The first way humans divide the wholeness is to understand the twofold nature of time and experience—the background movement that flows in and around all organizational processes. This can be expressed visually as the arrow of time—the movement of energy and life that moves in a direction and fluctuates between freedom and constraint, or energy and matter. This is illustrated

THE TWOFOLD NATURE OF ALL PROCESS

We live on the arrow of time in a pulsing rhythm between freedom and constraint, yin and yang, convergence and divergence, pull and push, top line and bottom line, breathing in and breathing out. It is a fundamental pattern of all life that lives in the thin envelope of our atmosphere between the solid earth and vast cosmos.

RELATIONSHIPS · STATES · ACTIONS

Past · Present · Future

ACTIONS, STATES, AND RELATIONSHIPS

This threefold way of viewing things distinguishes between actions, which are "future focused"; the states of being they affect, which are "present"; and our understandings about all this, which are of necessity "past" oriented since the action and results we are understanding have already happened. This threefold way of looking at phenomenon is a standard convention in physics and engineering. It also turns up as a very common way to think about process of any sort.

as a "top" and "bottom" line, and is one of the patterns that scales up and down the organization. Because human beings are upright most of the day and think of the ground as solid and "down" and the cosmos as expansive, open, and "up," I think that visual process maps and charts are more effective with this up and down orientation as a base map.

When you understand this idea, and can begin to discern when your team is converging toward agreements, or diverging toward more energized, high-performance states, your understanding of process will operate at a more sophisticated level than with simple, straight line process models that merely connect one stage with the next. This perspective assumes that your inner life and imagination—your spirit and soul if you want to use popular terminology—is as important as your thinking and operational expertise—your mind and body, to continue the comparison. Artists work on all these levels at once. They sustain both mastery and surprise. So do high-performance teams.

It is a feature of the twofold nature of process that it is felt and experienced more than it is calculated or observed. Energy and movement is shaped by intention, trust, and motivation—all very subjective qualities. While the TPM graphically emphasizes this in its "arc" design, your understanding must be rooted in feeling this pattern directly in the life of teams you are on.

The Threefold Operator— *Past, Present, and Future*

Being "in the flow" at a feeling level is not the only way humans relate to living on what Young calls the "arrow of time." We also move our attention between past, present, and future. In meeting design you will consider the before, during, and after parts. On teams the threefold shows up in the forward-moving actions of individual members, the consequences that are experienced in the present for other team members, and team understanding about the relationship between the two. In physical sciences the cause and effect links are described precisely. In human interaction, which includes conscious actors with free will, the understandings we form after actions have occurred will not be as precise, but nonetheless manifest as stories, excuses, and rationale.

All action happens in the present, of course, but sometimes we are focused on where that action is leading (a future orientation) and sometimes are experiencing the impact and "state changes" resulting from the action, and being present with what's happening. At other times we are analyzing and thinking about it all.

The Fourfold Operator—Thinking About Thinking

When humans do stop and analyze something for full understanding, four perspectives are required, Young reasons. You should recognize this as the "source code" for the Four Flows Model.

1. **The Knower**: Your intentions, projections, and "point of view," immaterial and nonobjective, represent one aspect you need to understand. You achieve this through self-awareness. Even modern science accepts that the perspective of the observer affects the observed in the more subtle realms of subatomic physics. Your intentions definitely impact relationship.

2. **The Known**: This is the other end of a spectrum, and includes what you can objectively discern from your senses—reading, observing, cross-checking, weighing, measuring, and describing. This is the realm of objective data and representations—scientific knowledge.

3. **Your Process**: Full understanding also involves being aware of how you interact with what you are trying to understand, and the feelings, values, and experiences that result. Memories of past interactions function as associations and connotations that have their own qualities.

4. **The Thing Itself**: You may not be able to prove in argument that something exists apart from your knowledge about it, but it is a very practical stance to assume that it does! The

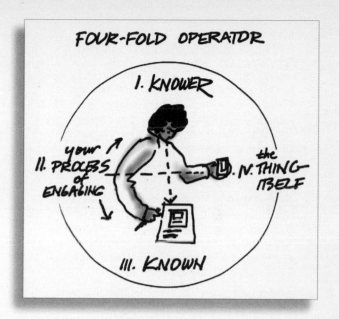

FOURFOLD IN USE

Assume you are choosing a type of smartphone. You can look at what is "known" objectively about the phone including its look, size, functionality, and so forth. The other side of this analysis is understanding of your own intentions and perspective—the "knower." Your needs and intentions will affect your choice. There are two other perspectives needed to completely understand the phone. You will experience what it is like to interact with the phone, how it feels, and how you feel about the quality of and rigor of your research. The fourth perspective is to actually get and use a real phone. It may or may not factually fit your other assessments. If a part is malfunctioning it won't work, regardless of what you think.

thing itself isn't what you think about it. It isn't your interactions with it. It isn't your intentions about it.

Young appreciated that the fourfold set of distinctions was mirrored throughout history when people tried to think about dividing the whole of life into some elegant parts. These distinctions are those Aristotle made describing four causes—Final Cause (intent), Material Cause (substance or quality), Formal Cause (plans), and Efficient Cause (the work itself). Carl Jung saw humans having four modalities of perception—Intuition, Feeling, Thinking, and Sensing. Alchemists in the Middle Ages divided things into Fire, Water, Air, and Earth, each standing as metaphoric symbols for the four distinctions Young describes. Even the Native Americans organized their thinking in the four directions on the medicine wheel with resonant meaning. In *The Geometry of Meaning* Young shows how modern engineering uses these same distinctions in its formal designations of four kinds of action—position (D or no action or location), velocity (DxT or constant change in position), acceleration (LDT2 or change in changing action), and control (DT3 or change in acceleration). Young's mathematical and scientific arguments are beyond the scope of this book, but are summarized in the Appendix, along with links to more resources. Young successfully makes the case that a fifth distinction is not necessary for thinking, because change in acceleration essentially stops the action and takes you back to the beginning.

Instances of fourfold models use different words and describe different phenomena, but are reflecting the universal pattern of a knower creating understanding of the known through some process—all relating to something that has a factual existence apart from the knowing.

Nesting the Models

I'm sure you can see by now that the fourfold way of breaking things apart is the background structure of the four flows framework that is implicit under the bouncing balls of the TPM.

When you combine the twofold way of experiencing process with this fourfold way of thinking about it, the seven-stage arc models is the result. (Four ways of thinking about creating the team, and four about how to sustain it, with the overlapping fourth distinction one and the same, because it is the manifest team itself—objective and particular.)

If you take the fourfold way of understanding, and apply it to each of the threefold positions, it results in a "Rosetta Stone of Meaning" with 12 distinctions. These map to what are called the "measure formula" of modern engineering. They also resonate with the 12 distinctions about process embodied in traditional astrology. This kind of integrated thinking has not been fashionable in science or in metaphysics, so Young has "resistors" in both camps. But the Theory of Process still represents the most sophisticated integrative thinking I am aware of in our times. His links to contemporary science are invaluable, and he uses graphics to explain it, which may be a key to making it possible.

Those of us who studied with Young knew that he successfully invented the Bell Helicopter, the world's first commercially licensed helicopter. His solution to the stability problem that all previous inventors encountered was to put a little, gimbaled bar on the rotating blade shaft at 90-degrees to the big blade. By combining two systems and integrating them he achieved a way to operate more flexibly. Those of us who are his students like to think of working out with his theory as developing "helicopter-quality thinking."

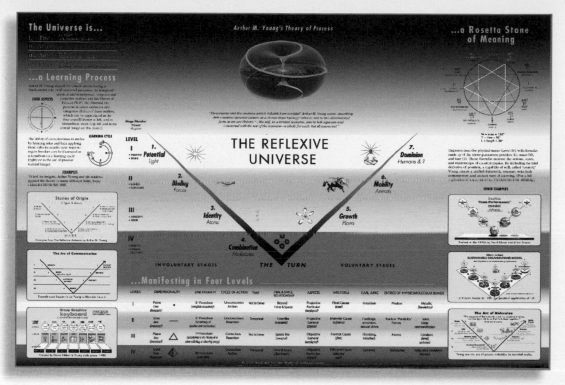

THEORY OF PROCESS SUMMARIZED

For those of you who are interested in Young's original thinking, a very complete website is available at www.arthuryoung.com. After he passed away in 1995, The Institute for the Study of Consciousness, Young's non-profit, created a canonical, four-color Storymap of his theory, shown here in two colors. It is available through The Grove, along with an abstract of the theory.

When teams begin to command dexterity in thinking, combining a strong process-model—like the TPM with a structure-model of the organization, or the little "nested processes" drawing at the start of this chapter (a fourfold)—they embody helicopter-quality thinking as well. Members can move big picture or drop into detail, move forward or backwards, and stay oriented to the integrated picture the whole time. What an advantage this is in a virtual world.

Process Theory, a Link Between Science and Organization

In developing a graphic interface for the Theory of Process, and developing and testing application programs based on this operating system, I've come to appreciate how much nature itself has given us templates for how to organize teams and organizations. Young developed his theory to make sense of our evolutionary process at the most general of levels, and show how the contemporary sciences themselves have shown that the phenomenal world is a dance between the open, free, and subjective realms of consciousness in humans, the constrained and deterministic realms of the manifest, physical world. He does not reject science, but expands its framework to re-include what historically has been relegated to the thinking of psychologists and metaphysicians. By using disciplined graphic language, in his case the language of geometry, he was able to hold distinctions in the visual space and achieve flexibility with language and labels. I think the same is possible with organizational thinking in a more focused way.

The last section of this book takes us back into the realm of tools for visualization that are available to contemporary teams. I stay focused on the practical ones, which you will be pleased to know if this chapter has edged out into territory that seems too "far out." I know, however, from the many scouts who send me the latest information about what people are doing with data visualization, interface design, video, and other dynamic media, that it won't be long before actually seeing processes in action will be possible—a development moving us far away from the structured simplicities of static, mechanistic models of organization.

VI. New Technology Tools
A Revolution in Visual Collaboration

VI: New Technology Tools

Chapter 17: Visual Tools Come of Age The Institute for the Future's Groupware Users Project in the 1990s defined the emerging field of collaboration-oriented software, the precursors of contemporary social media, game environments, and immersive environments. This chapter uses the lens of the high-performing Groupware Users Team to see the full sweep of visual tools available for teams.

Chapter 18: Graphics for Distributed Teams This chapter focuses in on practical ways to use graphics for regular web and teleconferences, including target documents, tablet recording, and video.

Chapter 19: Team Rooms & The Net The digital world provides "spaces" for teams to meet inside team databases, project management programs, dedicated websites, and virtual environments. This chapter explores what's possible with these kinds of tools.

Chapter 20: Mobile Technology Teams are working in a world that is more and more mobile, a development that is forging new possibilities and challenges. This chapter explores what that world might look like, and what thought leaders in management see coming for organizations.

17: Visual Tools Come of Age
Experiencing High Performance at the Institute for the Future

I remember vividly when the Groupware Users Project began. It happened in October of 1988 when Bob Johansen, then leader of the technology horizons work at the Institute for the Future (IFTF) in Palo Alto, and I were flying back from some work at Procter & Gamble (P&G) with the Management Systems Division (MSD). This was a group in P&G that was responsible for searching out and deploying new software tools for teams inside the company. P&G, without advertising this fact, was fully engaged in figuring out how to use computer conferences, video, total quality tools, and other kinds of technology to augment their teams. Bob and IFTF were leaders in exploring how to use video conferences for distributed teams, and were busy working with P&G as well as Hewlett Packard, Bellcore, AMEX, and other companies researching emerging technologies. I had been working with Bob on different client projects using visual meeting methods and what we called Group Graphics at the time.

Why Not a Project on Graphic Tools?

"Why can't we collaborate on a project on graphic tools for groups through IFTF?" I asked Bob on our flight home. We'd been talking for a while about the work we were both doing, and a lot of it involved helping with visual media of various kinds. Eight months earlier I'd been back at P&G helping them design a workshop on tools for total quality management (TQM). They'd had success with an initial course on the general principles as described by Edwards Deming, but now wanted practical tools for their TQM teams. I realized at the time that some 80 percent of what they were talking about was ways of using charts and graphs to literally see what metrics and data were indicating—Pareto charts, scatter grams, fishbone diagrams, frequency checklists, histograms, flow charts, and control charts were all visual tools! And much of the work Bob and I were doing helping MSD on strategy involved cocreating visual diagrams of the systems and process they were recommending.

I was highly motivated to write about this field. I'd started a consulting practice focused on providing

ENTERPRISE INFORMATION MANAGEMENT

The Groupware User's Project was conceived when Bob Johansen from the Institute for the Future and I were working at Procter & Gamble in the late 1980s. This picture shows how we were using graphic displays at that time to illustrate information systems and their possibilities.

graphic recording to strategy consultants in 1977, and then in 1988, incorporated a new company called Graphic Guides, Inc. with the intention of writing and publishing tools in addition to offering visual facilitation and consulting services. We'd moved into a downtown San Francisco office, sharing space with our partners CoVision, who were using video to help managers clarify their visions and voice of the customer. I'd met CoVision's founder, Lenny Lind, working at Apple Computer, and that experience was pushing both of us farther into visualization as we saw the power of graphical user interfaces transforming the computing world.

At the time I was studying the Theory of Process. Young invited those of us in his study group to test his theories in an area we knew inside and out. For me that was using graphic tools with groups. My work with Young resulted in the Group Graphics Keyboard shared in the last chapter. Bob attended one of my first workshops in 1980 using these ideas and became a convert. He'd followed my application of these ideas to teams as well.

A Groupware Project Is Born

Bob was interested in my proposal about a project on graphic tools for groups. Maybe we could plan conferences for project supporters in addition to doing the research. We could write a Group Graphics Guidebook. We could circle back to our respective clients and have them create a research fund to sponsor a joint team from IFTF and Graphic Guides (now The Grove Consultants International).

Bob made some calls. He and IFTF were used to multiclient projects like this and had a spectrum of influential client organizations already supporting different kinds of research. IFTF was created as a spin-off of the Rand Corporation, a leading think tank in Southern California, and at that time had 25 years of experience in forecasting and futures research. IFTF had staked out the areas of strategic planning, technology, and health care as areas to research, and every year published (and still do) a 10-year forecast of trends and

Our purpose and intention was clear. We wanted to define this new field and identify the opportunities for our client organizations. We also wanted to do this research from the perspective of users.

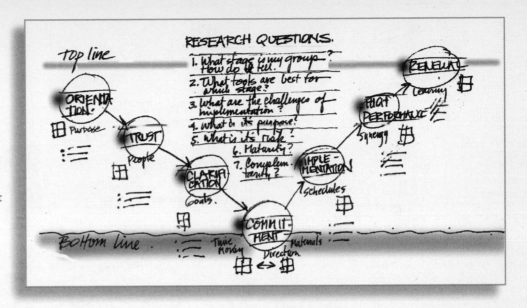

factors that could affect their clients, as well as specific reports in each of their three fields of study. Staff complemented this general research with customized work for individual clients, applying the research to specific, pressing problems of member organizations. In the technology practice that Bob headed, being located in the heart of Silicon Valley gave IFTF a distinct advantage in being in close touch with emerging trends.

Bob's reflections ended up broadening our idea beyond graphic tools to the embrace the larger, emerging phenomenon of groupware.

The map on the next page gives you a visual sense of what we were seeing.

Our First Groupware Team Meeting

"I think graphic tools are just one element in the broader phenomenon called groupware," Bob explained to four of us at an initial gathering at IFTF. He'd invited Paul Saffo, a lawyer by training and excellent writer and thinker about the future; Alexia Martin, one of the senior researchers at IFTF working on technology; and myself. "Clients will sign up for us making sense out of the larger field of group-oriented software, and it will build on IFTF's reputation in the video conferencing field. We can integrate the technological and paper-based practices in one combined project!" Bob suspected that HP, Bellcore, P&G, IBM, and several government agencies would sign up for this project, and indeed they did.

From this first meeting our purpose and intention was clear. We wanted to define this new field of groupware and identify opportunities for client organizations. We also wanted to do this research from the perspective of users, and not the inventors and vendors of the new tools, knowing full well how many hopeful

USING THE TPM TO IDENTIFY RESEARCH QUESTIONS

The Groupware Project team used the TPM to think through which research questions it needed to answer in the project.

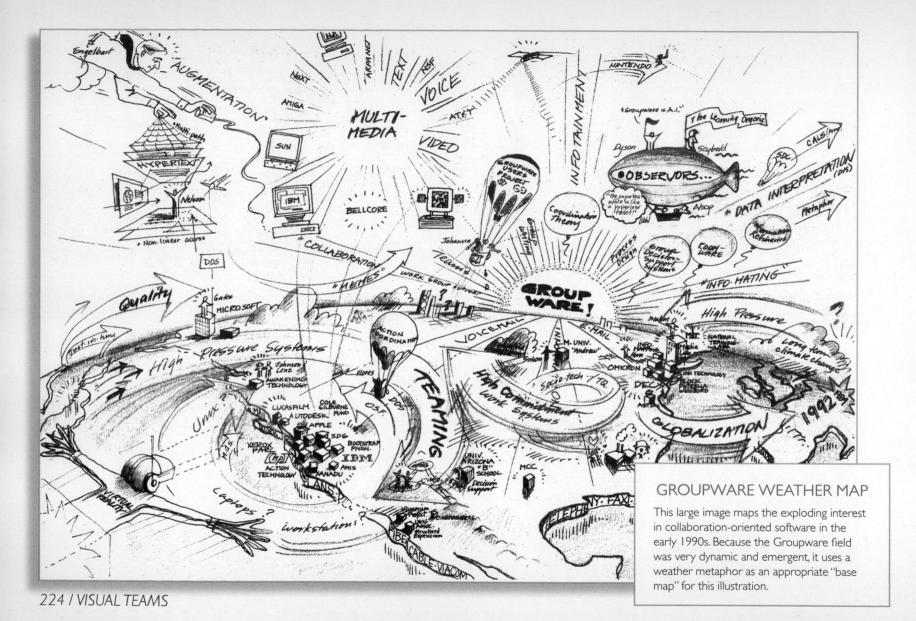

GROUPWARE WEATHER MAP

This large image maps the exploding interest in collaboration-oriented software in the early 1990s. Because the Groupware field was very dynamic and emergent, it uses a weather metaphor as an appropriate "base map" for this illustration.

claims are made as innovations emerge. We decided at that first meeting to use the TPM as a framework for our work, and held a special meeting to organize ourselves. We also agreed we needed Robert Mittman, an IFTF researcher with deep experience in computing technology, and Sue Bensen from my staff, a seasoned writer and editor working on our Graphic Guides, Inc. publications.

Soon afterward Bob and I worked out a joint venture agreement between our two organizations and our roles. Bob would head the project and I would lead on the organizational development aspects—the user exchanges, the process frameworks, and facilitation tools. We knew that the projects we were already working on with Apple, P&G, Bellcore, and HP would support us with real grounding in the field.

Moving to High Performance

Our Groupware Users Team took on four or five research projects that initial year and held our first user's exchange at the University of Arizona, a well-known source of experimentation with distributed learning and groupware. We planned and began writing our first big deliverable, the *Groupware User Guide*. We would write it collectively, with my firm responsible for design and production. At the time IFTF did not have graphic designers on the staff. Their reports were traditionally clean, well edited, text-based material with maps and diagrams as appropriate, but wouldn't have stood out as being highly visual.

Our Groupware team worked together for ten years on this project, with the group expanding to around 10 to 12 researchers. Our initial publication in 1989 was republished by Addison Wesley in 1991 in their OD Series and was called *Leading Business Teams: How Teams Can Use Technology and Group Process Tools to Enhance Performance*. It was one of the first comprehensive books on groupware.

Groupware User's Exchanges

Every year our project team organized and led two users conferences with state-of-the art groupware, getting hands-on experience with every conceivable kind of tool (see side story on the next page). Our first

LEADING BUSINESS TEAMS

Our self-published first year report became one of the first comprehensive books on Groupware in 1992.

was at the University of Arizona, known for its distance learning curriculum. They were using a new kind of software called Group Vision, which had what were called decision support tools like electronic brainstorming, rating and ranking, and grouping. This software was wholly text-based. We later went to Apple Computer and pushed their systems to the graphic limits doing group drawings 60-strong with MacDraw.

We discovered in these exchanges that technology can trump group process and result in meetings that don't have a lot of interaction and life. But we did experience the cutting edge of what have become much more supple and transparent tools today. Check the side story here for some of the other tools we explored in the project. They pushed our team to be very agile with process as well as content and technology. We had to work hard on all four of the flows of activity in a process. One of the principles that came out of all this experimentation was the deep conviction that group-oriented tools need to be simple and easy to disappear so that the group interaction can come to the forefront of everyone's attention.

Within our Groupware Users Project team, graphic recording and large Storymaps, diagrams, and visual conceptual models became standard practice. On the following page is a typical example of all the visuals used in our exchanges. It's interesting that in the midst of all the technology we were exploring, simply writing on paper and whiteboards and using sticky notes became our power tools of choice most of the time.

Visiting MIT's Capture Lab

While much of our research and most of the user exchanges dealt with software aimed at actually supporting and managing live group process, we also looked at how people were using computing and visualization to think about group dynamics conceptually. Our visit to the MIT Capture Lab in Cambridge, Massachusetts, stuck with me to this day. On page 228 is a picture I drew in my journal of the setup—a conference table with embedded screens for each person, on which anyone could type or draw. They projected up on two large BARCO screens that had been integrated so they could show two different images or one stitched-together image.

FIND THE VISUALIZATION TOOLS

This illustration I made in my journal at the time of our Groupware Exchange at Apple Computer shows the full array of things we tried there. See if you can find the following in the picture:

❑ Graphic agenda

❑ Visual mental model

❑ Group-oriented graphic rating system in MacDraw—projected

❑ A network of Mac SEs for group brainstorming

❑ A "techretary" taking notes in a word processor program

❑ Active graphic recording of discussions

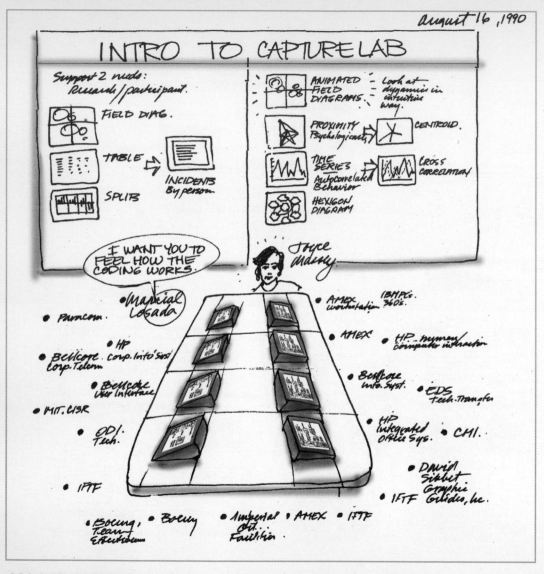

If you examine this drawing you will see a number of little drawings on the space representing the big screens. They represent ten different ways researchers were visualizing group process in their studies. While we met and discussed our experience, three researchers sat behind one-way glass windows and coded every group interaction by making tick marks on some special frameworks they had developed. This data was compiled overnight and the next day we were able to see animated movies of our group interaction like x-rays into our group process.

This book isn't about this kind of research, but it's interesting to see what visuals they chose for the different aspects of groups they were studying. Here's the list:

- Bubble maps on a four-box model to show four "fields" of activity—who was most active offering ideas, building on ideas, blocking ideas, or being passive.

- Tables of the same data.

- Bar charts showing splits in activity.

- Animations of the "field" maps.

- Proximity diagrams.

- Control diagrams.

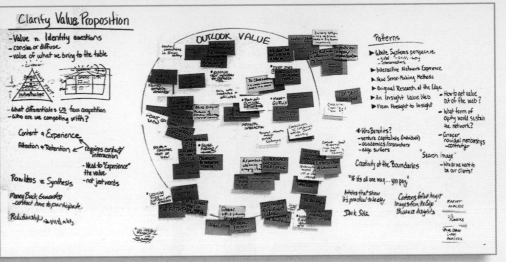

- Time series views.
- Cross-correlated time series views.
- Hexagon systems diagram of the group.

If you are familiar with the seven archetypal kinds of displays depicted in the Group Graphics Keyboard shown earlier, you will recognize that they were using five of the seven.

Lessons on Teamwork

The learning from this decade of teamwork is extensive, and includes much more than our visual explorations. Here are some of the highlights worth sharing:

- **Roles**: I marveled at how such a strong group of "egos" could cooperate like we did. I remember the meeting where we compared past team experiences and realized that our leader, Bob, had been a star center in college basketball, and was clearly experienced at doing "set-ups," "passes," and "jump shots" at the intellectual hoops we played against.

- **Metaphors**: Early on the women on the team complained that it was hard to get a word in edgewise in our meetings. We realized that the guys were playing a kind of verbal hockey and were quite comfortable chasing the puck of attention all around the room. The women on the team preferred a little more thoughtfulness. Coming to this metaphor markedly improved our meetings after that.

- **Audio is king**: Time after time in our virtual experiments we experienced the fidelity of audio being bottom line. In a large video conference connecting 90 people spread between Bellcore in New Jersey and Telia in Sweden we discovered from the engineers that the standards for voice telephony was set to optimize the male timbre. It is very difficult to balance microphones for both male and female registers.

MAKING SENSE OUT OF COMPLEX INFORMATION

This kind of cluster display was used regularly by the Groupware User Project team to take initial cuts at its research. In the original the sticky notes had four colors, each indicating a different kind of value. This chart was used during the annual planning to refine the value proposition of the project and see patterns in what clients wanted. I was fascinated that in spite of having all the technology, we still tended toward simple sticky note displays and active graphic recording.

MAPPING TECHNOLOGY HORIZONS

Kathi Vian, a former IFTF staffer who rejoined the Institute during the Groupware Users Project, is shown here in front of one the concept sketches for the visual maps that now characterize IFTF's reports. She is a gifted graphic visualizer as well as writer, fully using both sides of her brain. As of this writing she leads the 10-Year Forecast work at IFTF.

- **Magazine formats**: We were quite stymied trying to figure out how to write our initial book until we landed on the magazine format as a concept. Interestingly, this format has expanded to take over newspapers, blogs, and many websites as the format of choice. Magazines were the first print media to fully embrace full interdependence of text and image.

Fast Forward at IFTF

The Groupware Project was so successful it morphed into the Technology Horizons project that continues at IFTF as a multiclient project, heading into its third decade. Most of us on the original team have moved on to apply our learning to other pursuits. But we are still in touch with the new group at IFTF, which is exploring all the technology we associate with the twenty-first century—gaming, cloud computing, crowd sourcing, geodata, and social networking.

Visualization became such an embedded aspect of our Groupware Users Team, and subsequently of IFTF, that it was treated just like any other channel of communication, modeling many of the practices written about in *Visual Meetings*. It became and still is a signature way of working for IFTF, whose annual forecasts and reports are regularly accompanied by large graphic maps and accessible diagrams, supported now by a very sophisticated team of information designers.

At team meetings where IFTF focuses on making sense of research, large displays are the accepted way to do conceptual prototyping. Usually a smaller subgroup works out the key concepts and then reviews the maps with the larger group for refinement and input. These tools amplify the team's ability to think systemically and comprehensively as a group—no small challenge with information as complex as that being organized by IFTF. As the institute now explores social networking, games, and simulations in the 2000s it has actively explored how entire networks can help source the data, maps, and scenarios that help guide their clients in thinking about the future.

18. Graphics for Distributed Teams
Web & Teleconferences

Teams all around the world are increasingly using teleconferences and web conferences for whatever meetings they have. At The Grove, our work has steadily moved in that direction. We are fully engaged in exploring how these platforms can benefit from working visually and have discovered many strategies. This chapter will share some of our experience and ideas about where this work is heading.

What Are the Choices for Virtual Visual Work?

There is a spectrum of ways to work in real time from different remote locations. This is the "same time/different place" option on the four-square map described in Chapter 2. (The next chapter will deal with "different time/different places" platforms.) Here are your choices.

- **Teleconference without explicit visuals**: The simplest option is to have a telephone call and have one of the team participants keep notes and e-mail them to everyone else afterwards. If team members share common visual models like the TPM, the shared graphic language allows a team to make more sophisticated points regarding the process and work.

- **Teleconference with target document**. Far and away the most common way to work visually is distributing a set of documents via e-mail and having a telephone call.

- **Web conference with target document**: A common practice is to load key documents into a web conference platform and share them in a push mode with audio and chat feedback.

- **Web conference with graphic recording**: A standard web conference platform usually has desktop sharing, which allows everyone to see tablet recording on his or her screen.

- **Video conferences with chat**: Standard chat software increasingly incorporates simple video from cameras embedded in the computer.

DID I CATCH THAT CHANGE YOU SUGGESTED?

A BASIC RECORDING SETUP

This picture is of a MacBook Pro with a Bamboo Tablet from Wacom, with the Otis HR Roadmap loaded into Sketchbook Pro from a file saved from a PowerPoint slide of The Grove's Roadmap Graphic Guide. The conference platform is WebEx, a web conference service from Cisco that is one of the current leaders. It's a standard setup for graphically facilitating a distributed meeting with a single document focus. It combines the advantage of a target document with active recording of everyone's comments. No doubt all these capabilities will be superseded when integrated tablet computers start reflecting these same capabilities.

- **Video conferences with shared whiteboard**: It is possible to have a video chat window open while working on a whiteboard and tablet. Audio services can be integrated or separate.

- **Telepresence**: High-end video conference systems from companies like Cisco, AT&T, Siemens, and HP create a very high definition connection between participants that simulates sitting around a common table. These systems have ways to show graphic displays, interact, and present.

- **Interactive whiteboards**: Companies like Smart Technology in Canada now allow their interactive whiteboards to be multitouch and integrated across many different nodes. A central server can download client software that allows remote participants to see and interact with the working display.

- **Telepresence and interactive whiteboards**: A high-end team room can combine high definition telepresence with interactive whiteboards.

- **Virtual worlds**: Three-dimensional environments like Second Life and its many imitators provide a shared world for meetings. These solutions have a steep learning curve and require high bandwidth connectivity, but are increasingly available.

Some new teleconferencing services are emerging that provide greatly expanded options for real-time meetings. Maestro is an early leader offering the ability to set up audio breakout groups, facilitator-controlled muting and unmuting, and polling with the keyset numbers on the phone. These systems can support real-time audio conferences with hundreds of participants.

Teleconferencing With Target Visuals

Let's start by looking at the simplest of the choices. Some of the kinds of visual documents that are commonly used to focus a teleconference would be the following:

- **Agendas**: Taking the time to format these as time block agendas helps people see the amounts of time that different elements will take. I've included an example of a real agenda created in a word processing program with the client identification removed. By including clear headers, bold-faced names for different events, and bordered grid structures showing the time blocks, the design of the meeting is more visible.

- **Missions and Visions**: Include key documents that reference overarching missions, visions, and strategies that provide a context for teamwork. In many cases these are slide decks provided as background for the call. If your organization has a Storymap of its overall direction, that would be good to include.

- **Budgets**: It's almost impossible to have a good discussion of resource allocation in a teleconference without a visible budget. These are displayed as tables and spreadsheets. Graphic formatting to support scanning helps a great deal.

- **Action Plans and Road Maps**: Having a good graphic that illustrates the overall team process also helps orient people to communications about the parts. Any of the many examples in this book can be shared in advance and referenced in a call. It's also standard on projects to have an action list that shows specific items, due dates, and responsible parties.

- **Meeting Reports**: If you create graphic meeting reports that include copies of charts, photos, and the like, these can be sent as attached files and referenced in conference.

Web Conferences with Active Recording

The addition of active graphic recording to a meeting with reference documents transforms the levels of engagement your team will experience. This requires moving to a web conference platform from a simple teleconference. The good news is that these are readily available. There is a spectrum of choices from free to full service subscription services. Some of the considerations you need to take into account are listed in the side box on the next page.

TIME BLOCK AGENDAS

By adding visual blocks around items that spatially illustrate the time of an event you can increase understanding in web and teleconferences. Using graphic titles and subtitles supports scanning.

Challenges with Graphic Recording a Web Conference

There are some challenges that you can expect from working this way. These may seem detailed but they end up making a difference in the quality of the experience.

- **Getting a clean graphic effect**: The best tools to use are tablets that let you see what you are recording right under the tip of your electronic pen. A basic tablet computer works this way. So does a high-end tablet like the Cintiq from Wacom. Less expensive tablets that hook into your USB port show what you are recording on the screen. You have to practice working this way. Fortunately our brains adapt fairly quickly and can correlate hand movements to what you are seeing on the screen. The iPads and other consumer-oriented tablets are initially focused on being viewers and do not yet have the functionality to be used interactively in a web conference (although this may change quickly if demand increases).

- **Knowing what to record**: Basic principles that apply to graphic recording on paper also apply to working on tablets. *Visual Meetings* covers this thoroughly. In simplest form you record what is relevant to the stated objectives. One nice advantage to tablets is having air-brush capability on many of the sketching programs. This allows you to shade and highlight a display to pop out the relevant material, in the same way you would with chalk on paper.

- **Desktop sharing blocks chat**: On many of the services, when you activate desktop sharing so that everyone on the call can see what you are recording on a tablet or typing in a document, you then can't see the web conference dialogue box, chat window, and so forth. In those cases you will need to work with another person who is also logged in to the conference and fielding questions in chat, raised hands for voice activation, and other communications carried out through the main screen of the web conference software.

- **Chat windows block the graphics**: For participants, the open chat window in web conference programs can cover up part of the screen and possibly the graphic display you are creating. Most platforms allow you to close this window, but each participant must do this individually. This requires instructing everyone how to do this. On teams who aren't used to web conferences this might be a distraction. If you can't reduce the size of the chat windows you then need to test out what part of your working display people can see, and keep your recording to that area on whatever sketching program you are using.

- **Participants refer to prior displays**: A computer or tablet screen is a fairly small "window" within which to display information. Fifteen minutes of a meeting can easily fill one page, which then needs to be saved. The different sketching programs available for note-taking were not designed for graphic recorders in live meetings, and have different file saving commands, almost all of which open up dialog boxes right on top of your display. This requires you to be VERY familiar with how your program works so you can eliminate this annoyance and find the page you are looking for. Some programs create small thumbnails that ride alongside the main display and can be accessed by tapping on them. This kind of interface is preferable but not widely available, except in interactive whiteboard software design for meeting interaction. I personally set up all my files in advance with headers and page numbers so I can toggle back and forth between them rapidly. Another approach is to create pages in the layers that programs like Sketchbook Pro provide, and turn them on and off for access.

- **Cutting, pasting and resizing**: Sketching software usually allows you to lasso parts of your drawing or text and move it around. Sketchbook Pro also makes it easy to resize whatever you have lassoed. This is another way to deal with the small space on the display. Take your page, highlight it, and reduce it to a smaller space.

- **Making notes on predesigned graphics**: Many times on a web conference everyone wants to talk about a graphic or target document. There are several ways to do this. If you

WEBINAR RECORDING

A high-potential leadership team met in a conference room with the CEO of the company, but wanted to share the experience with all other graduates of the program on a web conference. These graphic notes of the questions and answers made it possible for the larger network to participate in real time.

have pulled an image into the web conference program, you will have rudimentary pens and markers for taking notes. Some don't word wrap and require lots of practice to do more than make check marks and boxes. Sketchbook Pro and other sketching software usually allows you to import a jpg or tiff image. Then you can record in the margins or directly on the target image. But this requires getting those pages set up in advance of the call in most cases. Another way to deal with this is to have the target image on one page or layer, and take notes about it on other pages or layers and toggle back and forth.

If you are using a special recording format, like time-boxes for an agenda, a grid, or a diagram, get group agreement that this will be a useful way to record so you can stay focused.

iPad Recording

The iPad opened up a new genre of tablets in 2010 and dozens more brands flooded the market in 2011. These new machines differ from traditional tablet computers in that they don't have keyboards, don't use standard operating systems, and are tailored primarily for web and entertainment in these beginning versions. The software and tools are evolving rapidly, and they can be used for recording virtual meetings.

During the first month of the iPad's release, Rachel Smith, Director of Digital Facilitation Services at The Grove, tested out four of the sketching programs that were available and made a graphic of each one's pros and cons. This information will soon be out of date, but provides a useful set of criteria by which to judge new software that will surely stay relevant. The images on the next page show her initial notes. Because the digital ink technology on these pads uses conductivity and not pressure, they don't work with pointed pens like tablet computers or tablet peripherals. It takes a little practice to get precise results. New styli with more pointed ends are reportedly on their way.

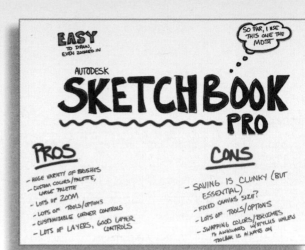

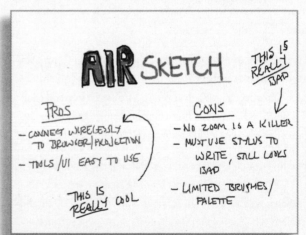

TABLET RECORDING

Rachel Smith jumped right on the new iPad platform when it first came out and tested out several available sketching apps. These will soon be outdated, but the pros and cons are a rich source of ideas of what to look for as the updates and new apps appear.

Computer projector for video

Headphones

MacBook Pro

Wacom Tablet

PC for Video Feed

Mac Monitor for WebEx

FIVE-CHANNEL VIRTUAL CONFERENCE

1. A basic **web conference** with slide presentations from the different country teams

2. A **video channel** over an internal company system

3. A **browser-based interactive system** from CoVision that allowed each country team to respond to questions pushed out to all the participants

4. A **graphic recording channel** consisting of screen sharing for a Grove computer and tablet

5. A **Skype backchannel** that allowed facilitators to talk to each other and make decisions on the fly during the conference

Multichannel Conferences

I recently collaborated on an innovative virtual project led by my consulting colleague Meryem Le Saget for one of her clients. She asked me and CoVision to help her facilitate a four-hour web conference that foreshadows the kind of conferences that will be happening more and more. This conference linked six sites in Asia to review country-specific action plans for implementation of a large multinational consumer goods company's vision, developed at a face-to-face meeting some months before. The conference operated on five different channels that were carefully integrated from the central site in Asia by the CoVision technical director in close collaboration with the client's HR and IT teams.

One of the CoVision consultants helped with their software from his office in the San Francisco Bay Area to support real-time responses to questions carefully designed by Meryem and the company design team. I was in San Francisco supporting with graphic recording of general manager responses to plans. Our two channels joined video and web conference connections to the six company facilities, from Japan to Singapore, with a Skype backchannel for facilitators.

One of the country meeting rooms had the top management and the HR VP, the lead consultant, the CoVision technical director, the IT project manager, and a few HR team members to support the process. Each of the outlying rooms had an IT technician and an HR facilitator and country manager. The central group controlled which channel was broadcasting to each site— either the team presentations or my graphics of general manager responses. Each meeting room also had an LCD for the video. Individual computers linked through the web used the CoVision software to support small group meetings and answers to questions. Extensive preparation and a full dress rehearsal led to a very successful event that was very empowering to the teams involved!

SmartBoard Networks

Leaders in interactive whiteboard technology, Smart Technologies in Calgary, Canada, now have the ability to connect up to 64 different boards, PCs, and iPads in remote conferences that support two-way drawing, and drawing on top of anything you have loaded on your computer—websites, slides, spreadsheets, design, or drawings. Text blocks group automatically and are resizeable and moveable with multitouch movements like those now possible on smartphones and tablets. Handwriting can be converted to type automatically. All this can happen on top of whatever you have up on your computer, or in the Smart software. It can then be saved at the touch of a button, and stored below the working area as little postcard-sized images, expanding to fill the screen at a tap of your finger. This kind of connectivity for teams will become standard, I'm sure, especially for design teams and anyone who has to produce something tangible that requires review of concepts and versions.

I've personally been waiting for entire rooms with this capability. It seems with Smart technology it is now possible. The company has built into its software special code that allows a user with multiple boards to literally flick one of the images to a second board by its side, and even a third, finally allowing the panoramic thinking that those of us who work with large paper regularly enjoy. Participants calling into such a multiboard meeting cannot see all them at once, but they can toggle between them quite easily.

As if this weren't enough, SmartBoard software has built-in capture of the drawing process and any audio that might accompany it. This means that with a headset and some rehearsal, the SmartBoards become a production platform for groups that want to communicate ideas to those who aren't directly in the meetings. This blending of face-to-face work with media creation and asynchronous reaction opens up vast new channels for collaboration. Rapid prototyping is

TWO-WAY WHITEBOARDS

SmartBoards connect together for interactive, remote drawing and conferencing.

central to most innovation methodologies, and this is what media creation allows. The next step is linking interactive whiteboards with telepresence!

Telepresence Rooms

At the high end of connecting technologies, an increasing number of organizations are investing in telepresence rooms. The cost recovery from saving airfare, hotel, and transportation pays for these rooms if the companies are large and the systems are used frequently. The sketch on this page illustrates what they look like in general. This particular image links four sites. You can see how the graphics are handled at the present time, with an LCD screen below the telepresence tables. An alternative way is to have a separate interactive whiteboard that is capable of showing displays and using the two together. I suspect that full telepresence will be quite popular with management teams, while design teams may prefer the interactive whiteboard capability.

The Challenge of Supporting Panoramic Thinking

When teams can see a room full of information and ideas on several different charts the whole group can move to a panoramic level of systems thinking. It operates in a completely different way than a meeting that takes on a topic at a time and keeps no overall visual record. Linear, analytic work sits side-by-side with evocative imagery and right brain panoramas. I keep working to achieve this same kind of support in virtual environments. It looks like it is almost here!

TELEPRESENCE CONFERENCES

High-definition video conference setups are making it possible to simulate a single meeting with several sites, like the four-site meeting illustrated here. Combine these units with interactive whiteboards and teams can truly go visual!

19. Team Rooms & the Net
Physical Places or Virtual Spaces?

In the early days of the Groupware Users Project when our team was developing ideas about how people might use collaboration software, it seemed increasingly clear that the idea of digital "spaces" was closely related to real-world, physical work spaces. The value in both is having a stable, consistent reference environment within which changes are meaningful. These operate in the "different time/different place" (or what is sometimes called "asynchronous" mode) most of the time, but could operate in "same time/different place" if everyone is in the environment at the same time. Social media sites, for instance, increasingly have chat functions that show who else is logged in at the same time so that you can connect in real time.

In this chapter I want to suggest some of the developments that are possible, extrapolating from some of the current uses of team rooms and virtual meeting spaces.

Virtual Team Rooms

Teams now have an explosion of software providing them with one-to-one and many-to-many communications, promising virtual meeting support, document storage, calendaring, presentation support, e-mail, profiling, and other features. Most large enterprises provide these kinds of environments for their teams. Here are some of the approaches being tried. This sector is changing very rapidly so I'm making no attempt to be definitive here. But I do want to represent the range of approaches:

- **Document management**: Some services, like Documentum's eRoom.net, have evolved from handling the problem of content management. The entire system interfaces with document servers that can produce any of the many items that are stored there. Google Docs is moving into this space on the consumer end. The various cloud-based services are moving into the document management space as well.

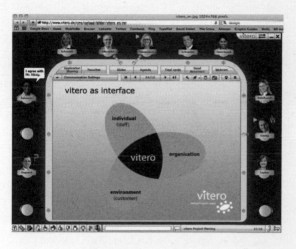

VITERO INTERFACE

As social networking sites grow in popularity team room interfaces are getting more visual and personal. Here is an example of a service from Germany and its welcome screen, with pictures of the team members on the home page. Search for Vitero.de/English.

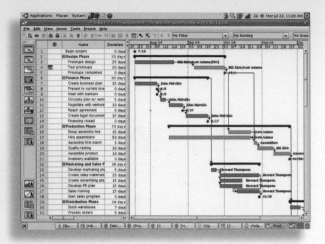

STANDARD GANTT CHART

Microsoft Project includes many kinds of reports, with this being the most graphic. It shows starts and stops for all tasks, and some of the interdependencies. These kinds of charts link to other kinds of tables and reports that these kinds of software produce for project managers.

- **Integrating social media conventions**: The explosion of social media sites has many organizations looking at how some of the same kinds of interconnections might be possible inside company firewalls. Vitero.de, a spin-off of Franhofer IAO, one of Germany's leading research institutes in the field of information technology and work organization, is focusing on the person-to-person aspects of teaming.

- **Technology support sites**: Some web conference platforms like HP Virtual Rooms provide a web conference platform with document storage, chat and other features, and have support versions that allow technology support teams to work virtually.

- **Virtual conference and forum sites**: The original leader in computer conferences, Caucus, is available as eCampus and represents a service designed to support web conferences that are not conducted in real time. These sites allow organizers to post key information, profiles, threaded forums, and alerts that tell you how many posts you have or haven't read.

Project Management Software

A more analytical kind of "space" for project teams includes the many different kinds of project management platforms, which are beginning to integrate virtual team room capabilities. Someone has posted a comparison of project management software on Wikipedia and lists 124 different applications. Two dozen of these are stand-alone programs that aren't web based, but the majority work on the web. Some two dozen are open source but most are proprietary. The full-featured ones include collaboration software, issue tracking systems, scheduling, project portfolio management, resource management, and document management systems. Many of these platforms are supporting software development teams, which are quite comfortable working virtually.

Some of the early consumer versions of this kind of software included:

- **Microsoft Project**: Primarily focused on scheduling and resource management.

- **MacProject**: Also focused on scheduling and resource management.

- **Basecamp**: Focused on collaboration, document management, and resource management, but not scheduling.

More recent, less expensive options include Tom's Planner and Viewpath. While most of these programs seem visually rooted in a very linear, left brain style of representation of data, the movement is toward a much more graphical interface. The scheduling reports usually have choices of lists, grids, and Gantt Charts—the ones that show bars of activity over time with milestones. I've included some screenshots here to give you an idea of the graphic conventions being used. Project management software tends to be used by project directors for control and documentation—not so much for team development and communications. But I think the trend will be toward integrating social networking features into the more formal programs as organizations continue to work virtually.

Working in the Cloud

Teams that work visually will find that file sizes get pretty large. Fortunately, a host of services have emerged to deal with this issue in a very focused way. They are similar in that they allow uploading and downloading for large files from the "cloud" and some level of file management. In working on this book with my daughter, a designer who lives in Portland, we used Box.net to share the In-Design files and Photoshop graphics. These services interface with e-mail and send alerts when there is activity.

Some predict that computing is moving heavily in the direction of having very mobile interfaces to these cloud environments, and thus seeing the decline of the personal computer. The forerun-

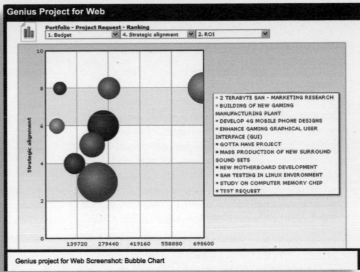

Genius project for Web Screenshot: Bubble Chart

GUI IS ON ITS WAY

Except for lists and grids, project management software hasn't really embraced having a GUI, or graphical user interface. There are a few exceptions, like this bubble chart option in Genius Project.

ners of these systems were the old light clients that linked into a large mainframe that contained all the software. As connection speeds continue to increase this kind of arrangement is becoming generally available.

Visual teams that work remotely will want some kind of support for large graphic files, either bundled into an e-platform or stand-alone and linked with e-mail. As teams move into video the pressures to increase storage and bandwidth will be steady.

Dedicated Websites

Along with the growth of the Internet has come the growth of website design software platforms that provide templates for easy construction of a dedicated website or blog. Visual teams have the choices of constructing one of their own environments if persons on the team either feel comfortable with this kind of design or have access to technologically savvy people. These kinds of services are usually quite easy to set up in regard to text communications, and usually provide challenges when it comes to managing imagery and large visual files.

If you want to have a visually flexible site on a consumer-level platform, you will need to develop imagery at several levels of resolution. Little thumbnail images are needed for the overview pages. Larger images need to be added that link to these so a user can click on the thumbnail and see a bigger image. Blog software provides this kind of functionality automatically. If you want to have the images be printable, an additional layer of PDF files or print resolution files will need to be created. The full service document management systems have this kind of capability built in but the easy-to-use website development programs often do not.

The advantage of a dedicated website is being able to establish a real identity for the team. The downside is it provides another service people need to check, especially if it doesn't link to e-mail.

Virtual Worlds

Since 2006 I have been a regular explorer of the possibilities of virtual worlds like Second Life (SL) for teams. I'm convinced that as power and bandwidth increase, these kinds of platforms will become options for visual teams. These environments are deeply connected to the world of gaming, which is already completely immersed in interactive 3-D. Environments like World of Warcraft (WoW) involve complex team interaction to manage the more challenging quests. A whole new generation of young people are coming into the workforce quite literate with these kinds of systems. As of the writing of this book, WoW alone has 11.5 million subscribers. SL reports 25 million. Both often have 50,000 to 80,000 people online at any given time, with SL supporting all concurrently, and WoW splitting them up in some 240 realms with 4,000 to 5,000 concurrent users in each realm. And this is only the tip of the virtual world iceberg. Look over the site map of a Virtual Worlds Research site on the next page for evidence of all of the blooming activity.

I'm already seeing evidence of their slow spread in business. The challenges of learning to navigate in these kinds of spaces is real for people who aren't gamers, and the current move to mobile computing is actually taking consumer attention the other way, toward more simplicity, texting, and such (topics I will treat in the next chapter). But some kinds of teamwork are being well supported by virtual environments.

- **Design projects**: Young architects are very active in Second Life and other virtual environments, creating all kinds of structures and environments to explore their ideas and skills.

THE GROVE GLOBAL CENTER

This is my avatar, Sunseed, welcoming you to the lobby of the Grove's Global Network Center in Second Life. It simulates our real life headquarters in the Presidio of San Francisco, and explores what might be possible in virtual environments when they become more widely available. It serves as a virtual HQ for any Grove associates that wish to show others how visual teams work. Visitors log into SecondLife.com, download the viewer, create an avatar of his or her own, and search for "The Grove." A map on the pier will allow you to teleport to this location. Touch the door to enter. It's open to anyone who wants to visit.

DIVERSITY OF VIRTUAL WORLDS

Even though many of these are entertainment sites, the extensive experimentation suggested by this site map points to a future with a bounty of choices for working virtually.

- **Simulations**: The company IBM has created environments where an in-world visitor can literally walk through one of their computer systems. I'm aware of ecologists replicating different kinds of natural environments. The Exploratorium in San Francisco has an in-world version called Splo that models all kinds of scientific and visual perception phenomenon.

- **Education**: Many groups are creating virtual worlds that reflect special interests, like Native American life, Masonic Orders, Buddhist practice, temple of Solomon, Christian cathedrals, Atlantis, and almost anything else you can imagine. One of the biggest "land owners," the New Media Consortium (NMC), has scores of islands and helps educational institutions create special labs in spaces rented from the NMC.

- **Community Building**: People with special needs and certain kinds of disabilities are finding creative release in virtual worlds.

- **Arts Projects**: Virtual worlds are brimming with visual artists of all sorts creating galleries, exhibitions, experiences, and all manner of experiments with animation, light, color, and shape. Many of these projects are collaborative.

- **Businesses**: Virtual worlds are creating economies and businesses within their own contexts. The manufacture of digital objects for sale is huge, as is the global commerce in these objects. Networks of creators, vendors, and marketers are learning to work these new channels of interest. Traditional businesses do not find these environments especially helpful, and the speculation that caught media's fascination in the early 2000s has died down.

- **Live Music**: Some musicians are finding their audiences through virtual environments. Lady Gaga, the pop singer with a real knack for being different, in fact, just produced a series of first releases that are only available to participants in Farmville. Certain challenges must be met in order to hear the music. You can bet that if a trend maven like Gaga is taking these worlds seriously, there is probably much more to come.

- **Seminars, Conferences, and Dialogue Groups**: This last category of activity has some real overlap with the world of visual teams. People who have managed to gather people in places like SL find that the levels of exchange and disclosure can be quite interesting and meaningful.

  I'm part of a dialogue circle that has been meeting 2.5 hours a week for three years, working with texting around a virtual campfire. We all know each other well and are finding that this kind of gathering is a real support structure for our work. All of us are consultants or in the visualization business of some sort so there is real affinity between the medium and our interests. One of our members is a leader in the application of World Café methods in virtual worlds, and has led many very effective meetings within that methodology.

If you look at the visual interfaces of the traditional project management sites I've reproduced here and compare them with the game interfaces and virtual world interfaces, you will be experiencing more than a metaphor about the differences in cognition and visual literacy that are moving up the generations. I have no doubt that the youngsters will win out eventually.

Is a Network a Team?

Our classical ideas about teams are shaped by experiencing them in fixed locations—factories, offices, research facilities, and hospitals. But the way people are working as contract employees, free lancers, and netizens may be evolving a new class of cooperation. The world of social networking allows for grouping in different ways, but are these kinds of relationships truly interdependent, or

GROVE GARDEN ROOM SIMULATION

In The Grove's Presidio headquarters is a room we call the Garden Room because sunlight streams in from the garden. It looks pretty much like this. It is where we can work with large, panoramic visuals like the Strategic Visioning Graphic Guides displayed here. In SL this room is in full color of course, and one can look up close at any of the displays and move around. The little computer on the table is playing a slide show case study of using these methods with an architecture firm. Search "The Grove" in Second Life to visit.

is this another kind of workgroup dedicated to swapping information and insights but not really having to pull together in one direction?

In my own experience, some of the networks I'm involved with do have a feeling of shared intention, and a kind of unstated commitment to work with a certain level of integrity in what we pass along to each other. Because I'm not a researcher, I've thought about this in more metaphorical terms, trying to come to some kind of clarity about what I'm experiencing. I am beginning to see the emergence of thought leader networks that resemble loose trade associations or a type of press service. But these comparisons really don't describe the experience of having a constellation of trusted "scouts" and reporters on different aspects of our business. It's the digital equivalent of the informal communities of practice that are said to be the source of richest learning by people who research these subjects.

Part of what makes the digital world so interesting is its openness and surprise. But I see it closing in. Eli Pariser made Internet history by posting online following the 9/11 attacks and creating MoveOn, one of the early successful online organizing networks. His new book, *The Filter Bubble*, outlines the growth of "personalization" and filtering. He says two searchers on Google will not get the same results any more. This job historically was filled by human editors in newspapers and magazines. What does this mean for the future, Eli asks?

I suppose it is inevitable that the wide open range land of the Internet will start getting fenced and corralled. But the implications for organizations that incorporate these tools and begin to learn how to have the help teams need to keep out the caution flags, especially if innovation and creativity are top concerns. These same tools can become tethers and boxes, isolating teams in interesting but incomplete information.

I am beginning to see the emergence of thought leader networks that resemble loose trade associations or a type of press service.

20. Mobile Technology
Reshaping Tomorrow's Teams

As I come to the end of this book on visual teams I find myself thinking about how many changes have and are about to take place in how teams do collaborative work. The information revolution of the last 20 years has transformed many organizations. Virtual work is commonplace. Visual communication is a norm. Global work is a given. Multimedia production and sharing is exploding. It's hard to believe e-mail only became ubiquitous in the 1990s. And now we all face mobility!! The implications for teams are enormous.

Team Challenges Are Universal

The good news is that the basic challenges teams must face haven't really changed. They are rooted in how human beings move through life as cooperating, social beings. You still need to orient to your purpose. You must learn to trust each other and be clear about goals. You still need to come to agreement on decisions, resources, and roles. You have to be disciplined about implementation processes to produce anything. It's still possible to occasionally find a groove and experience surpassing results and high performance. And given all the change and flux, you will want to learn from your projects and initiatives only to repeat the process all over again.

Practices Are Transforming

But best practices—the ways teams meet these challenges—the ways work actually gets done— these are very diverse, culturally sensitive, and transforming in the face of new technology tools. I believe we've just seen the start of it. I want to end this book speculating a little on what is possible, with special attention to what mobile communications have in store, and why I think visual teams will be even more advantaged in this kind of environment.

Lest this chapter worry you about too much change, there are many traditional team practices providing anchors in the storm. You will still want a good story about why you need to work

TRANSFORMATIONAL TOOLS

While writing the first part of this chapter I had the idea of showing just how radically smartphones are changing communications. Within minutes I was able to take this picture with my digital camera of me sending the TPM to a colleague (I have all our tools in my iPhone). You can see my MacBook Pro in the background and my Cintiq tablet that lets me draw whatever I want. I process drawings and pictures in Photoshop and pull them into InDesign for captions like these and now you are reading about it. This kind of plasticity in visual communication is having a HUGE impact on teams.

Lest this chapter worry you about too much change, there are many traditional team practices that will be anchors in the storm. You will still want a good story about why you need to work together and what you hope to achieve. You will still develop trust by having a meal and going out for a coffee as a way to get to know others on your teams. These are deeply rooted human needs.

together and what you hope to achieve. You will still develop trust by having a meal and going out for a coffee as a way to get to know others on your teams. These are deeply rooted human needs. But as you think about how to communicate, and what you can and can't communicate, and how the world of physical things is structured and how organizations actually work at the level of laws, finance, and systems—you know that it's a time of tremendous upheaval.

Recent Developments Fueling Change

Think about how the following developments are fueling mobility and other changes that are loosening organizational tethers.

- **Smartphones**: People the world over are moving to having one smartphone number, and a portable device that rivals some of the biggest computers 20 years ago. Digital money transfer by phone is already available. Airline boarding passes are transmitted by phone. E-mail, text, video, e-books, games, search, and thousands of apps are making these devices something unimaginably flexible.

- **Texting**: Young people are texting more than they e-mail, and many say they don't even use e-mail. This is a challenge for teams depending on e-mail.

- **Cloud computing**: The cloud is allowing anyone who can pay the (very inexpensive) service fees to store everything in remote servers, and access the information from whatever device can hook to the net. The cloud fuels the smartphone and vice versa and many believe is spearheading the next big revolution in computing.

- **Tablets**: Forecasters are suggesting that tablets will outsell personal computers in 2012 and that the number of consumers who want everything on one device will drive a fire storm of evolution in this new platform. If you can remember the very first graphic Macintosh computer, and appreciate the rapid evolution that followed, you can appreciate what is beginning to happen with tablets. I predict that within a few years you will be able to:

- Easily transfer documents from tablet to tablet
- Create group drawings integrating face-to-face and remote participants
- Control all your other devices from the tablet
- Project anything from your tablet
- Access and play in 3 D worlds
- Read, with permission, what is on another person's tablet
- Write by speaking
- Translate anything, in real time, into text or your chosen spoken language (early apps are already here!)

- **Artificial intelligence and data mining**: The debate is joined about when computers will satisfactorily mimic human intelligence, and it's about years, not a lifetime. Machines already do translations. Some are writing articles from news feeds. They already shape the markets with blindingly quick data analysis. They fly airplanes. They screen our Internet activity for preferences. They determine what ads you see. They are the other side of many satisfactory games. The link to mobility is the possibility of being able to access your auto-mated "coaches" from wherever you are.

- **Surveillance**: The increase in geodata, video data, tracking data, and the software that can analyze and make sense of these patterns is moving at a pace well out of reach of the everyday citizen to keep up. As mobility increases so will new kinds of links and tethers, as organizations attempt to keep track of distributed employees.

- **Voice-over Internet protocol and video chat**: Telephony as we knew it is gone. People expect to be able to call free around the world, and see video too! Mobile devices are also portable teleconference machines. Services that allow break-out groups to hold meetings and then reconvene are already available.

THE TABLET REVOLUTION

The new slates and tablets are letting people get their hands back on information directly. The sketching and note-taking functions are in their infancy and will improve rapidly. Here are some notes I took at the Institute for the Future's Horizon Conference. Jamai Caisco is comparing organizations to the "r" and "k" species defined in evolutionary biology, claiming that in very turbulent times like today neither has a strong upper hand.

Teams that take the time to visualize their mission and purpose, draw out maps of their competencies and resources, agree on goals explicitly in language and symbols everyone understands, pull this all together in detailed action plans and roadmaps, link over new media, and track themselves with visual progress reports will be much, much more productive and creative.

- **Video:** The tools to create movies and media are fully available to anyone, and the rocketing success of You Tube is testimony. The scale of content creation has never been seen before. No one knows where it will go, except that it is happening. You can search for almost anything you can think of fixing or making and someone has made a how-to video. Musicians, actors, speakers, and comedians now debut in this medium.

- **Video animation**: You may have seen the growing number of whiteboard talks where the graphics are accelerated, jumping out of the pen of the illustrator at lightning speed. See the caption on the next page for an example.

- **Social networking**: Was this even a term four years ago? Was there a time before Facebook, Linked-In and Google+? Facebook's world is bigger than many countries. It's morphing and changing so quickly organizations can hardly keep up. This phenomenon is generating huge attention and may well have the biggest impact of all the new technologies on teams. I'm not attempting here to speculate on where this is going, except to assert that it will have a big impact as organizations begin to bring similar systems inside to support relationship development and knowledge sharing.

This list is just some of the communication technologies. Materials science, neuroscience, astronomy, energy technologies, and field after field is being rocked with change and new discoveries.

Implications for Teams

I wrote earlier about my hypothesis that increased virtualization and decentralization of the workplace will require more highly developed and shared mental models. Traditional teams and workgroups that still work in the same environments, see each other informally, know a lot about each others' lives and habits, and can communicate a lot of things very efficiently, because there is plenty of support for making correct interpretations. Being able to understand what your teammates are requesting and needing is about this kind of understanding. It stands to reason that

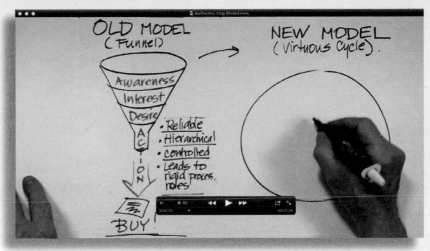

mobility will have a huge impact on this ability.

Imagine a soccer team that is required to wear helmets and only read texting on their visors. Laughable? It's not far from what we are expecting of teams. Now if that helmet happened to have an image of the playing field, and had data that corresponded to all the players as little icons or dots, and had some artificial intelligence (AI) backup anticipating where the ball would move, with appropriate suggestions for moving on the field—then you might have a game!

The Visual Team Advantage

Teams that take the time to visualize their mission and purpose, draw out maps of their competencies and resources, agree on goals explicitly in language and symbols everyone understands, pull this all together in detailed action plans and road maps, link over new media, and track themselves with visual progress reports will be much, much more productive and creative. All these things can be done remotely, but require spending the time learning some of the new tools and choosing a common set of platforms that everyone on the team understands.

Remember back in the beginning chapters when I wrote about Robert Fritz and his idea that tension between aspirations and realities drives human creativity, just like structural tension in the cables of suspension bridges seeks resolution and keeps up the bridge. It's easy to make a case that along with rising temperatures in our atmosphere and oceans, the heat is up in the kitchens of finance, government, and large enterprise. Our aspirations do not match current realities.

For some this stress drives simplistic thinking and true belief. I'm sure that some bosses think it will be easier to just give orders and demand compliance than deal with new media and changing

VIDEO ANIMATION

A new approach to graphic animation is getting the name "video animation." It involves video-taping a visualizer creating a sketch, and then speeding up the drawing so that the charting appears almost magically as the narration unfolds. I created this one in my own studio with original video integrated with narration in iMovie. Its purpose was to give feedback to participants in a summit on new models for the chief communications and chief marketing officers. The new model isn't ready for release, but I can show you a stop action picture of the video here. You'll see a lot more of these as regular kinds of communication in the future. I think it's a stunning medium for concept sharing and explaining new mental models.

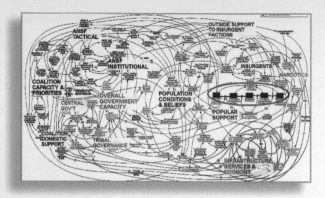

HOW COMPLEXITY LEADS TO SIMPLICITY

Using as an example of complexity a graphic on the front page of the *New York Times* diagramming the war in Afghanistan, Eric Berlow shows how, when you look at the entire system, and then eliminate the elements that you can't affect and don't change much, you can see a much greater simplicity. "Zoom out and embrace the complexity in order to zoom in and see the simple details that matter most," he says. (See www.ted.com/talks/eric_berlow_how_complexity_leads_to_simplicity.html.)

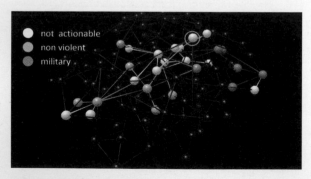

work styles. Why be stressed out when you can be completely right and tell everyone else what to do? It's an old human coping mechanism. But for others it will drive true breakthrough and innovation.

I'm personally biased toward creativity and change as a way to cope—and finding reasons for hope. The energy and drive of young people will always surprise us. Here are some of my hopeful examples.

Simplicity from Complexity

I recently talked with a young ecologist from the University of California Merced, Sierra Nevada Research Institute, named Eric Berlow. In 2010 he became a TED Fellow and was able to present a wonderful little talk in 3 minutes called "How Complexity Leads to Simplicity," applying his ecological graphing tools to social concepts. (If you don't know about TED it's one of the most innovative organizations around—holding a pricey conference on Technology Entertainment and Design every year that supports a giveaway of dozens and dozens of their "best idea" presentations over the net.) Eric's presentation has resulted in 200,000 downloads and requests coming in from large companies and even the government to help them make sense out of some of the mounds of data that they collect. He's realizing that his understanding of complex systems could be applied to social good. His projects are always collaborations with small teams that have access to data, and need his very special kind of visual facilitation (and creative brainpower) to find the simplicities.

Pioneers of Change

In Denmark Ole Qvist-Sørenson is part of a large (1,500), informal network called Pioneers for Change. He runs a small company called Bigger Picture and uses graphic facilitation (or "visual thinking, methods, and tools") to help create strategic engagement in complex change processes. Ole works internationally and focusses as much as possible on sustainability issues. He is married to Russian / Ukrainian Nataliya. This has brought his work and an expanding network to Eastern Europe where there is a growing need, interest, and use. The Pioneers don't do a lot formally, but all their members are still animated by the operating principles of the Pioneers they evolved. They are worth appreciating as a harbinger of future collaboration norms:

- Be Yourself
- Do What Matters
- Never Stop Asking Questions
- Engage with Other
- Start Now

Innovation Games

Gameology is a big deal and getting bigger, as young people are applying what they are learning about games to business and organizations. Luke Hohmann is founder of a young startup called Innovation Games. He cut his teeth doing procurement programming and operations analysis for big enterprises, but is now moving into the area of game-fueled collaboration. His development group is a visual team. They sit around a common table in Palo Alto. A large wall contains 24 feet of sticky notes that map out the logic of the game they are designing. They live and breathe what is called "agile software development," creating versions just good enough and getting rich feedback. He's got one called Prune the Product Tree (shown here) that allows teams to set priorities by playing interactively with sticky-note type elements they can move and rate on a symbolic tree as a way of determining the proper portfolio. They are fully engaged in making these kinds of learning games available on tablets. I know they are not alone in this respect. Tools like this will be widely available in the near future. The value of games is how powerfully they support fun-filled "playing around." Neuroscientists are convinced this helps creativity.

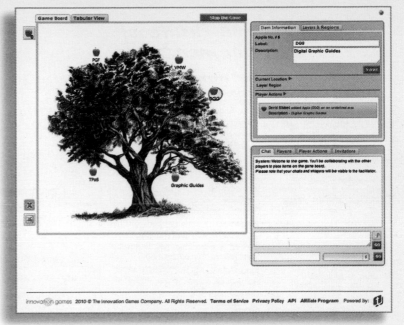

PRUNING THE PRODUCT TREE

Innovation Games provide a great way for teams to play around with complex decision making online. Our team at the Grove played with "Prune the Product Tree," where different players entered the products and ended up ranking and discussing which were the most important. This game is available for free on the public site. You can pull any background graphic in and use the same functionality.

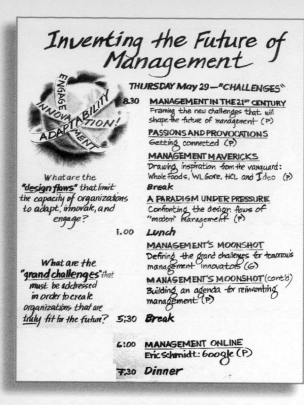

Inventing the Future of Management

THURSDAY May 29 — "CHALLENGES"

8.30 MANAGEMENT IN THE 21ST CENTURY
Framing the new challenges that will shape the future of management (P)

PASSIONS AND PROVOCATIONS
Getting connected (P)

MANAGEMENT MAVERICKS
Drawing inspiration from the vanguard: Whole Foods, WL Gore, HCL and Ideo (P)

Break

A PARADIGM UNDER PRESSURE
Confronting the design flaws of "modern" management (P)

What are the "design flaws" that limit the capacity of organizations to adapt, innovate, and engage?

1.00 Lunch

MANAGEMENT'S MOONSHOT
Defining the grand challenges for tomorrow's management innovators (G)

MANAGEMENT'S MOONSHOT (cont'd)
Building an agenda for reinventing management (P)

What are the "grand challenges" that must be addressed in order to create organizations that are truly fit for the future?

5:30 Break

6:00 MANAGEMENT ONLINE
Eric Schmidt: Google (P)

7:30 Dinner

LOOKING AT A TRULY BIG PICTURE

The first day agenda for MLab's Inventing the Future of Management summit gives you a sense of the ambitious aim of this gathering.

Inventing the Future of Management

The examples I just cited are all coming from the grass roots and the soil of creative people willing to step out into the unknown. I'm convinced there will be no shortage of innovations at that level. But I know that teams also need support from the tops of organizations. How receptive are leaders going to be to the new emergent, living systems-type patterns of organization?

In 2008 Gary Hamel convened a summit meeting in California called "Inventing the Future of Management." McKinsey, the strategy consulting firm, cosponsored the event along with the London Business School, and MLab, Gary's new nonprofit venture, which is focused on catalyzing collaboration and contribution to the field that has been his life. Gary is a true thought leader in the fields of leadership, management of organizations and businesses in particular. Thirty well-known thought leaders in management development, education, and consulting attended, including Chris Argyris, (double loop learning), Tim Brown (designer), Kevin Kelly (technology tracker for *Wired*), Tom Malone (educator-MIT), Henry Mintzberg (organization and strategy at McGill University), Jeff Pfeffer (org theory professor at Stanford), C. K. Prahalad (consultant), Peter Senge (learning organizations), Julian Birkinshaw (professor at London Business School), and Shoshana Zuboff (business professor at Harvard) to name just a few—as well as the CEOs of Whole Foods, W. L. Gore, IDEO, Google, Seventh Generation, and HCL (one of the fastest growing IT companies in India). Gary's gathering question was, "Why can't we bring as much innovation, adaptation, and engagement to our organizations as we do to our development of products and technologies?" The meeting framed some big questions for me that seem a fitting way to close this book.

1. Are We at a Momentous Turning Point in History?

Gary framed the meeting as a time when the old management paradigm is long in the tooth and

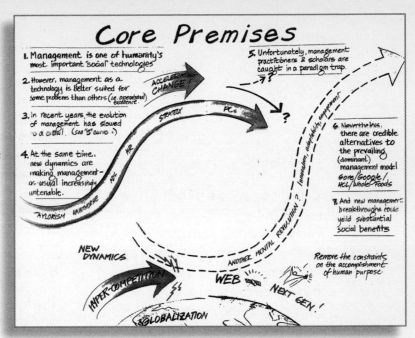

Core Premises

1. Management is one of humanity's most important "social" technologies.

2. However, management as a technology is better suited for some problems than others (i.e. operational excellence).

3. In recent years, the evolution of management has slowed to a crawl. (see "S" curve.)

4. At the same time, new dynamics are making management-as-usual increasingly untenable.

5. Unfortunately, management practitioners & scholars are caught in a paradigm trap.

6. Nevertheless, there are credible alternatives to the prevailing (dominant) management model. Gore/Google/HCL/Whole Foods

7. And new management breakthroughs could yield substantial social benefits.

ACCELERATING CHANGE — STRATEGY — PCs — HR — ADL — HAWTHORNE — TAYLORISM — INNOVATION, ADAPTABILITY, ENGAGEMENT — ANOTHER MENTAL REVOLUTION? — NEW DYNAMICS — HYPER-COMPETITION — WEB — NEXT GEN! — GLOBALIZATION

Remove the constraints on the accomplishment of human purpose.

ARE WE AT A TURNING POINT?

Gary Hamel identifies these premises of why a new effort is needed to invent a new future for management.

no longer viable given the forces at work in our times. He identified several that I had mapped up in a chart of core premises that was posted high on the wall in the session. The chart showed a traditional "S" curve arcing up and over from the early periods of Taylorism, through Hawthorne, McGregor, Sloan, and other pioneers (see next page). "Are we at an inflection where another management revolution is needed?" Gary asked the group. There is no question that hyper-competition, globalization, the web, next gen workers and accelerating change seem to be changing the game, but is the change historic? Some 80 percent of the attendees thought so, if only because of the revolution of the Internet and how it is changing business models. There were those who saw the credit crisis, globalization, and retiring boomers alone as imminent threats to the current order.

But some, like Henry Mintzberg, a professor at McGill University and author of many provocative books on strategy and organization, did not agree. He did not see momentous change happening, but people and organizations acting much as they always have, with power and control issues abundant. I thought it was interesting that the evidence for big change emphasizes external factors. That was until the management maverick panel started.

2. Why Aren't Innovations That Are Happening Catching On and Spreading?

Much of our first morning was spent listening to five CEO "mavericks" talk about their disruptive business models. John Mackey from Whole Foods, Vineet Nayar from HCL in India, Terry Kelly from W. L. Gore, Tim Brown from IDEO, and Jeffrey Hollender of Seventh Generation each talked for about 20 minutes, focusing on what was distinctive about their companies.

The management mavericks all had different models, but were similar in that all have departed radically from the command and control norm for large, successful operations. None of these people carry themselves like imperial CEOs. And none of them went to business school! They live and breathe the culture of their companies from the inside out.

The management mavericks all had different models, but were similar in that all have departed radically from the command and control norm for large, successful operations. None of these people carry themselves like imperial CEOs. And none of them went to business school! They live and breathe the culture of their companies from the inside out.

- **Whole Foods**: The group was rocked by its inventiveness. John Mackey talked about Whole Foods' focus on deeper purpose and core values, and the manager's role being to empower his self-managed teams and see that they are happy and well trained.

- **HCL**: Vineet Nayar shared about posting all 55,000 employees' 360-degree feedback scores on their intranet, in a culture that overtly puts employees first and is very open about what is going on. "Transparency creates trust," Nayar said. All requests for help and response times of teams are also posted and available for scrutiny by anyone with intranet access.

- **W. L. Gore**: Terri Kelly from W. L. Gore shared a deep team focus, within a strongly technical culture. Their belief in the individual, the power of small teams, being in the same boat, and taking a long-term view have generated such practices as calving off any group that grows larger than 200, insisting on leaders who live the culture, and practicing freedom in a box. (It's not an accident that they had The Grove spend a good part of 2010 training their HR people all over the world in the Drexler/Sibbet Team Performance System.)

- **IDEO**: Tim Brown shared about how they have built a culture of creatives by hiring learners rather than specialists, and supporting them to fully use their creativity. (IDEO is a leader in defining what it means to have a visual culture. His book, *Change by Design: How Design Thinking Transforms Organizations and Inspires Innovation* is seminal in this field.)

- **Seventh Generation**: Jeffrey Hollender is a supplier of Whole Foods, and shared about his philosophy of growing people to grow the business with a social equity approach.

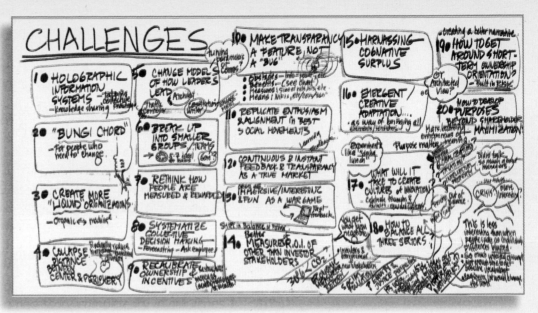

There were many more gems and conversations, of course. But what stuck with me is the extent to which—in each case—committed, trusting leaders were willing to experiment and adapt and change in the interests of their people and teams. While I'm sure each of these organizations has a shadow, as any entity does, there was a lot of hopeful light generated out of this maverick session.

When considering why these ideas aren't spreading, the group was back wondering about the influence of context, intention, timing, virtuous cycles, and other things. It's clear that most of the organizations we consultants work for aren't led by leaders with the kind of integrity, passion, and inventiveness we were seeing in the five Gary picked for this meeting. Big enterprises are organizations glazed over with history and procedures, best practices from earlier times, and tons of inertia. How can these organizations change—or will they?

3. What Challenges Need Attention?

In the design of this two-day conference Gary focused on the idea of identifying twenty-first century "moon shots" that in management might parallel the engineering challenges that galvanized a generation of inventors and technologists in the twentieth century. Small groups of mixed teams of five tackled this question in the afternoon. The challenges they emerged with are illustrated in the graphic on this page, a copy of the large wall mural created in the meeting.

At the end of this reporting back, the group had an unsettled feeling that they hadn't really come up with much that was new. These ideas have been around for a long time, and many have been

CHALLENGES CHART

Here is the graphic created at the Inventing the Future of Management summit from the discussion of what challenges to take on. See if you can imagine which could be addressed by better communications and systems level thinking.

addressed before. Something was missing. Several people tried to put their intellectual finger on it. Shoshana Zuboff, a professor at the Harvard Business School and author of books on industrial cluster theory and social support networks said, "This seems less interesting than when people this morning spoke as individuals. We haven't been together enough to even get our baseline vocabularies understood." This questioning catalyzed some to wonder why the group hadn't brought up equity and justice, an enormous problem, or the global warming crisis, or the role of diffuse networks. What about globalization, taxation, and intellectual property?

4. Is the "Inventing" Group a Mirror of What's to Come?

Native Americans have a concept that people are a "smoky mirror," in that our responses to each other are reflections, and we can see ourselves in others, but it isn't clear and precise. I began to get more and more interested in this meeting being a smoky mirror of what is possible in collaborative processes. As the meeting progressed, several people pushed back on the format of assigned topics and relatively short breakouts. Others challenged the metaphor of "taking on moon shot-level challenges." But everyone was completely engaged and turned on by the rich exchange. As the staff huddled late in the evening to think through day two, we began to get fascinated with the idea of practicing what the mavericks were preaching, and letting the group self-organize around their true centers of interest. We decided to hold an open space session in the morning and let the participants propose the topics. They foreshadow some important movements.

1. **Conscious capitalism**: John Mackey gathered a group focusing on purposes beyond profitability, stakeholder orientation, and the energy of engagement. The group brainstormed ideas for an initial conference on the subject.

2. **Creating the conditions of self-organization**: This group gathered to explore how living systems theories can inform organizations. They dove into ideas in evolutionary biology and the social patterns of termites.

I was fascinated that there was so much emphasis on networking, self-organization, and purpose-centered organization. These are all hallmarks of living systems.

3. **Maximizing the potential of the organization**: Terri Kelly led a group focusing on creating a systems-level architecture around clarity of purpose, guiding principles, role of leadership, how work gets done, knowledge transfer, and reward systems.

4. **Creating true internal markets**: John Malone headed up a group looking at how to apply prediction networks and resource auctions to internal organizational challenges.

5. **How can we use the psychological principles of multiplayer online games as a setting for all work?** Leighton Read, a successful biotech investor, headed a games group that actually invented a game that would teach hygiene in hospitals.

I was fascinated that there was so much emphasis on networking, self-organization, and purpose-centered organization. These are all hallmarks of living systems. I found in this smoky mirror evidence that we are indeed moving to a whole-system, ecological paradigm, albeit slowly. Interestingly, the younger participants were the most articulate in this regard.

5. What Is the Role of Visualization?

In my role as graphic facilitator I was completely absorbed in the challenge of reflecting this group's thinking back at itself. I couldn't help but have many thoughts about how visualization will play in the future of organizations, much like it was in this ad hoc group, coming together for two days to make sense our of very complex material. I realized after the fact that we had used the entire keyboard of possible display formats in this event.

FULL IMMERSION

Being surrounded visually by two days' worth of thinking creates a conceptual container that supports high levels of integrative thinking. With this kind of orientation the dialogue can flow deep and wide and circle back to core themes—and it's possible to track the results afterward. This is a picture from the end of day two of Gary Hamel's Inventing the Future of Management meeting.

OPERATING PRINCIPLES FOR VISUAL TEAMS

Throughout this book I have emphasized a set of principles about the value of visual teams.

1. **Imagine working like designers**: Designers solve problems by holding visions of possibility in creative tension with current realities, and consistently playing around with ways of "satisficing."

2. **Trust creative tension seeking resolution**: A team doesn't need to have all the steps laid out to map out visions and resources and start playing with possibilities.

3. **Learn tools for visualization**: There is a growing range of choices for working in both face-to-face meetings and virtually.

4. **Commit to a common visual language**: Visual mental models support more robust distance communications.

5. **Draw pictures of progress**: Visual tracking and coordinating is central to effective project management on any kind of complex team assignment.

6. **Expect surprises**: Stay open to new possibilities and ideas all the way along.

7. **Take time to learn and improve**: Teaming is a process and benefits from having a repertoire of practices. Unless you take time to develop these you will just cycle in place.

1. **Posters**: We had a logo, high up on the agenda—and directional posters and quotes.

2. **Lists**: Is there an easier way to do an agenda?

3. **Clusters**: Our "Passion and Provocations" introduction was a big popcorn diagram or cluster map—no connections, just clouds for ideas and sparkles for passions.

4. **Grids**: Our first small group template was a grid of questions, and my recording of the Management Mavericks was basically a grid across the front of the room.

5. **Diagrams**: All the groups that talked about seeing organizations as whole systems were drawing diagrams. It's the fundamental language of systems thinking.

6. **Drawings**: The Core Premises chart was a drawing of the familiar "S" curve, plus globe.

7. **Mandalas**: The way the mavericks talked about their companies, it was clear they think of them as unified around central purposes, and that was the way I drew them.

We Come Full Circle

This book is an extension of the ideas in *Visual Meetings: How Graphics, Sticky Notes & Idea Mapping Can Transform Group Productivity*. Here I have argued that it will be teams that make visual meetings and other kinds of multimedia their core way of working who will create our future. The wonderful thing about this movement is its spirit of collaboration, improvisation, and innovation. Playing with imagery, media, and all the new tools loosens up the mind at the same time it grounds ideas and proposals in visuals that build alignment and commitment. My hope is that more managers will have the insight and the imagination to let this revolution proceed, and invite in the play and possibilities that codesigning the future entails. My hope is that those of you who are finding your own creative spark growing brighter as a result of all these tools and stories will fan those flames into a forest fire of commitment, innovation, and high performance.

VII: Links, Tools, & Other Resources
Bibliography & Appendix

VI: Links, Tools, & Other Resources

Chapter 21: Websites & Bibliography This section contains annotated links to websites with key information about teaming and visualization, as well as a bibliography that is organized in useful categories.

Appendix: This includes background material on the team research of Jack Gibb, and Arthur M. Young's Theory of Process.

Index: Key names and concepts are indicated by page numbers.

21: Websites &
Bibliography

Team development is a rich and well-studied field, with many tools and resources available. An online search of "team development" will bring up nearly a half million links. *Visual Teams* focuses principally on how teams can use visual meetings and other visual media for communications, and how graphics can help understand team dynamics through useful interfaces like the TPM. I acknowledge the importance of interpersonal relations, conflict management, group dynamics, and such but did not focus on these practices outside the context of visual strategies. This resource section provides places that you can go to develop more insight and proficiency about the human dynamics aspects of teaming. The links and bibliography titles were chosen for practitioners who are seeking tools and methods across the full range of team development strategies.

Team-Oriented Assessments and Tools:

- **Drexler/Sibbet/Forrester Team Performance System (TPS):** The Grove has worked in team development since the early 1980s. It offers a full line of support tools for the Drexler/Sibbet/Forrester Team Performance System, including Team Performance Models (TPM) in all sizes from wall murals to handouts; a self-scoring Team Performance Indicator (TPI) and associated *Team Performance Indicator Application Handbook*; a Team Performance Online Survey (TPOS) available on request; a *Team Leader's Guide* with explanations of the TPM, 80 best practices and 12 key strategies plus support for leaders; a Team Performance Model puzzle; Team Theme cards; and a *Team Startup Guide*. The Grove also carries all the supplies necessary for working visually, including Graphic Guides in all sizes from wall templates to smaller worksheets, pens, paper, markers, Digital Graphic Guides, and associated Facilitation Guides. For more information explore the Grove Store.

THE GROVE ONLINE STORE

Choose the "click here to get started" line on The Grove Store home page about Team Performance to see a quick guide to getting started with the Drexler/Sibbet Team Performance System (www. grove.com).

- **Cog's Ladder**: Developed by George Charrier, an employee of Procter & Gamble in 1972, this model has persisted as a useful tool for thinking about group dynamics. (wikipedia.org/wiki/Cog's_Ladder; www.evergreenconsulting.com/stages6b.htm).

- **Council Processes for Interactive Meetings**: The most robust and simple to use system for supporting large teams and networks with highly interactive online tools is available through Co-Vision. This browser-based system works flexibly across platforms. (www.covision.com/index.html).

- **DISC Personal Profile**: A good resource is Geier Learning, originators of the DISC Personal Profile System (DISC stands for Dominance, Influence, Steadiness, and Conscientiousness). John G. Geier, PhD, first developed it in 1958 from the work of Dr. William Moulton Marston. The DISC profile has been specially designed to build a cohesive team in a multicultural environment, gaining insight into an employee's deviant personality attributes that can possibly provoke a conflict. People like this instrument because it can be applied to individuals in a team setting. (www.geierlearning.com).

- **Facilitative Leadership for Teams**: Interaction Associates, pioneers of professional facilitation and problem solving for groups, offers applications of its well-developed approaches to team leadership. The Grove and Interaction have been collaborators from the beginning of their businesses. (www.interactionassociates.com/services/leading-teams).

- **FIRO-B**: Stands for Fundamental Interpersonal Relations Orientation–Behavior. This is a questionnaire and model developed by William Schutz in 1958 for the US Military for team working in very intense situations. It is now a widespread, popularly used assessment. (www.youtube.com/watch?v=UCsGtSeWFiM; wikipedia.org/wiki/Fundamental_Interpersonal_Relations_Orientation, www.psychometrics.com/en-us/assessments/firob.htm).

- **Five Dysfunctions of a Team**: Patrick Lencioni, author of *Five Dysfunctions of a Team* and founder of the Table Group has an online assessment and collateral materials. (www.tablegroup.com/dysfunctions).

- **Myers-Briggs Type Indicator (MBTI):** This is a robust, over 60-year-old personality assessment tool based on the psychological types identified by C. G. Jung. The instrument identifies four modes of perception and judgment and 16 distinctive personality types that result from their interactions. People use MBTI because it is very robust and reliable since it has been established for such a long time. The Myers-Briggs Foundation is a good resource for more information. (www.myersbriggs.org/).

- **Trimergence Nine Doors Process**: Ward Ashman has created an adaptation of the Enneagram to business that identifies preferred intellectual styles—intuitive, rational, and emotional—and the nine doorways to perception that occur archetypally in groups. (www.trimergence.com/team_perf.html).

- **True Colors Personality Test**: David Keirsey refined the work of Myers and Briggs, and created work that was then designed into a color-based metaphor by Don Lowry in his book *Keys to Personal Success*. Several of my clients have used this system successfully in team-development activities. It associates blue with compassion, gold with responsibility, orange with spontaneity, and green with conceptual focus .(www.true-colors-test.com/).

- **Tuckman Model of Group Development**: There are many resources citing Tuckman as a tool. If you want a couple of good descriptions of the model check these links. (www.chimaeraconsulting.com/tuckman.htm; wikipedia.org/wiki/Tuckman's_stages_of_group_development); (www.e3smallschools.org/download/TuckmansTeamDevelopmentModel.pdf; www.infed.org/thinkers/tuckman.htm).

Bibliography

Austen, Hilary. *Artistry Unleashed: A Guide to Pursuing Great Performance in Work and Life.* Toronto: University of Toronto Press, 2010. This is a terrific application of research on artists to organizations and management.

Axelrod, Robert and Michael Cohen. *Harnessing Complexity: Organizational Implications of a Scientific Frontier.* New York: Basic Books, 2000. Pulls together applications of complexity theory to organizational work.

Bennis, Warren G., and Patricia Ward Biederman. *Organizing Genius: The Secrets of Creative Collaboration.* Reading, MA: Addison-Wesley, 1997. These case histories read like short stories—sagas of driven, creative collaboration.

Bois, Joseph Samuel. *The Art of Awareness: A Handbook on Epistemics and General Semantics.* Santa Monica, CA: Continuum Press & Productions, 1996. This has been a seminal book for me on thinking about language.

Boulding, Kenneth. *The Image: Knowledge in Life and Society.* Ann Arbor: University of Michigan Press, 1956. This seminal work shaped my perceptions about mental models and their importance.

Brown, Tim. *Change by Design: How Design Thinking Transforms Organizations and Inspires Innovation.* New York: Harper Collins Publishers 2009. As CEO of IDEO, Brown has been at the vanguard of Silicon Valley design.

Daniels, William R. *Group Power.* San Diego, CA: University Associates, 1986. The ability to lead a task force comprises a set of skills that a manager must deliberately set out to acquire. Offers well-tested, practical advice.

Drexler, Allan, and Russ Forrester. "A model for team-based organization performance." *The Academy of Management Executives* 13, no 3 (August 1999). (www.jstor.org/pss/4165563). Summarizes the TPM.

Fritz, Robert. *Path of Least Resistance: Learning to Become the Creative Force in Your Own Life.* New York: Fawcett Books, 1984. Fritz was a key influence for Peter Senge when he wrote the *Fifth Discipline.*

Gibb, Jack. *Trust: A New View of Personal and Organizational Development.* Los Angeles: Guild of Tutors Press, 1958. This is Gibb's description of his TORI model and underpinning assumptions—theory behind the TPM.

Goleman, Daniel. *Emotional Intelligence: Why it can matter more than IQ.* New York: Bantam Books, 1995. Breakthrough book applying neuroscience to human relationships and leadership.

Hackman, J. Richard. *Leading Teams: Setting the Stage for Great Performances.* Boston: Harvard Business School Press, 2002. Hackman identifies five conditions that set the stage for great performances by teams—a real team, a compelling direction, an enabling team structure, a supportive organizational context, and the availability of coaching.

Hagel, John, John Seely Brown, and Lang Davison. *The Power of Pull: How Small Moves, Smartly Made, Can Set Big Things in Motion.* New York: Basic Books, 2010. The authors make a solid, well-researched case about people who use connections, knowledge and resources to solve problems.

Hofstede, Geert, Gert Jan Hofstede Hofstede, and Michael Minkov. *Cultures and Organizations: Software for the Mind,* 3rd ed. New York: McGraw-Hill, 2010. Based on research conducted in more than 70 countries over a 40-year span, examines what drives people apart.

Horn, Robert. *Visual Language: Global Communication for the 21st Century*. Bainbridge Island, WA: 1998. This is a comprehensive history of the emergence and applications of text/graphic, visual language.

Jaffe, Dennis, and Cynthia Scott. *Getting Your Organization to Change: A Guide for Putting Your Strategy Into Action*. Menlo Park, CA: Crisp Publications, 1999. Two very experienced colleagues share their best insights.

Johansen, Robert, and Mary O'Hara Devereaux. *GlobalWork: Bridging Distance, Culture and Time*. San Francisco: Jossey-Bass Publishers, 1994. Mary wrote this book while working at The Grove during our partnership with the Institute for the Future. I contributed quite a bit of the writing and graphics to this effort. It remains a very good overview of the challenges of working globally across cultures and time.

Johansen, Robert, David Sibbet, Suzyn Benson, Alexia Martin, Robert Mittman, and Paul Saffo. *Leading Business Teams: How Team Can Use Technology and Group Process Tools to Enhance Performance*. Reading, MA: Addison-Wesley Series on OD, 1991. This was the first-year report of the Institute for the Future/Grove Groupware Users Project making sense out of the emerging collaboration-oriented software for groups and teams. It is still a very useful exploration of the drivers of collaboration-oriented tools.

Kahane, Adam. *Power and Love: A Theory and Practice of Social Change*. San Francisco: Berrett-Koehler, 2010. Following *Solving Tough Problems*, Kahane digs in on the need to deal with power as well as trust and cooperation.

Kaner, Sam. *Facilitators Guide to Participatory Decision Making*. San Francisco: Jossey-Bass, 2007. This book is a rich unpacking of the process dynamics underlying collaboration, with ample illustrations and diagrams created by Lenny Lind of CoVision.

Katzenbach, Jon R., and Douglas K. Smith. *The Wisdom of Teams: Creating the High-Performance Organization*. Boston: Harvard Business School Press, 1993. This classic provides a manual for creating what executives say they want: high-performance teams. Insights and guidelines have a lot of stories of real-world teams

Kelly, Kevin *Out of Control: The New Biology of Machines, Social Systems, and the Economic World*. New York: Persesus Books, 1994. Kelly is founder and Senior Maverick at *Wired* magazine. He is as good a tech pulsetaker as there is.

Kleiner, Art. *The Age of Heretics: A History of the Radical Thinkers Who Reinvented Corporate Management*, 2nd ed. San Francisco: Jossey-Bass, 2008. Kleiner's freewheeling portrait gallery focuses on corporate mavericks of the 1950s, 1960s, and 1970s who pioneered self-managing work teams, responsiveness to customers, grassroots organizing, and other ways to tap the value of human relationships.

Kouzes, James M., and Barry Z. Posner. *The Leadership Challenge*, 3rd ed. San Francisco: Jossey-Bass, 2002. Authors debunk the myth of the leader as a maverick rather than a team player.

LaFasto, Frank M. J., and Carl E. Larson. *Teamwork*, 2nd ed. London: Sage, 2003. The authors explore the eight properties of successful teams based on a three-year study including the space shuttle Challenger investigation team.

_____. *When Teams Work Best: 6,000 Team Members and Leaders Tell What It Takes to Succeed*. Thousand Oaks, CA: Sage Publications, 2001. Probes deeply inside the workings of hundreds of teams.

Lencioni, Patrick. *The Five Dysfunctions of a Team: A Leadership Fable*. San Francisco: Jossey-Bass, 2002. This best seller focuses on relationships and how they get challenged.

_____. *Overcoming the Five Dysfunctions of a Team: A Field Guide For Leaders, Managers, and Facilitators*. San Francisco: Jossey-Bass, 2005. A follow-up to *Five Dysfunctions of a Team*, with many exercises and examples.

LeSaget, Meryem. *Le Manager Intuitif*. (French Edition). Paris: Dunod, 2002. One of the chapters is on the Drexler/Sibbet Team Performance Model.

Lipnack, Jessica, and Jeffrey Stamps. *Virtual Teams: People Working Across Boundaries With Technology*, 2nd ed. New York: Wiley, 2000. Serves as an excellent primer of both theory and practice about the challenges and imperatives of learning to work virtually. This book has a model similar to the Fourfold Model of Groupware with six distinctions.

MacGregor, Steven Patrick. *Describing and Supporting the Distributed Workspace: Toward a Prescriptive Process for Design Teams*. Doctoral Thesis at University of Strathclyde, Glasgow, Scotland, 2002. Explores the Drexler/Sibbet Team Performance Model among others . See www-cdr.stanford.edu/~macgregor/MacGregor2002.pdf.

Mader, Stewart. *Wikipatterns: A Practical Guide To Improving Productivity and Collaboration in Your Organization*. Indianapolis, IN: Wiley Pub., 2008. This book provides practical, proven advice for encouraging adoption of your wiki project and growing it into a useful collaboration tool.

McGoff, Chris. *The PRIMES: How Any Group Can Solve Any Problem*. New York: Victory Publishers, 2011. This unpacks the key consulting concepts of Chris and my mentor, Michael Doyle, co-founder of Interaction Associates.

Miller, Brian Cole. *Quick Team-Building Activities for Busy Managers: 50 Exercises That Get Results in Just 15 Minutes*. New York: Amacom, 2004. Describes simple team-building activities for managers, supervisors and team leaders.

Minahan, Matt, Judy Vogel, Lee Butler, and Heather Butler Taylor. "Facilitation 101: The Basics to Get you on Your Feet." *OD Practitioner*, 2007. Features the TPM. See www.ntl.org/upload/ODP_Facilitation_101.pdf.

Morrison, Richard, and Brian Sullivan. *The Team Memory Jogger: A Pocket Guide for Team Members*. Methuen, MA: Goal/QPC, 1995. This pocket reference guide helps with communication, productivity, and decision making.

Neal, Craig, Patricia Neal, and Cythia Wold. *The Art of Convening: Authentic Engagement in Meetings, Gatherings, and Conversations*. San Francisco: Berrett Koehler, 2011. Pioneers in consciousness, deep dialogue, and engagement.

Pariser, Eli. *The Filter Bubble: What the Internet Is Hiding from You*. New York: Penguin Press, 2011. Pariser started MoveOn and knows what he is talking about regarding the networked world.

Peterson, Brooks. *Cultural Intelligence: A Guide to Working with People from Other Cultures*. Yarmouth, ME: Intercultural Press, 2004. Explains how to manage broad cultural differences and cultural egocentrism.

Pink, Daniel. *A Whole New Mind: Why Right-Brainers Will Rule the Future.* New York: Riverhead Press, 2006. Brings neuroscience to bear on the six senses of design, story, symphony, empathy, play, and meaning.

Reina, Dennis, and Michelle Reina. *Rebuilding Trust in the Workplace: Seven Steps to Renew Confidence, Commitment, and Energy.* San Francisco: Berrett-Koehler, 2010. Authors' long experience results in very practical advice.

Rath, Tom. *Strengths Finder 2.0.* New York: Gallup Press, 2007. This book is the follow up to Gallup's *Now, Discover Your Strengths* and includes a revamped version of the Strengths Finder test.

Roam, Dan. *The Back of the Napkin: Solving Problems and Selling Ideas with Pictures.* New York: The Penguin Group, 2008. One of the best, practical primers for getting starting with visualization.

Scholtes, Peter R., Brian L. Joiner, and Barbara J. Streibel. *The Team Handbook,* 3rd ed. Madison, WI: Oriel, 2003. A reference of choice for team leaders and team advisors for many years. The new edition of this classic takes you beyond improvement teams to work teams and the teams of today.

Schrage, Michael. *Serious Play: How the World's Best Companies Simulate to Innovate.* Boston: Harvard Business School Press, 2000. At such firms as Walt Disney, Microsoft, 3M, Sony, and Hewlett-Packard, serious play is serious work. Schrage, is a research associate at MIT Media Lab and a *Fortune* writer.

Senge, Peter M. *The Fifth Discipline: The Art and Practice of the Learning Organization.* New York: Doubleday/Currency, 1990. Presciently identified and described the learning organization. Senge has the ability to apply breakthrough ideas to concrete practices that businesses can emulate. It is a great introduction to systems thinking.

Sibbet, David. *Best Practices for Facilitation.* San Francisco: The Grove Consultants International, 2002.

____. *Graphic Facilitation: Transforming Group Process with the Power of Visual Listening.* San Francisco: The Grove Consultants International, 2006. Definitive book for persons wanting to become professional graphic facilitators.

____. *Principles of Facilitation: The Purpose and Potential of Leading Group Process.* San Francisco: The Grove Consultants International, 2002. This book provides ideas for addressed each of four flows of facilitation.

____. *Strategic Visioning Agenda Planning Kit.* San Francisco: The Grove Consultants International, 2009. Card based.

____. *The Theory of Process Poster.* San Francisco: The Grove Consultants International, 2002. This large, full-color, folding poster is a summary of Arthur M. Young's Theory of Process, cocreated with a working group from the Institute for the Study of Consciousness.

____. "Visual Intelligence: Using the Deep Patterns of Visual Language to Build Cognitive Skills." *Theory into Practice* 47, no 2, (2008): 118-27. I argue that practicing with the Group Graphics Keyboard formats builds perceptual ability.

____. *Visual Meetings: How Graphics, Sticky Notes & Idea Mapping Can Transform Group Productivity.* New Jersey; John Wiley & Sons, 2010. This best seller provides a foundation for understanding the visualization strategies elaborated upon in *Visual Teams.* It shows how graphics are used for inspiration, engagement, thinking, and enactment.

Sibbet, David, and Ed Claassen. *Team Leader Guide: Strategies and Practices for Achieving High Performance.* San Francisco, CA: Grove Consultants International, 2003. Comprehensive guide for first line managers with 80 best practices.

Smith, George. "Group Development: A Review of the Literature and a Commentary on Future Research Directions. Group Facilitation." *A Research & Applications Journal. International Association of Facilitators.* no 3, (Spring 2001). Smith's book is a very thorough, academic comparison and analysis of a wide range of team models. Download pdf from citeseerx.ist.psu.edu/viewdoc/download?doi=10.1.1.131.1981&rep=rep1&type=pdf#page=17.

Tapscott, Don. *Grown up Digital: How the Net Generation is Changing Your World.* New York: McGraw-Hill, 2009. Selected as a 2008 Best Business Book of the Year by the *Economist*, it is based on a $4 million, multiyear research project including nearly 10,000 interviews. Good for wondering how to integrate Net Gen into the workforce.

Trompenaars, Alfons, and Charles Turner. *Riding the Waves of Culture: Understanding Cultural Diversity in Global Business,* 2nd ed. New York: McGraw-Hill, 1998. The authors write for managers and businesspeople who are looking to understand cultural differences and how to deal with them in a variety of circumstances and situations.

Tushman, Michael L., and Charles A. O'Reilly III. *Winning through Innovation: A Practical Guide to Leading Organiztional Change and Renewal.* Boston: Harvard Business School Press, 1997, 2002. This is a classic primer for leadership teams interested in leading change and innovation.

Von Oech, Roger. *Creative Whack Pack: Success Edition—Two Powerful Creative Thinking Tools.* Stanford: US Games Systems, 1992. An illustrated deck of 64 creative thinking strategies.

Warkentin, Merrill, and Peggy M. Beranek, "Training to Improve Virtual Team Communication." *Information Systems Journal* 9, no 4:(October 1999): 271–289.

Wheelan, Susan A. *Creating Effective Teams: A Guide for Members and Leaders.* Thousand Oaks, CA: Sage Publications, 1999. A best seller in previous editions—intended for team leaders, members in organizational studies, management, human resources, social psychology, education, group studies, leadership, sociology, and communication.

Young, Arhur M. *Geometry of Meaning.* New York: Delacourt Press/Seymore Lawrence, 1976. Young integrates contemporary science with traditional wisdom about how human make sense of the universe.

____. *Reflexive Universe.* San Francisco: Delacourt Press, 1976. Anodos Foundation, 1999 Revised Edition. This is Young's seminal work on evolutionary process and how nature reflects universal principles.

If you are interested in resources relating to visualization, graphic facilitation, and visual thinking, check the extensive list of links, books, and articles in *Visual Meetings* (see reference on prior page).

Appendix

A THEORY OF TRUST FORMATION

GROUP CONCERN	INDIVIDUAL CONCERN	IMMATURE OR POORLY FUNCTIONING GROUP	WELL-FUNCTIONING GROUP
ORGANIZATION How will we form to accomplish our goal?	**CONTROL** Who is in control? Will I have some control?	Dependence / Counterdependence	INTERDEPENDENCE
PRODUCTIVITY What can we do together?	**GOAL FORMATION** What do I want to accomplish?	Hostility / Apathy	PRODUCTIVITY "We can do it!"
DECISION-MAKING How do we make decisions?	**DATA-FLOW** Will I be heard?	Politeness Caution Closed STOP	DATA FLOW "I hear you"
MEMBERSHIP Who will belong?	**ACCEPTANCE** Can I be me?	Mistrust Fear	TRUST "I accept you"

Jack R. Gibb's Original Research

Jack R. Gibb is one of the pioneers of applied behavior science, publishing research on groups, control, and trust that influenced many in the field, and was an inspiration to Allan Drexler. Jack Gibb's distinguished career as a psychologist and consultant spanned five decades. He was a pioneer in humanistic psychology, and the originator of Trust Level theory (TORI Process for Trust, Openness, Realization and Interdependence). Often called the grandfather of organizational development, he applied TORI theory to all forms of organizations, from corporations and governments to schools, churches, and hospitals. He was the original proponent of the importance of trust in team dynamics and organizational behavior, and of the effect of trust on creativity.

Gibb was an early innovator at the National Training Laboratories (NTL) in Bethel, Maine, where behavioral scientists performed the pioneering work in team dynamics, communication, sensitivity training, and leadership training in the 1940s and 1950s. Jack was one of the first and most highly regarded T-Group (training group) leaders at NTL, and served as Director of Research. His seminal book is *Trust: A New Vision of Human Relationships for Business, Education, Family, and Personal Living.*

Jack consulted for IBM, AT&T, General Motors, Dow, DuPont, the State Department, the IRS, TVA, YMCA, and the National Council of Churches. He held a doctorate in psychology from Stanford and has taught at Brigham Young, Michigan State, and the University of Colorado, where he also directed the Group Process Laboratory. He is past president of the Association for Humanistic Psychology, a diplomat of the American Board of Professional Psychology, and a fellow of the APA, ASA, the NTL Institute for Applied Behavioral Sciences, and of the International Association of Applied Social Sciences. He contributed chapters to 26 professional books on management, organizational development, group dynamics, human potential, communication, and education, and over 350 articles to professional journals on those subjects and on learning theory, therapy, and counseling. His classic article, "Defensive Communication," written in 1960, continues to be the standard in the field. His work focused on formulating a new vision of a more trusting world.

In Gibb's scheme, trust concerns remain throughout the life of a team. They cannot be completely resolved. The concerns are highly interdependent; success in dealing with one set of issues clearly affects the ability to deal with others. For example, when a team has not resolved basic membership issues, it can hardly have the kind of free flow of data that supports good decision making. In theory, the four primary categories of concerns are neat abstractions; in real life, they are messy and do not come compartmentalized, arranged in a fixed hierarchy or sequence.

TORI PROCESS

Jack Gibb illustrated his TORI Process with this graphic depiction of the stages of trust formation. It plumbs some of the psychology under the early stages of the TPM.

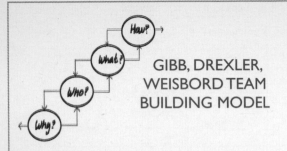

GIBB, DREXLER, WEISBORD TEAM BUILDING MODEL

Jack Gibb studied a large number of groups and discovered that people bring the following four basic concerns to all social interactions: These form the underpinnings of his TORI Process and the team model described here.

- **Acceptance concern**, which is related to the formation of trust, the acceptance of oneself and others, a decrease in anxiety, and an increase in confidence (this concern in part involves membership and degrees of membership on a team).

- **Data concerns** about the flow of perceptions, feelings, and ideas through the team and the individual, and the social system for expressing them.

- **Goal formation concern**—the process of team goal setting, problem solving, and decision making—and the integration of the intrinsic motivations of individuals (goal setting in part involves productivity, having fun, creating, learning, and growing).

- **Control concern** for mechanisms by which activities are regulated, coordinated, and put into a useful sequence.

Arthur M. Young and the Theory of Process

Arthur M. Young received a degree in mathematics from Princeton in 1927 and studied relativity and quantum mechanics with Oswald Veblen. Young set out in the early 1930s to develop a unified theory of how universal systems relate to each other, caught up in the general efforts of the early twentieth century to describe a unified field theory integrating the major findings of science. In the process he spent a good number of years in the 1930s and 1940s grounding his thinking in the practical process of inventing and developing the world's first commercially licensed helicopter, the Bell 47.

He emerged from his work with Bell and parallel research believing that the unity of things cannot be found by examining forms and structures and deterministic rules, but by appreciating the nature of process—the actions of the photon and fundamental particles upon which all else is based. He came to see that all process in the universe is playing out a creative tension between freedom and constraint, between the potential of the photons of light and the constraints of cause and effect at the molecular level. When matter finds the combinatory rules at the molecular level, it can then turn back toward freedom through the evolved structures of plants, animals, and humans.

The Theory of Process presents an integrated set of tools for understanding the evolution of life and consciousness in many fields of study. Students have applied the theory effectively in everything from the healing arts to international relations. Young evolved his theory of process by working deductively from basic principles and testing his ideas against both scientific fact and accepted theories over a period of 30 years. He was able to show that the process of nature is more fundamental than the structures it forms. He identified seven distinct phases of process that express themselves throughout seven kingdoms in nature.

In practice, Young's ideas are clear and sensible, once you appreciate how to bring the role of purpose back into the scientific method. The fourfold aspects of nature and the seven-stage arc pattern, key elements in the theory, turn up not only in mathematics, quantum physics, chemistry, and biology, but also in philosophy and religion. The following brief outline can only begin to touch on the richness of Young's ideas. It is included here as an invitation to further study of Young's books, publications, and videos. See a very complete website at www.arthuryoung.com for links to further resources.

The Photon as a Universal Quantum of Action: Perhaps Young's most profound insight was that physicists had found, but not yet fully acknowledged, an active agent that continuously sets process into motion in the universe. This is the photon, a quantum (unit) of light holding in its spin an infinite capacity to store energy. A photon's energy varies in direct proportion to its frequency. It took one of the twentieth century's most famous physicists, Max Planck, to discover that photons in nature always package their energy in units, or "quanta" of action, of constant invariant size. Planck's constant also happens to be exactly the same size as the minimum uncertainty in Werner Heisenberg's uncertainty principle, suggesting that it is equivalent to a quantum of uncertainty. Young reasoned that since photons come in whole units, and are basic and "prior to" force, time, space, and matter in the universe, the photon fits the definition of what philosophers would call "first cause." He correlated it with conscious action and human decision, both of which also come in wholes. He also knew that photons are intimately associated with all molecular and chemical activity, and provide an access point for will to effect matter. So what appears to be uncertainty to a scientist looking outside in, can be interpreted from the inside out as freedom to act for the photon, and freedom to act on purpose for humans. Young concluded that all process in the universe is set in motion by purposive action. Light, as a radiant point source, becomes an icon for the monad of consciousness.

Universe as a Learning Process: From this starting point, Young then reasoned that the universe is fundamentally a dynamic learning process—a forward thrust due to time being irreversible. Process moves "toward a transcendent goal" in the sense that evolution demonstrates both direction and the property of continued transcendence of constraints. But first, a system of cause and effect must be created from what is initially present, namely light, with its potential and freedom. These are sacrificed to obtain the determinate means that make experience and learning possible. In the findings of physicists, it is possible to trace the path by which light (the photon) transforms into matter by a gradual investment of its freedom (or uncertainty). It first becomes mass and force by creating protons and electrons, then confines its energy within the atom, and finally combines atoms into molecules, materializing as the physical world we experience. In becoming force and then atom and then molecule, the photon learns firsthand the constraints of matter and the laws of cause and effect. But this "descent" is not the end of process; rather it is a preparation for learning-through-becoming, and using what has been learned to ascend back to freedom. In doing so the photon (or "monad" as Young liked to call it) develops the complexity and understanding embodied in the more evolved forms of plants, animals, and humans.

Fourfold Reality: The theory of process shows how the four basic entities of physical science just

THE OPERATORS IN THE THEORY OF PROCESS

Young used geometry to illustrate basic distinctions. These are three of the foundation operators.

Twofold Operator

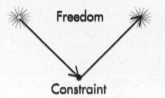

Threefold Operator

Fourfold Operator

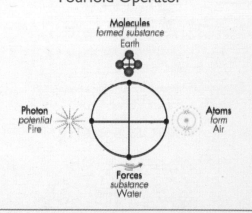

THE SEVEN-STAGE ARC OF PROCESS

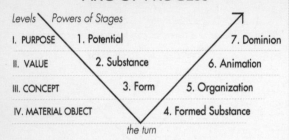

Levels	Powers of Stages	
I. PURPOSE	1. Potential	7. Dominion
II. VALUE	2. Substance	6. Animation
III. CONCEPT	3. Form	5. Organization
IV. MATERIAL OBJECT		4. Formed Substance

the turn

PRINCIPLES IN THE ARC

- The universe is a process put in motion by purpose.

- The development of process occurs in stages, seven in all.

- Each stage develops a new power, retaining powers learned from prior stages.

- Powers evolve sequentially—in the natural world as kingdoms and substages.

- Early stages take on constraints until the "turn"; later stages regain freedom.

- Levels of constraint are the same on both sides of the arc.

- Stages of process alternate between innovation and recapitulation.

THE TORUS PATTERN

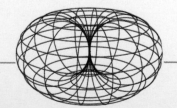

276

described—the photon, forces, atoms, and molecules—are an important expression of the ancient fourfold—fire, water, air, and earth. These are aspects of reality that Young illustrated as angular directions on a circle. He identified the general qualities reflected in this fourfold and correlated examples across many fields of study. The four causes of Aristotle are an example—final cause (intent), material cause (substance), formal cause (plans), and efficient cause (fabricated work). The four modalities of perception and judgment by Carl Jung—intuition, feeling, thinking, and sensing—are another.

Seven-Stage Arc of Process: Young called the point when process has fully manifested in molecular form, "the turn." Even though process is now constrained by three dimensions, it still retains some freedom of action (in molecules, through the emission and absorption of photons within molecular bonds) and can ascend back to freedom through new levels of organization as it learns to apply the rules. Illustrating the descent and ascent pattern across the fourfold displayed as levels, rather than angular relations, Young creates a a seven-stage pattern he called the "arc." He saw it describing the evolutionary stages of the kingdoms of nature, a reflexive universe. He also saw it applying, at a general, paradigmatic level, to any process, including ancient myths of origin around the world.

The Torus: The arc illustration shows how process folds back on itself reflexively as it learns the rules of nature. This movement, in three-dimensional space, is illustrated by the donut shape—what mathematicians call the torus. A torus form allows the center and periphery of a system to be completely connected. Young concluded that all substances in nature solve the problem of achieving dynamic equilibrium between inert and chaotic states with this vortex pattern. This includes magnetic fields, water, air, and human energy fields. He also developed a formal mathematical argument about why seven distinctions are necessary to fully describe toroidal patterns where only four are needed to describe spherical shapes.

David Sibbet joined Young's study group in 1976 and worked for seven years applying these very general theories to Group Graphics and teams. The patterns Young articulated confirmed Gibb's field-based research, and provided Drexler and Sibbet a pattern for the sustaining stages of team development. It also helped them understand why the formative steps are so important and persistent throughout a team's life. Young's notion that freedom can be regained by mastering the initial constraints provides a conceptual template for understanding the conditions necessary for high performance.

For a complete explication of these ideas see *The Reflexive Universe* and *Geometry of Meaning* in the bibliography, or search www.arthuryoung.com.

Index

DAVID SIBBET is president and founder of The Grove Consultants International, a firm leading strategy, visioning, creativity, future-forces, leadership development, and large-scale system change processes worldwide since 1977. He is author of the best-selling *Visual Meetings: How Graphics, Sticky Notes, & Idea Mapping Can Transform Group Productivity.*

He was involved with the growth of Apple Computer in the 1980s, facilitated the change management team at National Semiconductor during its turnaround in 1990, and worked at HP and then Agilent Technologies for many years, leading strategic visioning sessions for groups and divisions, helping develop leadership programs, and designing Grove Storymaps for special kickoffs and change projects. He and The Grove facilitated the community visioning processes and planning fairs connected with the conversion of the Presidio in San Francisco to a national park. As a founding director of Headlands Center for the Arts and tenant in the Thoreau Center for Sustainability, he has long experience as a park partner.

In addition to corporate and government work, David has sustained a diverse involvement with foundations, nonprofits, schools, and professional associations. Over the years David has helped design and lead many board/staff retreats, strategy sessions, and cross-organizational projects working on social change.

David is author and designer of many of The Grove's integrated process consulting tools and guides, including the Grove's Visual Planning Systems, the Drexler/Sibbet/Forrester Team Performance System, the Sibbet/LeSaget Sustainable Organization Model, The Grove's Strategic Visioning Process and related graphic templates, and The Grove's Facilitation Series. In 2007 the Organizational Development Network awarded David and The Grove their Membership Award for creative contributions to the field of OD.

David holds a master's degree in journalism from Northwestern University and a BA in English from Occidental College. He was awarded a Coro Fellowship in Public Affairs in 1965 to study metropolitan public affairs in Los Angeles. For eight years in the 1970s he was executive director and director of training for the Coro Foundation, designing experience-based education programs for young leaders. He began his own organizational consulting firm in 1977. David is a longtime affiliate with the Institute for the Future in Menlo Park, a member of the Global Business Network in San Francisco, a longtime member of both the Organizational Development Network and the International Forum of Visual Practitioners, and a member of Heartland Circle's Thought Leader Network. He is president of the Argonne Community Garden and currently on the board of Coro. David lives in San Francisco with his poet/teacher spouse, Susan.

For additional information, explore www.grove.com and www.davidsibbet.com.